Acclai

MW00831019

Move over, Lon Cheney. Pack your bags, Boris Karloff. Kane Hodder - the baddest big screen monster of the bunch - is ready to share his amazing and surprisingly intimate story. What's most impressive about Unmasked is not only what Kane has accomplished as an actor and a stunt man, but what this self-effacing screen legend has overcome as a person. Read this book. You will love getting to know the man behind the mask!

-Bruce Campbell
Burn Notice, Evil Dead Series, Bestselling Author of
If Chins Could Kill: Confessions of a B Movie Actor

"After years of hanging out and working with Kane I thought I'd heard all his stories but his book is a surprisingly honest and revealing peek behind the mask of one of horror's busiest stars. Ch-ch-ch-ch-check it out!"

-Robert Englund
Freddy Krueger, The *Nightmare on Elm Street* films

If Kane Hodder ever takes the business of killing people as seriously off the screen as he does on it, my advice would be this... Run for the hills! Trust me on this. No one would be safe.

-Doug Bradley
Pinhead, The *Hellraiser* Series

Kane came up from the ground, being a stunt man paying his dues... to being one of the best horror icons in the business. I know that on any location I'm on with him that he has my back.

-Tony Todd
CandyMan

This is a gripping account of Kane's transformation from kid to killer. Now I dream of one day swinging a machete, too!
-Gunnar Hansen
Leatherface, *Texas Chainsaw Massacre*

Kane looked me right in the eyes with intensity I have never seen before. He *really* wanted to kill me. Taking step after step towards me, he never broke his gaze or intensity. It was an amazing performance... the fact that he was complete engulfed in flames the entire time... made it amazing. Kane really is fearless.

-Lance Henrickson
Aliens, Terminator, Millennium, Near Dark

Kane Hodder frightens me. I'm not joking...
-Angus Scrimm,
The Tall Man from *Phantasm*

Kane always scares the hell out of me, but I love him.
- Linda Blair
The Exorcist

Kane Hodder is the real deal. He's a horror icon who talks the talk, and has personally walked the walk. Having been through his own personal hell and back, Kane brings a true understanding of torment to every role he plays. Kane Hodder is horror."

- Dee Snider
Rock Legend from Twisted Sister,
Actor/Writer/Director of *Strangeland*

Kane always made me feel safe, even when chasing me with a knife.

-Jensen Daggett
Rennie, *Jason Takes Manhattan*

Genuine...Honest...Real...AKA "JASON"

-VC DuPree
Julius, *Jason Takes Manhattan*

Kane was the best serial killer I ever worked with.

-John D. LeMay
Jason Goes to Hell

In this business there are people I will never work with again. And there are people I'll work with if I have to. Then there are those I WANT to work with again. I want to work with Kane again.

-Todd Farmer
Writer, *Jason X, My Bloody Valentine,
Drive Angry, Hellraiser (2012), Halloween 3 (2012)*

Kane Hodder, if you research the history in the annals of horror films, that name continues to appear either as a stunt coordinator, stunt man, actor, and the quintessential monster of all time. A lifetime of work that continues to expand...the man will go on forever!

-Ken Foree
*Dawn of the Dead (1978 and 2004)
The Devils Rejects, Water for Elephants*

Kane Hodder is a hell of an actor as well as the baddest stuntman I've ever worked with. The scene in "The Devil's Rejects" where I kill Banjo & Sullivan is a testament to Kane's grit & genius. He's a great guy to boot. We always have fun together at horror conventions. The only difference between us is that he doesn't mind killing the willing fans (guess he has a good lawyer)!

-Bill Moseley
Devil's Rejects, Texas Chainsaw Massacre 2

Wouldn't want to meet Kane in a dark alley, movie or not.
- Daniel Logan
Young Boba Fett from *Star Wars* Series

Kane is the nicest bad guy in Hollywood.
- C. Thomas Howell
E.T., Outsiders, The Hitcher

Kane is more psycho without the mask on.
- Edward Furlong
Terminator 2

People are always afraid of Jason, but what they really should be afraid of is Kane Hodder.

-Sean S. Cunningham
Director, *Friday the 13th, Deep Star Six*

UNMASKED

The True Life Story of The World's Most Prolific Cinematic Killer

By

Kane Hodder & Michael Aloisi

ISBN: 978-0-9852146-7-8
Library of Congress Control Number: 2012948757

First Published by *AuthorMike Dark Ink*, 10/13/2012

www.AuthorMikeInk.com

AuthorMike Ink, Dark Ink and its logos are trademarked by *AuthorMike Ink.*

Printed in the United States of America

I dedicate this book to anyone who has ever suffered a *serious* burn injury.

And to my Mother,
For always being my biggest supporter
and never giving up on me.

-Kane Hodder

TABLE OF CONTENTS

Part I: Youth

Fight Intermission I

Part II: Burn

Fight Intermission II

Part III: Stunt Man

Fight Intermission III

Part IV: The Rise and Fall of Jason

Fight Intermission IV

Part V: The Birth of a New Killer

FOREWORD

By
Adam Green

I was 15 years old the first time I almost met Kane Hodder. Growing up in the Boston area and being the self-proclaimed king of the holy holiday of Halloween, "Spooky World" was a yearly tradition each Fall that I never missed. Scary hayrides, haunted houses, horror celebrities… it was the Halloween event of New England each year. I had met Alice Cooper there the year before and while that was a huge moment for me, I can't even express the excitement pumping through my young wannabe filmmaker heart when I found out that Kane Hodder would be appearing at "Spooky World." I got into the autograph line that night filled with glee, turning to my friends, and reminding them every few minutes, "We're about to meet Kane Hodder!" as if they didn't know.

For almost two hours I stood in that line with my VHS copy of John Carl Buechler's *Friday the 13th Part VII* in my nervous and sweaty hands. Finally the time had arrived. I was at the end of the roped-off line with only two fans left between me and Mr. Hodder. Is that what I should call him? "Mr. Hodder?" Or would he be cool if I referred to him as "Kane?" Is that disrespectful? How do I do this? Holy fuck, I'm about to meet Kane Hodder!

"Sorry kid, line's closed."

What? Are you kidding? I had my parents drive me all the way here just to meet my horror hero and I waited in this line for two hours and now you're gonna what?! The huge "Nnnooooooo!" I was screaming inside my head rivaled that of Louis Creed's in *Pet Sematary*.

"Spooky World" was closing. I watched Kane get carted away by event security while I stood there in absolute disappointment. Like Ralphie choking up when he finally met Santa Claus in *A Christmas Story*, I watched my moment crumble before my eyes. Only there was no department store Christmas slide to stop myself from sliding down. There was no turning back to get a second chance and yell what I really had to say to Kane. The moment was over. It was not meant to be.

Little did I know then, but about 15 years later I would be sitting down with Kane to discuss his potentially starring in my screenplay for *Hatchet*, a story I had come up with when I was only eight years old, and a film that I had fought tooth and nail for to actually bring to fruition. I wouldn't be meeting him as a fan in an autograph line, but as an actual filmmaker.

The first piece of the *Hatchet* puzzle came together in special effects master John Carl Buechler who was the first credible piece of talent to believe in and come on board with my (then) scrappy and unproven team of filmmakers known as "ArieScope Pictures." Sure, I had written a few television pilots, booked a few studio writing jobs, directed some local cable commercials, made about half a dozen short films, and even directed a micro budget feature film, but I had nothing that proved I really knew what I was doing and that I wouldn't totally fuck everything up and waste everyone's time and reputations. When Buechler offered to get my script to Kane and see if he would consider playing the film's villain (Victor Crowley), you can only imagine how excited I was.

A few days later, I found out that Kane had responded enthusiastically to my script. We spoke on the phone briefly and he said that he was willing to sit down for dinner and discuss the Victor Crowley character with the producers and me. As we prepared to drive to the meeting, I asked Cory Neal and Sarah Elbert (*Hatchet's* producers) if it would be cool if I brought some of my Jason stuff to have Kane sign while we were there.

"No," they said. "That would so not be cool."

So my movies, posters, action figures, and hockey mask stayed behind in my little Hollywood apartment while I walked into the meeting armed only with my 90 pages of screenplay titled "Hatchet, First Draft, January 27, 2004." Surprisingly the whole fan boy thing went out the window within seconds of sitting down to begin the meeting. As I was soon to learn in the making of the movie, even though I was getting to live the dream and work with so many of my childhood heroes on *Hatchet* (Kane Hodder, Robert Englund, Tony Todd, John Carl Buechler, etc.) there was never a point where I let that excitement overtake my role as director or the job at hand. It was all business. I instantly forgot that I was probably being sized up and tested in that meeting and instead I just let my passion, confidence, and vision flow freely with no fear.

Something those outside of the industry need to understand is that known actors (especially within the horror genre) are approached with about a dozen projects each week. Unfortunately it's just the nature of the business that very few of those projects will actually get made. It's not because the filmmakers or producers are devious people or that they're bluffing. I'm sure they truly believe that their project is indeed real and that they won't be wasting the actor's time with it, but sadly this is the most unpredictable business there is. Overnight I've seen budgets just disappear, investors back out, and any other number of ridiculous problems blindside a production and knock it out of commission. Personally, I once watched a project I was making unravel mere days before rolling camera.

The investors literally ran away and dropped off the face of the earth, leaving my crew and me without a paycheck for all of the work we had done and with no answers for why the film was suddenly not happening. Years later I learned that the investors (there were two of them who were co-financing the picture together) were brilliant con artists trying to pretend they actually had financing in order to screw the other one out of money. When they both realized they had been had, they split. No explanation. No phone call. Not even a courtesy e-mail from an assistant. My production was merely caught in the middle of two terrible entities trying to play "Hollywood Producers." That shit happens in independent film every day. So the fact that Kane was willing to take *Hatchet* seriously on nothing but faith and his belief that I would deliver what I was claiming I could deliver… well, that was pretty amazing. Yes, I did have my cards in order before ever contacting him. But who was I? What track record did I have? What had ArieScope ever produced that he would have known at that point? However, as fate would have it, something clicked between us that day. When I left that meeting it wasn't the usual "Sounds good, let's talk again when you have a start date." It was Kane saying, "I'm in. I'm Victor Crowley."

I guess not bringing all of my toys to be autographed was probably a good idea on my producers' behalf.

Now, as Kane tells the story, when the subject of him also playing a more dramatic role in the film came up (a role that was not performed in the extravagant Victor Crowley make-up) he made himself start crying right there at the table just to show me he could do it. However if I recall, that's not exactly what happened. At the end of dinner, I had challenged him to a fight outside of the restaurant and said that if he could beat me up I'd consider giving him that role. We stepped outside of the restaurant and while he did indeed get a few good punches in at first, I literally destroyed him in front of everyone in the parking lot. At one point during the end of the fight I had him by the throat against an SUV and, as I choked him out, he begged me to stop the beating and then started crying. Seeing him on the ground in tears I thought to myself, "Fine, I'll give him the role." I felt bad having leveled him like that, you know? You see a grown man crying like that and something just tears at your heart. It was the least I could do.

Note about the conflicting stories: One of us is lying.

The rest, as they say, is history. Not only did *Hatchet* go on to become a success with genre fans, but the sequel was just as big of a hit, and (at the time of this writing) the third installment has been green-lit. At horror conventions you'll see fans walking around proudly in their "Hatchet Army" colors or displaying their tattoos of Victor Crowley on their skin. Even cooler to see is that Kane now fields more questions about Victor Crowley and moves more *Hatchet* memorabilia than he does for Jason. For me it warms my heart not just because it's amazing to see my first real film take off like that but because of a much bigger emotional accomplishment that comes with all of it. An accomplishment that you'll read about from the man himself in the following pages, but something I'd love to take this opportunity to really make clear.

Kane Hodder is Jason Voorhees. Let me say it again. Kane Hodder is Jason Voorhees. Yes, other people successfully played the character before him and yes, other people have successfully played the character after him, but any *Friday the 13th* fan that has stuck with the series through thick and thin knows that no one personified and embodied that iconic character more so than Kane. This is no slight to the other actors who donned the hockey mask. I am friends with most of them and fans of all of them and their performances in the role. In fact, in interviews and documentaries on the series many of the other actors who have played the character have testified to this. Kane is inarguably the actor most tied to Jason no matter what anyone says or who your personal favorite may be. When he was unceremoniously taken out of that role for *Freddy vs. Jason*, no one was more confused by the decision than Kane. As you'll read in this book, it was a devastating blow not only to Kane but to legions of Jason fans, and it is a choice that to this day there is still no clear reasoning for.

When I sat down with Kane to discuss playing Victor Crowley, I was meeting with a man who was at a crossroads in his career and dealing with an incredible loss, having just been booted out of his career-defining role. Now, I'd be lying if I said that there was never a conversation about casting someone else in the role of Victor Crowley. No specific other actor was ever in mind, but even though I had always dreamed of Kane playing the character, many of the higher ups in the production played devil's advocate at some point (just doing their due diligence as any good producer should) and suggested that I at least entertain the thought of putting a fresh face in the role. Their reasoning was twofold. There was the train of thought that there are some in the genre fan world who are so narrow minded that simply because *Hatchet* was a slasher film and because Victor Crowley was an unstoppable killer that no matter what we did we would be called a *Friday the 13th* rip off and that having Kane in the movie would only solidify that opinion. There was also a train of thought that we'd get a better performance out of an up-and-comer who was out to prove himself rather than an actor who had already "been there and done that." My producers and investors wanted to make sure that I was casting Kane because he was the right actor for the role and not because I was a fan boy or because I thought his name gave the film some sort of street credibility. Truth be told, they made good points. There was a risk casting Kane because we already knew we'd be facing the *Friday the 13th* comparisons even though *Hatchet* was tonally completely different, and Victor Crowley (being a paranormal repeating ghost) was not the same as Jason Voorhees. It's just how it goes with this genre. However, if you're going to direct a film you need to make your decisions with conviction and not care what the inevitable naysayers will say because believe me, they'll naysay no matter what. (Look up *The Dark Knight* on IMDB and you'll see that over 16,000 brilliant people have rated it a "1" for "worst film ever.") Be true. Put your heart in it. Everything else is just bullshit. And I mean that sincerely. The awards, the money, the fame, the critics, the haters... none of it really matters. It's the film that lives on forever, and it's the true fans that carry every film's torch from generation to generation. So when I was asked to consider casting someone who wouldn't come with any baggage and someone who would "want it" as badly as I did, my answer was simple.

"I *am* casting that person."

Kane was out for blood and just as hungry to prove himself as I was at that time. If there is one scene in *Hatchet* that embodies how badly Kane wanted it and how much he had an equal amount of heart and soul in the film, it's when we first see Victor Crowley in all of his glory. He runs out of his house shaking and screaming and then mows down an elderly couple right before our eyes, chopping a man in half (the long way) and then ripping a woman's face in half at the jaw. The scene brought audiences to their feet in theaters and is quickly becoming an absolute fan favorite kill in the world of slashers. That is sincere and pure rage beyond a mere performance. Sure I wrote and directed it, and the film's camera department, make-up effects team, composer, and sound designer all pulled it off... but no one could have done that like Kane. Period.

With Victor Crowley, Kane finally got to not just portray a terrific character, but build that character from the ground up. No one had played the character before and the choices were his to make. Here was a guy who had just lost the most important role of his career but then seized the opportunity to not just go with the flow and jump into any old role he could cash in on, but to truly create a new character and show that he could really act. As they say, when one door closes another door opens and no one is a better example of that than Kane and how he handled *Hatchet*. I don't want to spoil everything that happened for him after *Hatchet* as it's all in this book, but these days when I do a convention appearance and I look over to see Kane being hailed not only as "Jason" but as "Victor Crowley" to a whole new generation of slasher fans... I'm beyond proud of him. He not only deserved that. He earned it. And he's just about the only working iconic genre actor who has successfully pulled that kind of feat off.

Right before we started shooting *Hatchet*, Kane turned 50 years old and also lost his mother, thus adding a huge amount to the weight that was already looming on his shoulders. While I'm not there yet myself, I know that 50 is a big number and a point in life where people really analyze where they've been and where they're going. Though we never really got into it then (we weren't as close on a personal level yet) I sent 50 ice cold Coors Light beers to his house for his birthday. It was the most "manly" way I could think of to let him know I was thinking of him and knew what he was going through. Someone in the production office had suggested flowers, but we all assumed he'd just eat them. Cheap beer seemed like a better option. Point is, when we started rolling on *Hatchet* we all had a lot to prove to ourselves and that is probably why for so many who worked on that film, it still ranks as one of the most important moments in our lives.

Note: while some fans speculate that Kane Hodder is such a badass that he exists on a diet of Jack Daniels and the souls of young children, his drink of choice is actually Coors Light, and he requests peanut butter and jelly sandwiches on set. He is also a fan of Insane Clown Posse. You know, the rappers who paint themselves like clowns and write lyrics like "Fucking magnets, how do they work?" Them.

When it came time to shoot *Frozen* I was facing an absolutely terrifying production. Three young principal actors all suspended 50 feet off of the ground on the side of a mountain at 8,000 feet in blizzard conditions, with some truly dangerous stunt work. The way independent film works, when you shoot out of town on location, the production's goal is to try and utilize as much local crew as possible. It helps stretch the production's meager budget in a number of ways, most of all protecting the precious local tax incentive. But in the months leading up to shooting *Frozen* I was literally having night terrors about someone on the production getting seriously hurt or possibly killed. As qualified as the local stunt coordinators in Utah were (and trust me, there are some amazing stunt coordinators working in that area), I insisted that I absolutely needed Kane supervising all of the stunts and safety on the film. I needed someone I could trust with my own life and not have to get to know and learn to believe in on that crucial level. Sadly, the initial reaction was "Sorry, Adam, but we can't afford that." The nightmares and anxiety continued to the point that I was starting to doubt if I could even pull off what I was hoping to achieve with the film.

Now Kane probably wouldn't want anyone to know this, but seeing what I was up against with *Frozen* he took it upon himself (without even telling me) to call the film's producers and tell them that he would come and coordinate the show for whatever they were going to pay a local stunt coordinator; minus his travel and accommodation costs, minus his required per diem, and minus any losses against the local tax incentive. In short, he offered to take on a job that most sane stunt coordinators wouldn't take for all of the money in the world... and to do it for next to nothing. Now I'll never know what they actually settled on, but what I do know is this; he didn't do that to be a hero or because he had nothing better to do. He did it for me and he did it for my crew. That's the kind of guy he really is. That's the kind of friend he is. In fact he's such a tremendous stunt coordinator that his mere presence on set made everyone involved feel at ease while we suffered through one of the most challenging and grueling shoots since *March of the Penguins.*

There's this weird feeling you have when Kane is around that nothing can go wrong. Like if the chair had suddenly plummeted 50 feet to the ice with the three actors helplessly on it, Kane would have suddenly jumped in and caught them like some sort of superhero. It makes me laugh when I think that I feel safest when the guy who's killed more people on screen than any other actor alive is standing behind me. But that's Kane.

There are a lot of great stunt stories contained in this book. Some are triumphant while others are tragic. One thing that has always irked me is the completely asinine perception that stunt performers are not real actors. How many times have you heard someone say that when casting a film's masked villain, all you need is a big hulking brute who can withstand physical punishment because playing the killer can't be that hard to pull off? Well, in the shitty movies where no one involved really cares, perhaps that is the case. But every time you've seen a movie where you truly respected and feared the film's villain, that's because there is a very good performance going on behind the prosthetics or behind the mask. As someone who has done plenty of acting work in front of the camera, I can assure you that it is much, much easier to convey a performance when you have facial expressions and dialogue at your disposal. Take away those things and many actors whom you love and adore would watch their skills crumble like a deck of cards. Stunt performers are one of the most underappreciated and most crucial components to any production. Think about it, when a horrible accident happens or you are in harm's way, whom do you call? The police, right? Well on a production as soon as there is anything that could result in discomfort or an injury, whether it be a simple punch or even just standing in a spot of the shot where a piece of balsa wood *might* potentially hit someone, the actors step out and go to their trailers while the stunt performers bravely put themselves in harm's way. I've even seen stunt performers double actors because the water they were shooting in was too cold or the conditions were uncomfortable. The stunt performers don the actor's costumes, channel the actor's performance, and do what no one else on the set is willing to do. More importantly they do it without the recognition, without the fame, and for far less money. I love when I hear actors say they always do their own stunts simply because they took a fake slap or threw a stage punch once or twice. Don't believe it. Though it is true that some actors would *like* to do more of their own stunts, the production (if it's a smart one) usually won't allow it.

True story: on *Hatchet* there was a stunt where Joel David Moore and Deon Richmond's characters bump into each other and fall down in the grass as Victor Crowley chases after them. Doesn't sound that hard, right? Joel David Moore was adamant that he wanted to take the fall on his own, but Kane rightfully refused him. When the stunt performers did the first take they just so happened to land at an angle where Deon's stunt double's foot was where Joel's stunt double's face landed.

The result was a very bruised and very bloody split lip for Joel's stunt double.

It was our first week of shooting at that point. So what would we have done if Joel's face had been damaged? Shut down production for three weeks while it healed? Recast him and reshoot everything we had already shot with him? Either of those options would have ended the production of *Hatchet* because we couldn't have afforded it. So my point here is this: always listen to your stunt coordinator and the next time you hear someone try to say that stunt performers aren't real actors, tell them to eat a bag of dicks. Yes, Kane Hodder began his career doing stunts. He still performs and coordinates stunts in many of your favorite films. But he's an actor. He's a "real" actor. And he always has been.

In closing I'd like to say that I've read most every 5entertainment autobiography and biography out there. From directors and actors to rock stars and porn stars, I've read them all. The book you're about to read truly ranks as one of the best. Kane Hodder and Michael Aloisi have done an exceptional job. This book is raw, real, honest, and most of all, it has no publicity agenda. It reads as if you're a fly on the wall in a psychologist's office where there just so happens to be a guy on the couch who hurts himself and murders characters on screen for a living. Some books simply tell the same old stories you've read a million times ("I woke up and the needle was still in my arm so I went to rehab again.") or read like a narcissistic and almost defensive list of why you should look upon the celebrity in a higher regard ("Here's a list of every famous person I'm friendly with, a photo of me with the President, and an appendix of all of my awards."), but you're not going to get that here. You're about to witness one of the industry's biggest tough guys bare his soul and truly tell his story honestly. From his childhood beatings, to his risky chances, to his tragic burn accident that contains detailed suffering the likes of which will make many of you have to take a break and put the book down... what this book contains most of all is the true story of a kid with a dream who bravely paid his dues and honestly suffered for his craft.

In my years working with Kane, I've tortured him with hours of make-up appliances. I've made him dance on screen. I've broken a shovel over his head. I've stabbed him with a pitchfork. I've smacked him across the face with various household items. I've shot him several times. I've bashed his face to a pulp with a sharp blade. I've lit him on fire. I've thrown him into rancid freezing waters filled with everything from snakes to animal feces. I've watched him tear his entire bicep muscle to shreds and then continue working. I've watched him (almost) get knocked out. I've watched him continue working even though the very costume he is wearing is poisoning the skin on his back and turning it into bloody shreds. I've made him have his first sex scene. I've placed real lives in incredible danger and then put those lives completely in his hands. I've blown his entire head off point blank with a shotgun. I've even watched him break down and cry. However throughout all of that I've never seen him let down his guard as completely as he does on these pages.

Maybe you've watched Kane rip a person in half on screen. Maybe Kane's choked you in a photograph at a convention. Maybe you've witnessed him throw up more than a gallon of vomit at will. Maybe he's shown you the "KILL" tattoo on the inside of his lower lip. Maybe you've watched him set himself on fire. Maybe you've had the privilege of working with him. Or maybe, like me, you're one of the lucky few who can truly call him a friend.

Whatever the case, you ain't seen nothing yet.

And to Kane, my friend, all I really wanted to say to you that night at "Spooky World" when I was 15 years old was… thank you.

But by now you know that.

~Adam Green

INTRODUCTION:
DEAD IN THE WATER

Jason Voorhees was picked on as a child for being "different." He was endlessly teased and tortured and eventually left alone to drown… I almost met the same fate as a child.

I was a normal kid, though a bit skinny and small for my age. My size caused taunts and teases from the kids I went to school with on a fairly regular basis. I got in my share of small fights and feuds in my youth, but nothing out of the ordinary. Then one summer day when I was in fifth grade, my friend, Tracy Morgan, and I were at Deer Park in Sparks, Nevada, swimming at the neighborhood pool playing some games after taking some swimming lessons. There were people all around, and we splashed and played like all the other kids. My father was in Korea for an extended period of time working for the U.S. Army Corps of Engineers, so he wasn't around, and my mother was working. We were there by ourselves, but back then, that was normal. We rode our bikes wherever we wanted to go with no worries. When we finally got tired and hungry, the two of us got out and started to dry off. Our bikes were parked down the hill, outside of the pool, as they were not allowed in the pool area. Walking down the steep slope with our towels over our shoulders towards our bikes was when we first saw *them* coming.

Three of whom my mother called the "big kids" were suddenly circling around our bikes in the grass. Something about them made me nervous. I looked over my shoulder back at the pool to see if anyone was watching, but with the pool up on a hill, no one could see us. I nudged Tracy and gave him a look that said we should get out of there, fast. Our bikes were only about 20 yards away, lying in the grass. Without saying a word, we started to walk across the moist grass toward our bikes, our feet slightly slipping with each step. I started to wish I had kept my shoes next to the pool and not the bikes so we could just run and hop on. Before we could reach them though, the three teens, which at ten years old looked like men to me, formed a wall in front of our bikes. They didn't smile or laugh like they do in the movies when they are about to tease the little kids; instead they stood with stone cold faces staring at us. In my memories and nightmares from that afternoon I could see a couple of their mouths moving as if they said something to us first, but I can't recall one word said between any of us. What I do remember is the absolute terror of seeing two guys twice my size run right at me. My whole body cringed and braced for the impact... as the first fist made contact.

The first punch I remember well; it was to my left temple. The impact shot brilliant sparks of light in front of my face and twisted my head around towards the pool. I remember thinking how odd it was that there wasn't any pain; it just felt like a numb thud. The impact was so intense, though, that I couldn't tell myself to run or even fight back. I had never experienced a situation like this in my young life. I didn't know what to do. Before I could even think about blocking my face...another blow came. This one hit my right cheek as I was still spinning around from the first impact. After that, it was a series of repetitive punches to the head with the two teenagers taking turns beating me (a scenario that would occur again later in my youth). Over and over again, every punch landed on my face or skull. The beating was brutal and relentless. Even when

I was on the ground, they didn't stop. Instead of my head snapping around freely, it was now being crushed between fist and the ground, and sharp pebbles pierced the back of my skull. The will to fight back shut down, my arms flopped to my sides, and the punches kept coming. I was like a rag doll, moving only from the force of each blow. I just waited for my head to cave in and for everything to go black. Just as I thought it was about to… the punches stopped. I honestly believe that the only reason that they stopped was that they got tired of punching. By the time they were done, I was left gasping for air, bleeding on the ground next to Tracy…with whom I had just played Marco Polo.

After lying there, drifting in and out of consciousness, praying someone would come and help, I realized I had to get up, or I might choke on my own blood. It was hard to open my eyes, and even when I did, my vision was horribly blurry. For some reason I remember seeing the reflection of the water of the pool flickering on the grass a few feet in front of me. The gold light shimmered and rippled as kids laughed and played happily above us. I wanted to crawl up there and fall into the pool, sink to the bottom, and let the water wash away the throbbing in my head for good. My thought was interrupted when my vision clouded even more. After blinking a few times, I realized it was blood dripping into my eye.

I don't know how, but we eventually got ourselves up and walked our bikes home. Amazingly, no one came down from the pool and found us. We probably should have gone to the hospital, but we were kids. I was more embarrassed than worried about my well-being. Tracy and I didn't even bother saying goodbye when we parted ways for our houses. When I arrived home, I was thankful that my mother was in the backyard. I snuck into the house and locked myself into the bathroom. Looking into the mirror I was horrified at what I saw; it was not my reflection staring back. Instead it was some lumpy, bloody monster out of some movie. Seeing my image was when the excruciating pain started to seep in to my skull. Fighting through the hurt, I cleaned myself up as best I could. I didn't want my mother to see me that way.

An hour later I was in bed with a stomach full of aspirin and saltines that my mother made me take after checking every inch of me and talking to the doctor. At least I had the blood washed off when she found me hiding under my covers. Everything throbbed and ached with a pain I had never experienced. I wanted nothing more than to fall asleep, but every time I shut my eyes, I saw fists coming at me. The next day it hurt to blink, breathe, or even move my lips to talk. There was massive scabbing all over my face. My eyes were both almost swollen shut. Chunks of my hair were missing. My lips were the size of sausages, my nose looked like someone took a cheese grater to it, and even my temples were purple. The image of what I looked like that following day is burned into my memory; to this day I can see every cut and lump. I have seen people in head-on car crashes who had less damage to their faces... it was horrific. It took weeks for the swelling and bruises to go down enough for me to look normal.

The kids who beat us were never caught, nor did I ever see them again, which just added to the terror of the situation. Three kids, who were nameless to me, appeared out of nowhere and destroyed my childhood, only to disappear. Not only did the incident leave massive bruises, lumps, and cuts all over my face, it left me mentally scarred for life. For years through my childhood I would have nightmares about that afternoon. I avoided the pool as much as I could, and I was extremely cautious any time I saw a stranger approach me. The hardest part as a child to understand (and even today as an adult) was why? The attack came out of nowhere, for no reason. I never got answers as to why they did this to me and, in some respect that was harder to take than the beating.

When I play a killer, the rage and anger comes naturally to me. The director says *Action*, and I snap into this bloodthirsty monster ready to destroy whoever and whatever is in front of him. Though I inherited a lot of my temperament from my father, part of me believes this anger and rage comes from that incident. I was so angry, hurt, and scarred by it, that I always wanted to get revenge—hurtful, angry, violent revenge… that I never got. Thankfully, I am allowed to act out that revenge frequently and get paid for it.

PART I

YOUTH

HANGMAN

Man has been fascinated with death and horror from the beginning of time. It's a natural part of our biology and lives. Gladiators getting eaten by lions, and public executions were the highest form of entertainment in the old days. Now, we enjoy our horror without real death, in movies. Some grow to love the shit, others fear it. As for myself, I was born with a taste for the dark side. I'm not sure where it came from or how it came about, but regardless, I have always loved scaring people and every other aspect of horror. Some of my earliest memories are of living in Sparks, Nevada. As a kid, my best friend was Tracy Morgan (not the comedian) whom I like to think was a bad influence on me, but it could have been the other way around, or maybe we were just two souls who ignited the worst in each other. Over the years, Tracy would be a good friend and my partner in crime.

When I was around nine years old, I decided I wanted to build a haunted house in my garage for Halloween. Tracy agreed it would be a great idea, so we set about building our chamber of horrors. My parents gave us permission and just said to not break anything or get hurt. We promised to follow their rules and immediately blacked out the windows and made the garage as dark as possible. We set up some dummies using old clothing stuffed into my dad's shirts to make them look like dead bodies. I hung all of my toy snakes and monsters from strings and rigged them so they would swing down in people's faces. We didn't have a strobe light so we cut a hole in the bottom of a box, lined it with tin foil, and stuck a lamp into the hole. We then turned it on and off really fast thinking it would have the same effect.

As we were setting up, Tracy had an idea to use some of his mom's yarn to make a spider web so he ran home to get it. Alone, I had my own idea, what would be creepier than to have a dead body swinging from the rafters? I could hang myself and when someone came through, jump and scare them. It was going to work great. Wanting to test it on Tracy, I quickly grabbed some of my dad's rope and tied it around my neck. I didn't want to choke myself, so I put a towel around my neck, thinking that would save me. I was nine after all. With my safety gear in place, I threw the rope over the rafter, got up on a chair, and grabbed the other end of the rope. I figured, instead of tying it off, I could hold the end and then let it go to drop down and scare my victims.

Holding the rope in one hand, the other end over the rafter and around my neck, I stepped off the chair. The air in my lungs was suddenly cut off. I felt my tongue instantly slap the roof of my mouth gasping for oxygen. My eyes strained from the pressure, and the skin on my throat burned—shit, this was not going to work. Thankfully, all I had to do was let go of the rope. Realizing how much I loved and missed air, I let it go... only I didn't budge. I was stuck hanging, swinging back and forth. I tried to look up to see what the hell was going on, but my vision was getting blurry, and my head was throbbing. Reaching above my head, I grabbed the rope and tugged several times, I slid down an inch or two, but I still couldn't reach the floor.

As the room started to dim, I saw bright flashes in front of my eyes. I was going to die. I was too young for my life to flash before my eyes, but I did think of my parents and how much I was going to miss them. Then all of a sudden, the rope let go and I slammed into the floor, falling flat on my back. Air burst into my legs and tears shot out of my eyes. Lying on the ground, scared to move, I stared at the rafter above me. There was one single nail sticking up, with a few stray pieces of rope stuck on it. I cursed the nail, but then started to laugh… I was alive.

After a few minutes I felt well enough to stand up. I quickly bundled up the rope and put it away. The towel I hid behind a box. I didn't want Tracy to know what just happened, because I was embarrassed as all hell. Yet at the same time, something about my stupid stunt made me feel invincible. The fear was a rush, even if I only scared myself.

When Tracy came back I didn't mention what had happened. We just went about finishing up our haunted house, which we called *Spook House*. We invited our friends over and had them screaming; our parents even went through it and yelled a few times. Even though I was only nine, I knew there was something amazing about scaring people. Little did I know you could do it for a living.

ISLAND BOY

My father was a project manager for the Corps of Engineers which meant that he was gone for up to a year at a time during my youth. Most of my early childhood years are filled with memories of waiting and counting down the days until my father would be home. When you're seven, five minutes feels like an eternity to wait, and having to wait for over a year was gut-wrenching. I remember sitting, looking out of my bedroom window in Sparks. I'd stare at the sidewalk and driveway just waiting, hoping my father would come home early and surprise us. Of course being that he was in Korea or some other far-off country, meant that he couldn't just pop in for a visit.

My Dad and Me

Though I had two older half-sisters, they were more like aunts to me. Being that they were fourteen and fifteen years older than me meant I was going to their weddings when I was five. Basically I was an only child, sitting home with my mother, waiting for Dad to come home. By the time I was 11, I was used to my dad being gone for a year at a time, though being used to it didn't make it any easier. It wasn't easy for any of us, in fact. Mom had to raise me on her own for long stretches. She could only communicate with her husband through letters that took weeks to get. Phone calls were few and far between and usually filled with static, missed words, and heartache of wanting to be together.

Every time the phone rang, I ran into the kitchen to watch my mother answer, just in case it was Dad. She'd always smooth her hair and pat down her shirt before answering as if whoever was on the other line could see her. Her voice would always be smooth and lovely when she answered. My eyes would always be wide as I watched her lick her lips and answer with a soft *Hello*. Of course, most of the time I'd see her shoulders slump, her smile fade, and her voice change to her normal tone as she realized it wasn't Dad.

Then one night, a few months before my 12th birthday, I watched with excitement, as her voice didn't change. I edged closer to her when she gave me a big smile, I was going to get to talk to Dad. At the time, it had been over two months since we last spoke. My mother put her hand on my head and gushed for a few minutes before leaning down and offering the phone to me. I answered with an excited *Hello*; my father was obviously excited, as well, for he started to talk before I could.

"Doc! I got a new assignment; it's on a tiny island somewhere in the Pacific. It's a big job, might be there a few years." When I heard him say that I gripped the phone more tightly so I wouldn't drop it and run out of the room. I was

7

hoping to hear he was coming home, and instead I found out he was leaving for even longer.

"You know what though… you and Mom are coming with me." At that point I did drop the phone. I loved our house and had many friends, but none of that mattered if I could be with my dad and mom all the time. I didn't care if we were shipped to the moon. I was also happy to be leaving Sparks because the first half of seventh grade had been terrible. I had suffered more abuse at the hands of a bully again. It wasn't as severe as the swimming pool beating, but it was traumatic nonetheless. I was walking to school one day when I saw one of the school bullies get sick. For some reason he puked inside of his lunch sack instead of on the school grounds. His friends who were standing around all laughed, so I joined in, thinking nothing of it. After school that day, he and his friend jumped me, held me down, and poured the bag of puke on my face. The bag that had been sitting by a bush, in the sun, all day. It covered my eyes, dripped in my mouth, found its way into my ears and worst of all, when I had to suck in air, a stream of bitter, hot, chunky bile was sent up my nose. The two yelled at me and said things like *who's laughing now?* They also made it a big point to ridicule the shoes that I was wearing. Since my family didn't really have too much money when I was young, most of my clothing that I wore came from the lost and found items from Sparks High School. I had a family member that worked there and she would grab things that were my size and give them to me. I felt very fortunate to have that option, but these guys thought it was very funny that my shoes didn't exactly look new. When they finally let go, I got up gagging and wiped my face off. It was no good though; the smell was in my nose and taste on my lips for the entire walk home. It was so disgusting, sick, and traumatizing, I think I would have rather been beaten up again. I snuck in the house that day and showered… I was too embarrassed to tell my mom or anyone else that day. The humiliation that I felt because I did nothing to defend myself was overwhelming. I hated myself for years after that, because I didn't defend myself at all. I never told anyone that it had happened. I will never forget his name—Kim. I always thought that was an odd name for a tough bully. When my dad said I was going to be with him and out of Sparks, it was like a miracle.

In fact, I hate admitting it, but I got the shit kicked out of me a lot in my youth. I was bullied so much and so harsh that it's a wonder that I'm not more screwed up than I already am. In Sparks in the winter we got little snow, but when we did get it, it was great. All the kids would play in it until our fingers went numb and our parents dragged us in by the ears. When we were at school and the snow was melting, there was always this nice skinny, long patch of snow that survived in the shade of the fence. All the kids would walk on it and it would harden up like ice… just like we wanted it to. One by one we would get a running start, jump and land on the ice and see how far we could slide. After we did it a few times the school bully, Hank, decided to come over and watch. I didn't like his beady, evil little eyes staring us down, but I wasn't going to let that stop me from getting the farthest slide of the day.

Building up speed I ran as fast as I could at the patch of ice… just as I started my slide, a warm, slimy glob of something hit me right in my damn eye. I lost my balance and went flying face first into the ice. Getting to my knees I shook my face trying to get the glob off. I could hear laughing all around me as the viscous slime slapped against my cheek and slid over my lip instead of off my face like I hoped. He had spit a huge snot right in my face. The salty glob slipped in between my lips, I tried to blow it off but inhaled part of it instead. Giving up with the head shaking I wiped my face with my gloved hand. I was so damn humiliated that I was filled with so much rage that I unleashed it on Hank in the form of two words, *Jerk Ass!* I called him the foul name, still on my hands and knees, not even loud *or* to his face. I couldn't even believe such a foul word came out of my mouth; my mother would have been appalled. Instantly I wished I hadn't said it, as I saw Hank turn toward me and take three giant steps in my direction. I tried to get up but the ice was too slippery and I was in a panic.

Unfortunately, I went nowhere, leaving my face as a perfect target.

The top of Hank's wet boot slammed right into my face. As the inside of my lip split open I felt the soggy shoelaces dig into my skin. Before I could even open my eyes another kick came, this time the wet ropes hit my eyes, the third… crushed my nose. Everyone saw it and laughed…and laughed. No one helped.

Almost ten minutes late to class I strolled in, my face a bloody pulp. The teacher ran over to me and yelled at me as if it was my fault. After examining my face she grabbed my shoulders and asked who did this to me. I knew Hank was sitting in the third row, staring at me, daring me to say it was him. Hell, *everyone* knew it was him… but I refused to say his name. I was too scared, too embarrassed. *I fell…* I lied to my teacher. It was one of the most humiliating moments of my life. I feel so terrible inside when I hear about some poor kid committing suicide after enduring an extended period of bullying. It's heartbreaking, because I know that feeling. I don't feel that a kid kills themselves to escape the violence and pain of bullying, but rather to escape the utter humiliation and disgust that they feel from not doing anything to stop the bullying themselves.

Kids can end up actually hating themselves because of never doing anything to defend themselves against bullying. I can say from experience that the feeling of utter disappointment within can be absolutely overwhelming. That is the saddest part. After being beaten, abused and picked on so often... I couldn't wait for my dad to get home so we could leave.

Thankfully, a few weeks after the call, Dad was home and we were packing. I don't think I stopped smiling the entire time. I boasted to all of my friends about how I was going on a secret mission with my father to work on missiles and that I didn't know when I would be back. After a small farewell party, we headed out on our journey to the other side of the world...little did I know my life was going to be very, very different.

The project in Kwajalein was big; it would last for years, therefore, Dad decided to move us with him this time. At that age I really hadn't been out of Sparks. The thought of going to a tropical island was appealing, especially if I would get to be with my dad every day.

Kwajalein, Marshall Islands
Arrow Points to Where We Lived on Kwaj

Kwajalein, Marshall Islands
Arrow Points to Where We Lived on Kwaj

On the long journey, which involved about every mode of transportation possible, my dad told me about the island we were going to live on. The name was Kwajalein, and it was part of the Marshall Islands in the South Pacific. He said it was a coral atoll, which meant that the entire island was made of coral and that one side had a big lagoon I could swim in all the time. The part that really fascinated me was that he said we wouldn't have a car on the island, that we wouldn't need one. The entire place was only three miles long and a half a mile wide, which meant we could ride bikes across the entire place in a matter of minutes. I liked this idea, being 12, because a bike was my only mode of escape back in Sparks, though there, I was only allowed to ride in certain places. Dad said on the island I could ride around the entire thing. This idea amazed me; I couldn't wait to go exploring.

The flight over from Hawaii was exciting as we were told it was only the second jet ever to fly to Kwaj; before then, it used to be little propeller planes. As the plane started to descend, I looked out the window for the island that was to be my new home. I knew my father said it was small, but I couldn't believe it—what I saw down below was a tiny spot of land. I pointed and asked Dad if that little blotch was it. He nodded proudly, not looking away from the view. I started to get nervous, I heard some other people on the plane talking about "rock fever." I didn't know what it was, but I didn't want to catch it. Speaking up, I asked my Mom what it was; she looked a bit confused—my father on the other hand laughed at the question. Leaning over a bit, he answered me.

"Don't worry, Doc; you won't get the fever. There are plenty of kids for you to play with. There are two movie theaters and a beautiful beach; you are going to love it." I was still nervous, but I trusted my father. As we came in for a landing, my hands clenched onto my father sitting next to me. We came so close to the water, I thought we were going to crash. The second we flew above land, the wheels touched down, and I let go of my father, feeling embarrassed at being nervous. As we walked off the plane, it became a circus of confusion as boxes, bins, carts, and bags were thrown around as dozens of people got off. I was instantly struck by the humidity; it felt like a blast furnace. A man met us with a car, one of the few on the island (I was expecting to get on bikes when we got off the plane), and others grabbed our stuff and threw it onto a trailer being pulled by a tractor. A man told us it would be delivered to our house. Before I knew it we were whisked away and dropped off at our new home, a trailer in the "new living section" of Kwajalein. There was row after row of trailers, all the same. As we got out of the car, I wondered how I would ever remember which one was ours.

A few hours later we were treated to a "tour" of the island. Again it was by car. I was starting to wonder why my dad said we wouldn't drive anywhere, but after that day I didn't sit in a car again for years. The tour was short and when it was done, my parents asked me how I liked it. Looking back at both of them smiling, holding hands, even if it wasn't the truth yet, the only thing I could answer was... *I love it.*

Our Trailer on Kwaj

The Beach of My Youth

Riding Bikes with Mom and Dad on Kwaj

We settled in to Kwaj (the slang term I quickly learned to call the island) rather easily. A few weeks after moving in and exploring every nook and cranny (that I was allowed to at least), school started. There was only one school on the island that housed all the grades, K-12. I was about to start the 8th grade, and with all the bullying I suffered, I was worried about being with the older kids, but I adjusted quickly. The following year, they built a new junior/senior high school, so there was some separation. Though I was housed that first year with all the grades, with the small classes and excellent teachers, I quickly felt at home and made numerous friends.

Within a month of living on Kwaj, I couldn't imagine going back to Sparks or living anywhere else for that matter. In fact most of the people who lived on the island never wanted to leave.

It's a small close-knit community with absolutely no crime. Crime is not even tolerated on the island; on the off chance that someone does something bad, they'd soon be shipped off the island, sometimes with their entire family. Growing up I saw that happen a few times. It was a place where you didn't have to lock your doors or worry about your children wandering the streets after sunset. Best of all, there was no income tax, housing was provided, most of the entertainment was free, and you didn't have to own or pay for a car, so you could live there rather cheaply.

It was a paradise of sorts…and I was getting used to it. One remarkable thing about Kwaj was that for the first couple of years that I lived there, you could walk out on the reef at low tide and find remnants from World War II. Bullets, shrapnel pieces from exploded bombs, and other things. They weren't that hard to find in 1968. It was incredible. I collected the stuff for a while, but I have no idea what became of it. I wish I still had it now. Every once in a while, when they would be digging for construction purposes or whatever, they would even uncover an undetonated bomb. It was always a big deal when that happened. You could re-live so much history on Kwaj.

By the time I was an upper classman in high school, the world outside of Kwaj didn't seem to matter or even exist. We were in our own little bubble. There was a tight-knit group of friends I hung out with, not that we could be choosy with friends there

One of Several Japanese Bunkers on Kwaj

as there were so few of us. When my friends and I used to ride our bikes, I would let myself slip behind the rest and then slam my hand on a stop sign and throw myself off my bike. They'd all turn around, and think I hit the sign. After a while they caught on, but they still loved it. Really, I would do anything to get a laugh back then.

As time went on, I did well at school, excelling in French (not that I can remember a damn word of it today), and I played sports…everyone played sports, because there was no television to watch. Sports and the two movie theaters on the island were our main entertainment. I played varsity basketball, but I wasn't that good at it. Baseball, or more so mountain-ball, was my game. Mountain-ball was your typical baseball, except that the ball is thrown up in the air and has to land on the plate, which is bigger than your normal home plate. After playing for a few years, I became the pitcher on the varsity team, even made MVP my sophomore and junior years, and the All-Stars in my junior and senior years. The problem with being on a small island was that there were no other high school teams to play against! Therefore we ended up playing the men's leagues on the island, over and over again, which really wasn't fair being that they were adults, though we did beat them from time to time.

During my Sophomore year at Kwaj High School, I was suddenly left on the island without my parents for about a month. I was alone. My Dad had been battling heart disease for a while and he finally had to have a quadruple bypass open heart surgery to save his life. Since Kwaj didn't have the medical expertise for an operation like this, he had to go to Honolulu with my mom to have it done. This was in 1971 and it was a very new operation, so it didn't have the incredible success rate that it has now. It was a little scary and strange to be on my own at 16 for a month, but knowing my dad was in more capable hands made it worth it. I think I grew up a lot during that time.

STEVE SAVES THE DAY

While living on Kwaj there was one particular guy I got along with more than the others, Steve Nappe. Steve came along in my high school years, and we instantly became best buds. We hung out every day, caused trouble, played sports, and became a regular team. Through the years we became such regular buddies that we had many adventures together, starting on the island.

My Best Friend, Steve Nappe

In the early days of our friendship, he saved my ass numerous times. As I have seen often, a bullied kid will later become a troublemaker when he finally decides he won't put up with people picking on him anymore. That is exactly what happened with me. I'd get into fights in high school, and Steve would pull me away. He'd be the one to calm me down and talk some sense into me; basically he acted as the rational side I didn't have. Really, he is one of the only people who could settle down my anger when it boiled to the surface.

One time we were just hanging out at the snack bar on Kwaj. There was this gruff, old chef named Lee who didn't take too kindly to the kids on the island. He'd serve us, but act up once, and he'd kick your ass out. One day we were hanging out and goofing off like always. Lee was behind the counter boiling a giant pot of chili he had just made. As Lee turned around to focus on some stuff on the counter, I grabbed a salt and pepper shaker and threw them both into the pot, containers and all. I have no clue why I did it, just one of those jackass spur of the moment things that I did without even thinking.

Steve moaned and snorted a laugh at the sight of the glass shakers disappearing into the pot. Lee turned toward the noise and saw me sit back down. Instantly he knew what I had done. An ex-military man, he was at the pot scooping out the shakers in a second. When he saw what it was that I threw in, he lost it. An eight-inch chef's knife suddenly appeared in his hand. Some people pick up knives when they are mad, but they just want to look menacing; they would never use it. With Lee, I could tell he would stick me without thinking twice *and* that he would be able to talk his way out of doing time. Knife in hand, Lee thrust it forward over the counter—I jumped back and got pissed. Steve, being the smart one, wanted to run. I picked up a stool and started to swing it at the burly man. I was ready to take him down, to fight him! Steve, being the calm one, knew I would be no match for the military-trained man. Here I was, a stick-thin teenager, trying to go up against a man three times my size. Not the brightest idea, but I was not going to back down.

I would swing the chair, Lee would jab the knife. Having enough of it, Lee grabbed the stool out of my hands, threw it, and started to climb over the counter. *Come on, you fuck!* I yelled, taking up a fighting stance. Steve came up behind me, grabbed my arms, and started to pull. He was bigger than me and able to get me back a few feet. *Are you nuts? He has a knife—he is crazy.* For some reason, Steve's words got through to me; the knife Lee was holding suddenly looked sharper and more dangerous than before. As Lee's face puffed up red, he spit at me. Realizing this guy wasn't going to give up, I turned and ran with Steve by my side. Steve likes to say he saved my life that day, and damn well might have, as well.

Practicing For My Future Profession, Knives in Trees

Through the years, Steve was always by my side. Even when we left the island and went our separate ways in life, we stayed in touch. Over the years we planned trips together, and we hung out and got into trouble. When I started to get more recognition, Steve came and hung out with me at conventions, keeping me company in the dull times, and making the exciting ones even more exciting. There was one point where we lost touch. His wife thought I was an asshole and kicked me out of his house one day. After that, we stopped talking for almost six years. I was angry at losing my best friend, but I guess I understood. Some people just can't take my personality, or maybe more accurately, my attitude. We eventually mended the situation and are still best friends to this day... and he still keeps saving my ass.

During our high school years together we played on the same sports teams. We were both jocks of sorts; hell, there wasn't much else to do on the island; besides, it kept us out of trouble. Our Senior year I made the varsity basketball team, while Steve didn't. I was bummed out that he couldn't go on the big trip to Hawaii with us to play some other high schools. Even though Steve wasn't there, that trip had a subconscious effect on me that set about my career in life.

SPORTS AND BALCONIES

Kwajalein High School wanted us to experience what it was like to play against other teams our age, so my Senior year they flew us to Honolulu, Hawaii, to play basketball against some other schools. We had a few games and played decently, but the games didn't really matter to us. The fact that we weren't on our island was all we could think about. We wanted to do nothing but explore. My teammates and I ran around the city like crazy kids at Disney World for the first time. It was exciting for us to see cars, stores, televisions, and countless other things we didn't have. When we saw the high-rise Ala Moana hotel, we knew we had to go to the top of it, for the tallest building we had on Kwaj was only three stories high.

Cramming into the elevator, we pushed the button for the 35th floor. Our ears popped, and finally it came to a stop and the doors opened. We pushed each other out of the way as we ran down the hall to the stair tower's balcony. Each landing of the stair tower had its own little open-air landing which overlooked Honolulu. One by one, we each squeezed ourselves into a tiny spot on the railing. The view was spectacular, so much so, our teenage mouths actually shut for a few seconds. After taking in the view, I looked down to see that all of my friends had white knuckles as they were holding onto the railing so tightly... this gave me an idea.

"Back up guys!" I barked with urgency. They must have thought something was wrong because they all fought their way to the back of the balcony. As they did this I made my way to the railing, grabbed it, and hopped over to the other

BASKETBALL 1973

TOP ROW: Kami Hodder, Lynn Winterstine, Sam Ice, Jack Bartholomew, Griff Stelzner, Ron Katz, Coach Dave Larson. BOTTOM ROW: Jeff Roberts, Ken Graton, Phil Thames, Dennis Grason, Kelly McMinn.

My High School Basketball Team

side. Yes, that's right! I said I was standing on the OUTSIDE of the railing now. I heard several gasps and swears. I was now standing with the tips of my shoes between the thin posts, holding onto the railing...35 floors above the ground. At the

24

time I didn't think anything of it, besides the fact that I was going to get a hell of a laugh out of my friends. Instead, all of them stayed back from the railing. I looked down between my legs at a few tiny palm trees swaying in the wind and then back at my friends to see their faces were white.

"Shit, Kane, get back on the balcony," Ron Kain said, which was followed by mumbles of agreement from the rest of the guys. I laughed as I watched them start to huddle together like they were scared to walk through a haunted house.

"Fuck, just grab him."

"I'm not grabbing him, he could fall—you grab him."

"Jesus, he is going to die." I couldn't help but smile at their panic. Seeing their fright gave me another idea.

"Guys, what's the problem?" I asked as I released the railing and brought my hands up to gesture that nothing was wrong. As I started to tip back I quickly grabbed the railing, right before I would fall 350 feet down, just in time to see all of my friends' backs as they ran down the hallway. I was left by myself on the outside of the railing, and only then did it occur to me that maybe this wasn't too smart. But I still couldn't stop laughing as I climbed back over the railing. By the time I got to the elevator, they had already disappeared.

When I arrived down in the lobby, I saw Jack Bartholomew and Ken Grason sitting on a bench with their hands in their faces as if I was dead. Outside of the glass doors, I saw Griff Stelzner looking up at the sky as if he was ready to catch a pop fly. Sam Ice was at the guest services desk flailing his arms and talking frantically; his arms dropped to his side as he looked over his shoulder and saw me. When a security guard came into the lobby, we all ran in unison and didn't stop for several blocks. When we all caught up to each other, they burst out laughing. Jeff Roberts punched me in the shoulder and, as he laughed, said I was an idiot. It didn't occur to me then, but looking back now, I can say this was the start of my passion for stunts. The exhilaration I got from doing it, and the reaction I got from my friends, gave me a feeling that was addictive, to say the least. If I knew people got paid for that shit, I probably would have left high school to pursue a career in stunts. I wouldn't find that out for a long time, though.

BULLETS AND FIRE

While living on Kwaj, my parents and I would make a trip back to Sparks once a year to visit family and take care of some business, as they maintained ownership of their house. On those trips I would spend most of my time hanging out with my old troublemaker buddy, Tracy Morgan. Together we would cause more and more trouble. One summer he had a couple .22 caliber rifles. I was probably around 15 and loved going shooting, so we went into the hills behind his house and started shooting everything and anything we could. These rifles were cheaply made and terribly inaccurate. When it started to get boring, we would try to outdo each other by shooting at harder and harder targets. As this started to get boring, we saw someone down the hill off in the distance riding a dirt bike towards us... What a perfect opportunity.

Tracy bet me he could shoot closer to the guy than I could. I wasn't going to lose a bet, so I said *yes*. The first shot sent up a puff of dirt about five feet behind the guy. Second time, same thing. Tracy aimed his gun and shot twice, his shots landed in front of the kid about the same distance. Our shots kept hitting closer and closer. The guy saw *those* shots and panicked. He looked to the hills, didn't see us and hit the gas, which made us shoot faster. Shot after shot we both sent up puffs of dirt. With both of us shooting at the same time, there was no way to tell who it was who hit the guy, sending him off the bike.

As the guy lay on the ground, my heart stopped. I dropped the gun and sweat drenched my body. Tracy stood up, ducked back down and then yelled at me. *What the fuck is wrong with you!* We both started arguing at whose fault it was when the guy stood back up. We fell silent. *He's back from the fucking dead!* Tracy and I watched in awe as the guy kick-started the bike and rode away leaving a small dust trail behind him. I didn't touch his gun again after that.

The next day we were walking around town when we bumped into an old school friend of Tracy's. He was all frantic and went on to tell us a story about how someone was shooting at him from the hills the day before. His dad, who just happened to be the sheriff, was pissed and was looking for the shooter. He also went on to say that he was lucky to be alive. He said if he hadn't been wearing a helmet, that he would have been dead. He wanted to show us the bullet hole in the helmet, but his dad had it at the station as evidence. We promised to stop by and see it when he got it back. After talking to him, Tracy and I dipped into an alley and ran home, fearing the police were out searching for us. I was more than thankful that I was leaving in a day, but what a long day it was, sweating, waiting to be arrested. Though nothing ever came of it, I realize, even now, that it is on my list of the stupidest things I have ever done and probably ranks about number eight on the list.

The next year, on my annual visit home, Tracy and I once again were up to no good. Only this time we actually got caught. I would love to blame him for this one again, but I can't remember whose idea it was. We went to this empty parking lot where tractor trailers parked while in town. There was only one truck there at the time, Tracy's stepdad's. Being teens, we were fascinated by fire. With a pack of matches, we would light a match and flick it on the dry weeds. We'd watch it burn for a bit and then stomp it out. We figured the truck would keep us from the view of people driving by so we stayed close to it. Match after match, we lit a fire and kicked it out. Then one fire we let go a bit too long, and no matter how much we stomped, we could not put it out.

Within a second, the fire spread towards the truck, licked at the tires, and fought to climb up the truck. We kicked dirt, fanned our shirts at it, and even picked up handfuls of gravel and tossed it on the fire, but it was no use. Being gentlemen, we decided to run to a store and call the fire department instead of just running away and letting the thing burn. An hour later the truck was out, but practically destroyed. We got in some major trouble with our families, but the law let us off with a slap on the hands since we were minors and had apologized profusely.

I didn't make too many smart decisions as a kid, but for some reason I couldn't help it. I just always wanted to see how far I could push buttons before I blew something up. Thankfully where I was about to move didn't have many buttons to push.

KWAJ PLACEMENT

Growing up in Kwaj really affected my life, in a good way. The place was a protected paradise. Even if there wasn't much to do, it was wonderful. I love the place so much that I have subtly slipped it into countless movies of mine.

A lot of my fans know that Adam Green, the great director and writer of the *Hatchet* series and *Frozen*, graciously put Kwaj in all of his movies for me. In *Hatchet,* the tour guide says *that is Kwaj Island over there.* In *Hatchet II*, Beuchler's character mentions Kwaj Road. Adam even snuck it into *Frozen,* though even before Adam's movies, I have slipped Kwaj in here and there when I could. In *Jason X* the cryogenics chamber that I get frozen in has KWAJ written on the outside as if it is some acronym. In *B.T.K.* it is on Dennis' desk. In the *Chillerama* segment, *The Diary of Ann Frankenstein* where I play a Frankenstein type of monster, Joel Moore, playing Hitler, yells out, *Kwajalein!* There are numerous other little places you'll find the word in my movies, but I'll leave it up to you to find them, to make it more fun.

The only bad experience I have had in Kwaj was with a former classmate. He went from being just some guy I went to school with, to being an obsessive, lying, scary fan. In school, I hardly knew the guy. He had the locker beneath mine, but most of our contact was made when I would accidentally drop my books on his head. Other than that, we almost never spoke. Years later, when I became more well-known, he started to tell everyone what great friends we were, that we were buddies.

At a premiere for one of my films, I was walking the red carpet when I heard someone yelling *Kane, Kane! It's me, from Kwaj!* Of course hearing Kwaj got my attention. Going over to see who it was and remembering the guy, I brought him into the theater with me to watch the movie. We didn't sit near each other or even talk, but I figured us Kwaj kids should look out for each other, which is why I let him in. A few years later I went to a Kwaj reunion. About once a year they have a reunion in various places around the US where all Kwaj kids, regardless of what grade, get together (our classes were too small to just doing it by grades). I went to the reunion and people started talking about the guy and how we were such good friends. I told them we weren't really that close, but they would start to tell me stories about how this guy was on the sets of movies with me and how he used to visit me in the hospital when I was burned, all of which was a straight out lie—no one ever visited me in the hospital except for my immediate family.

At first I was annoyed at this guy making up stories, but I figured he just wanted the attention, so I ignored them. Then later that night, someone asked me about how they replaced my nipples after I got burned. I didn't know what they were talking about so I asked them to repeat the question. They said that this guy, who will remain nameless, told them how they had to reconstruct my nipples with skin from my anus. I was shocked and pissed. Where did this guy get off making up these fucking stories about me? Especially crazy ones like that. Everyone at that party thought I had ass nipples!

I never really got to confront the guy about it, but it really bothered me—the fact that someone would just make up stories for who knows what reason. I understand about being insecure, trust me, but I would never make up stories about other people just to get them to like me or something. The guy pissed me off so much I stopped going to the reunions for a while. Other than that one incident, Kwaj has been great to me. I'll always be sure to give it props in all of my movies, so keep an eye out for the nod to the slice of heaven where I grew up.

A NEW HOME AT THE ROACH MOTEL

The years slipped by on our peaceful island without much incident. We were a happy family; had good friends and a great life on our own piece of heaven, but like always, all good things come to an end.

Most people never want to leave the island; it's too beautiful and cheap to leave—hell, why would you want to leave a place where you paid no taxes, didn't fear crime, and could lounge on a beach any day you wanted? In fact, some of my classmates are still on the island to this day.

Really, I never thought much about leaving the island, but my high school graduation just happened to coincide with the end of my father's assignment, the work was done, so it was time to move on.

My graduating class had 47 students, and to my knowledge, the biggest in the island's history (it is now around 19 students a year). For years my world existed of nothing but the island and my friends. I didn't want to leave, but staying really wasn't an option. College was in my future, but before I went, I wanted to take some time off from school and get a closer look at what my father did for a living. Therefore, I decided to follow my parents to the location of his next assignment, which just happened to be another island, only…this one wasn't as modern as Kwaj.

KANE WARREN HODDER

KANE alias "Doc," alias "Hank," alias "Bosco," has lived on Kwaj. for five years. He is an active member of the French National Honor Society and the Lettermen's Club. He enjoys mountainball, golf, and football. His home town is Reno, Nevada and he plans to attend college after high school.

Kwajalein High School - Senior Yearbook

A few months after graduation, we arrived in American Samoa. We flew into Pago Pago and then took a tugboat seven hours to our new home on the island of Ofu. The island had no port or docks for large boats, which was why my father was there. He was to work on putting in a port so boats didn't have to drop anchor a half-mile off shore, which they had to do because it was too shallow to get any closer. The big boats would drop anchor in the deep waters and wait for large canoes, called longboats, to row out and take the passengers ashore. Resting my forearms on the sticky steel of the boat, I watched the longboats row towards us. The island looked desolate, like a jungle from some B movie I saw back on Kwaj.

Ofu Island
Arrow Points to Where We Lived

Ofu Island
Arrow Points to Where We Lived

I started to wonder if I had made the right decision to go with my parents. I could have stayed on the island with my friends or gone back to America for college like my parents wanted. When I saw that the longboats were filled with big, mean-looking, shirtless Samoans, I was sure I had made the wrong decision.

Rocky Beach, Ofu Island

Through a small door on one of the lower decks, the crew handed out all of my family's belongings to the natives. I watched silently from above, as I would get in the way down on the deck. Canoe after canoe floated away with my family's luggage and furniture. When I watched the crew try to handle and load our refrigerator onto the tiny canoe, I couldn't help but laugh out loud. One of the men glared up at me with such sharp eyes, I swore I felt them punch me. Here I was, a 140-pound white boy with long hair; I must have looked like some punk to him. Embarrassed, I backed away from the railing. After a few minutes I dared another look over. The canoe with the fridge was heading back to the island, the lip of the boat dangerously close the water as it bobbed back and forth. I wanted to see the boat tip over, to pay the man back for the glare he gave me, but at the same time, I wanted nothing more than for that fridge to make it to dry land. I couldn't believe it when my father told me that we had to take our fridge because they didn't have many on the island. The thought of not having cold food made me hold my breath until they got safely to shore.

When it was our turn to get into the longboat, I didn't want to. I wanted to stay in the boat and go back to Kwaj. The Samoan who rowed our boat had his back to us. I was amazed that he wasn't sweating when I was dripping wet just sitting there. As we approached the shore, a line of what could have been our rower's twin brothers stood stoic waiting for us. They didn't want us there, and I knew it. As the boat hit the sand, four of the monstrous guys ran over and pulled the boat farther onto the beach so we could get out. I was ready for more piercing looks, maybe some comments about how they didn't want us, but instead, I was greeted by bearlike handshakes and smiles which made me laugh. The men introduced themselves, helped us with our luggage, and started to tell us about the island in voices that made me know that we were more than welcome.

Unfortunately the joy of being welcomed wore off a little when I saw our "living quarters." We were to be temporarily housed in the old missionary dispensary building while they built us a new home. Having been built to house sick people, our living area was laid out like a letter H. The center was a small sitting area that used to have a desk and a small kitchen; then off to each side was a long skinny room with a bed at one end and a tiny bathroom at the other. As we first walked in, none of us spoke. I could tell Dad was trying to think up some positive thing to say; in fact, he opened his mouth and got out *Well...* just as a giant cockroach scurried across our feet. The Samoans bringing in our stuff didn't seem to notice or really care about it. Looking at my mother, I saw herself fanning her face, a forced smile on it.

"It's only temporary," Dad said. As I walked to one side of the tiny building, I looked around and realized, with horror, that there was no air-conditioning. In fact, the entire building was open to the air; only a thin screen and a squeaky screen door kept the bugs out or, depending on how you looked at it, the cockroaches in.

During that first night I had a hard time sleeping. The heat had subsided, but the humidity was so strong it felt like a wet blanket draped over me. I thought about taking a shower, but I hated the idea of standing under the bare pipe that shot out only cold water. Instead, I stared at the grimy ceiling and the broken fan with one single blade above me. Every once in a while it would move slightly from some unseen and unfelt breeze. *I should have stayed on Kwaj or gone to college in the States* I kept telling myself over and over again. After a few hours, with exhaustion pulling at my consciousness, I tried to tell myself that I would get used to the heat and that the island might not be that bad— after all, I had only seen a fraction of it. Then, just as I started to drift off for the first time, I heard my mother scream.

As my feet hit the floor I felt a crunch, but I ignored it—my mother was in trouble. After two more steps I felt another crunch, then another. By the time I made it to the lobby area of the dispensary I had to stop; whatever I was stepping on hurt my feet and was gooey. Thankfully the light came on from my parents' side; it gave me just enough light to see the brownish splatters on my bare feet. *What the hell?* I scraped the bottoms of my feet on the wood floor and carefully took the last few steps to my parents' room.

"What's going on?" I asked as I saw tiny dark spots scurrying away in every direction. My dad sat on the edge of the bed keeping his feet a foot off the ground. Mom was standing on one foot in her nightgown with that fake smile, once again, plastered on her face.

"Guess we have cockroaches... lots of them." I lifted my foot to look at it again. My stomach churned a bit as I realized that I had just crushed a few dozen bugs.

"It'll be fine, Son, we'll get something to...keep them away from the beds and the toilets tomorrow," Mom said as she gritted her teeth, grabbed a washcloth, and wiped off the bottom of her feet.

The next morning I couldn't help but examine the big crusty splotches that made a direct line from my bed to my parents' room. As I slowly walked next to the parade of dead bugs, I found one partially intact. I couldn't believe my eyes, it was huge, and at least three times the size of any cockroach I had ever seen. The thought of one of them crawling over me at night gave me the creeps. Thankfully, my mom found some chemical powder that killed them. The only pain was you had to make a line of the powder around everything you wanted to keep them out of. It was like some sort of voodoo ritual. Each night we had to take the box and pour a long line around our beds and to the toilets so we could get up and go to the bathroom in peace at night. The only problem was, each morning we'd wake up and find dozens of dead roaches along the powder lines that we'd have to scoop up and throw outside. It was a new life and going to take some getting used to.

THE SHIRTLESS WONDER

It took a while, and it was hard, but we slowly got used to the island. The worst part for me was that I had nothing, and I mean nothing, to do. There was no TV, no other kids my age; I was out of school, yet I wasn't allowed to work. I spent the days just wandering around throwing rocks into the ocean and trying to occupy my time with something, anything, every day. I adjusted to the heat by not wearing a shirt, ever. It was around the second week of living there that I realized wearing a shirt was useless because it would be soaked by sweat by eight in the morning; therefore, I wore no shirt. There was one stretch of over four months that I did not put one on. Ever. Not even once. The only reason I put a shirt on after four months was because we were invited to one of the Chief's houses for dinner. That night I sat, itching and scratching my body as I had become accustomed to nothing being on my skin. It was hard to get used to.

During that long stretch of shirtlessness, I became more conscious of my body for the first time. Growing up I was normal, a bit on the skinny side, but an average teen. Being in American Samoa, I felt like a twig. The men there were all massive, strong, and thick. Being one of only 12 white people on the whole island, I stuck out like sore thumb. Being self-conscious and bored beyond belief, I started to work out. I had nothing but time on my hands, so why not work on my body? Not really knowing what to do, I ordered some issues of Joe Weider's *Muscle Builder Magazine* (which eventually turned into the *Muscle & Fitness* that you see today). Using the magazine's tips and what knowledge I had from my old high school gym class, I started my own workout routine.

The routine started with pull-ups, push-ups, and sit-ups. I had to use a tree branch for the pull-ups. As I started to get a bit stronger, I added in curls, though not having any weights, I had to be creative. I took a broomstick and filled a bucket with sand. I would then put the stick through the bucket's handle and lift it. I would do different variations of this to hit different parts of my arms. When I noticed the first signs of muscles beginning to form on my body, I got even more ambitious. I started eating everything I could. At meals I would force myself to choke down plate after plate of whatever was on the table until I could eat no more. *I needed to gain weight.*

In one of the magazines I saw an ad for Joe Weider's weight gain supplement. I mailed off an order for it and waited...and waited. Mail on the island was horribly slow. We'd only get it once a week by boat, along with the groceries that we ordered. Every week on mail day, I would go down to the dock and do push-ups as I waited for the tugboat to arrive. As the longboat came in, I would splash through the water and ask for the mail before it even got to the beach. Every time, the big Samoans would laugh at me and say there was nothing. Then finally, after almost two months, the supplement arrived. It was wrapped in brown paper and had customs stamps all over it. Tucking it in my arm like a football, I ignored all the rest of the mail and ran back to our house to take my first dose.

Breathing heavily, I could hear my mom laugh at me as I tore open the package. Underneath the brown paper, I saw a man flexing his enormous muscles, with the tag line of *Gain a Pound a Day!* (By the way, it was a young Arnold Schwarzenegger on the label). Without delay I followed the directions and mixed up a glass. With one last look at the muscular man, I swallowed down the chalky, foul-tasting concoction, knowing I'd look like him soon. Finishing the glass I stood there as if waiting to transform like some sort of Dr. Jekyll/Mr. Hyde universal monster. Of course it did nothing in that moment. I was about to mix up another glass when my mother kindly reminded me that it took months for me to get that one and I should make it last. Reluctantly I put the canister away and ran outside to do another set of pull-ups.

In my boredom, working out had become my obsession. No longer was I going to be the skinny kid who got teased for his size, no longer was I going to be that kid who anyone could beat up—I was a man now. Every meal, I ate until I thought I would throw up, hoping to put on weight. The eating, the weight gain along with the working out... worked. After only six months on the island, I put on over 25 pounds of muscle. That discipline I taught myself on the island has lasted through my entire life. Working out wasn't just a fad or something I did to kill time. It became a daily way of life, to keep myself healthy and fit, especially in a stunt career.

Without friends, television, stores, theaters, or basically ANYTHING, time ticked by slowly on Ofu. The only excitement on the island was the weekly telecast of wrestling. Being there were only several televisions on the island, all the natives would go to the local schoolhouse, which was open air. They would put on the TV, turn it towards the outdoors, and everyone would sit in the sand and watch the matches. For some reason the big guys loved watching the matches. They especially loved watching Peter Maivia wrestle, who was an American Samoan himself. The natives would go nuts for him. Everyone would jump up and hoot and holler during his matches. He was one of them, and every time he slammed someone against the mat, it was like he was doing it for everyone on the islands.

Being that these community-wrestling outings were one of the only sources of entertainment, I looked forward to them and loved watching the matches. I would cheer and root for the *High Chief* along with all the others. Many years later, I would find out that Maivia was the grandfather of The Rock, Dwayne Johnson. When I met Dwayne, I told him how I used to watch his grandfather's matches from American Samoa; he seemed to really get a kick out of it.

The other nights of the week, when there was no wrestling, I would go to the beach and walk around. One of the first nights I was there, I saw these massive black objects flying above me. They dipped and dived, freaking me out. I started to run back to our house when I ran into one of the natives; he saw that I was a bit shaken and stopped me. I explained to him that there were these giant monsters flying around by the shore—he laughed at me, patted me on the back, and walked me back to the shore.

With his arm around my shoulders he pointed at the winged monsters in the sky and said, "Pe'a, they are a type of bat, one of the biggest, six-foot wing span, face like a dog. Samoan history says that Nafanua, the goddess of war, was rescued by these *flying foxes* when she was stranded on an inhospitable island. They are good-natured, only eat fruit and bugs. Nothing to worry about little palagi." With that, he patted me on the back and walked away. I was getting used to being called *palagi*, which was Samoan for a white man. Usually it annoyed me because I thought they meant it as a slang term, but this time, it was said with such care that I actually liked being called it. Knowing more about these creatures, I felt more comfortable, but I still couldn't help but duck when they swooped down. Eventually I sat down in the sand and watched them until the sun had completely set over the horizon.

Dwayne "The Rock" Johnson

The next night I went and watched them again. They moved so fast I wondered if I could hit one with a rock. I picked up a small stone and tossed it at the swarm, and I missed. I tried again, and this time the rock went right at one of the beasts, but the pe'a swerved at the last second, sending the rock whizzing by it. I didn't want to hurt the thing; it was just a way to occupy time—hell, they were so big I didn't think a rock would even hurt them, so I kept trying. Rock after rock, I missed the giant flying creatures. I kept trying until the sun went down, and I couldn't see them anymore. I was so frustrated that I couldn't hit one that I went back the next night and the next. It became my nightly hobby and entertainment. And for you animal lovers out there, don't worry, I was never able to hit one of those bastards.

It was during one of those long rock-throwing sessions that I realized I needed to leave the island. Throwing rocks at freakishly huge bats was not going to get me anywhere in life. I needed an education. When I told my parents that I was ready to leave and go to school, I was greeted with teary hugs. At first I thought it was because they didn't want me to leave, but then I realized it was because they were so happy that I wanted to go to college. That was all they ever wanted, for me to get a good college education. They also must have planned this all along, for that very night my father pulled out brochures for the University of Nevada, Reno. It was one of the schools that I had been accepted to earlier in the year. In fact, I'm proud to say that I was accepted to 100% of the colleges that I applied to...BOTH of them. I know, I didn't really put myself out there too much, but hell, I knew what I wanted. The other college I got into was the University of Hawaii. We still had the house in Sparks, so Reno was a better fit.

Maps had always fascinated me. Even now, give me a map and I can look at it for hours. There is just something about mapping out the lines of the earth, elevation, lakes, and roads. At that time in my life, it was the only real passion I had. Therefore, I decided to go to school for cartography. After being with my parents for so long, it was hard, really hard saying goodbye, especially since I couldn't do much to contact them on the island besides writing letters. The day I left, half of the island came to say goodbye; it was nice, but I really wanted to be alone with my parents. Even when I got on the tugboat to leave, half of the natives stood on the shore to say farewell. I don't necessarily think they cared about me leaving; I was the crazy palagi who threw rocks at the bats, after all. I think it was a gesture to thank my father for helping the island out.

As I watched the tiny island shrink in the horizon, I was excited, yet heartbroken. A new chapter in my life was beginning, but at the same time, I didn't want to leave my parents and the only life I ever knew.

BACK TO CIVILIZATION

After a full day of traveling by air, water, and land, I was back in America. The first few hours back felt like a giant explosion in my mind. Going from not wearing shoes or shirts in the jungle to the bright lights and cars of the *Biggest Little City in the World* was disorientating. I took in the sights, the joy of riding in a car, and even the noise like a starving man devouring a buffet. I wanted to see and feel everything. Part of me worried that I was going to overload, that it would be too much to take in, but after a mere few hours... it all wore off and it was like I had never left.

My first semester started in January, being that I decided to start late. When I arrived on campus, I was a bit creeped out, but thrilled at the same time, to find out my assigned roommate had died of a drug overdose. The happy part was because it meant that I had the dorm room to myself the entire semester.

As the semester began, I did well in classes and I dated off and on. The grades I got were good, but nothing special. I was enjoying the geography and cartography courses and life seemed pretty normal as the months ticked by. That summer, my parents even came back to Reno. The job in Ofu was done; my father took the opportunity to retire. I ended up moving back in with them to save money on dorm costs. My parents never did have too much money. Though the house was small, it was nice being back with them, even if I was getting older.

During that first summer break, I got a job doing maintenance in a nursing home. The title of "maintenance" might have been an over-glamorous title considering most of the times I ended up scrubbing old people's toilets with a pumice stone, without gloves. Great fucking job. It earned me some money, though, and that is all that really mattered to me at that time. Stock up enough money so I could get through the school year. When I went back to school after summer break, I couldn't have been happier—no more Tuesday "mystery meat" splatters to clean up every day.

The second semester was going well, though I was failing my ass out of French Honors. I had aced French back in Kwaj, but this was a whole new level that I didn't care to achieve. One day while dreading going to French class, I saw a flyer in the dorm hallway. *Extras needed for movie filming in Reno!* The idea of getting to be in a movie *and* missing French was too good to pass up. I hopped on my borrowed ten-speed bike (even with all the shit I cleaned I still couldn't afford a car) and headed down to the strip where they were filming.

I was nervous when I arrived. I didn't think they would let me in—they were filming in a casino, and I wasn't old enough to be in one yet. It didn't matter, though; I signed up and they threw me into the casino and told me to look natural. After whispering to another extra, I found out the movie was called *California Split*. As they set up the cameras and lights I watched in awe like a kid seeing Mickey Mouse for the first time. I had to keep reminding myself to shut up and not talk, especially when George Segal and Elliot Gould walked onto set. They were the first real celebrities I ever saw. Their presence, along with the hot lights, made my face flush with joy. *This was a cool life* I thought to myself. Though I was there for countless hours, was treated like shit, and made hardly enough money to buy dinner, I loved every second of it.

That day was my first taste of Hollywood, though at the time, after I left and told all of my friends about it, I didn't think about having a career in the industry. I went back to the books and learned more about how to map the earth. That is until I took a trip out to California to visit a friend.

THE WILD WEST...HOLLYWOOD

After my third semester of college during summer break, I went out to California to visit an old friend of mine whom I graduated high school with on Kwaj, Mike Cutchshaw. Being almost 19 at the time, the thought of taking a trip on my own to see my old buddy and to get to go to Hollywood was more than exciting. Mike had been living out there for two years at the time, so he wasn't too much into the whole tourist thing, but I made him show me the sites anyway. Being young and in love with movies made the town all that more magical. Back on Kwaj, Hollywood couldn't have seemed farther away.

Mike drove, bored, as we went on our own tour of the stars' homes. House after house that we drove by, I'd slap Mike on the shoulder and say something stupid about how I couldn't believe we were outside of so-and-so's house. I truly was fascinated by the lives of the people I had watched for most of my youth. Thankfully, Mike put up with me and kept showing me around. On one of the days, we walked down the Hollywood Walk of Fame, stopping and looking at each star, taking pictures. As we were about to leave I remember walking over one last marker and looking down. It was Boris Karloff. Seeing his star, I bent down and touched it, thinking back to how much I enjoyed his movies. As a kid, the local outdoor theater in Kwaj would play the Frankenstein movies every now and then; supposedly, one of the military higher ups loved Karloff. Unlike the other kids my age, I wasn't scared of the big monster on the screen, I thought he was...cool. One particular Halloween I even dressed up as Frankenstein's monster; I remember trying to walk like him for days before, until I got it just right. My mother told me how good of a monster I made…little did we know.

Mike was tired of showing me around all the "tourist" stuff. He wanted to show me the beaches and try to pick up some chicks. Though it was tempting, I couldn't leave Hollywood without going to Universal Studios. I begged him to take me—I told him that if he did, the rest of the week we could hang at the beach. Thankfully, he caved in. In the park I did my best to act cool and not like an excited little kid as we ran from ride to ride and show to show. While watching the *Animal Actors School*, the two of us got bored and left the show just in time to see the *Wild West Show*'s doors closing. As we ran in, the show was just about to start. The green seats in the stadium were packed, but we found two a few rows from the front. Not caring about the people who had been sitting and waiting a half hour to see the show, we crowded our way through the aisle and took our seats.

I had just enough time to catch my breath and to take in the set before the show started. It reminded me of the set of *Bonanza*, one of my favorites as a kid. There were three Old West-looking buildings, an old hotel and general store on each end, and the *Silver Slipper Saloon* in the middle of the outdoor set. Barrels and bales of hay were on the sides; old horse carts, props, and all sorts of other things were set out. Looking at Mike with a big smile, I could tell he was excited as well—this was going to be cool. Little did I know… this stunt show was going to change my life.

Guns fired, people fell, flipped, fought, got dragged through the dirt, things exploded, the audience clapped, and the actors were getting paid to do this! When the show ended and the crowd applauded, something in my mind clicked. All the stupid things I did in my youth to make my friends laugh flashed before my eyes. I did shit like this all the time to make people laugh. These guys got paid to do it! *I could do this... I had to.* Mike turned to me and said something about how cool the show was, but I ignored him. I had my eyes on the actors who were hanging around the exit, shaking people's hands and taking pictures. I *had* to talk to them—I *had* to find out how to do what they did.

Racing down to meet the actors, I left Mike behind me wondering what I was doing. After a group in front of me took a picture, I darted in and shook each of the four actor's hands. Their western costumes were dusty, and they had sweat on their brows—I was jealous. I wanted to be sweating from falling off a roof. Like a kid, I rambled on about how amazing the show was. More people came in for pictures, but I was able to pull one of them aside to talk for a bit. After introducing myself, I found out his name was Kent Hays. I told him that I wanted to...no—needed—to be a stuntman. He laughed for a second, which told me that probably every 12-year-old boy who saw the show told him that, but when he looked in my eyes, his tone changed; he could tell I was serious.

"Well, there is a stunt school in Santa Monica. If you go there, you'll get the training you'll need to do stunts, though there is no guarantee that you'll become a stuntman. You'll have to prove yourself first." I instantly told him that I would, that I was going to be a stuntman no matter what. He smiled at me, patted me on the shoulder, and sauntered off to take a few more pictures with the dwindling crowd. Kent, himself, left the live shows after a while and moved on to do stunts in dozens of major films like *The Goonies*, *Big Trouble in Little China*, and *The Thing*.

From the second I learned about the stunt school, it was all I could think about. Though I still loved maps, I no longer wanted to go to school to learn how to make them. My entire trip home from California, all I could think about was how to tell my parents that I was going to stop going to college to go to "stunt school." Amazingly, they took it better than I thought they would. My mother seemed to hold back some tears, but my father seemed alright with it, though I think he was only alright with it because he thought it wouldn't last. In fact, he made me promise to him.

"Listen Doc, you do this. You do what you have to. But you promise me, if this doesn't work out that you'll go right back to school. You got it?" I agreed with a handshake and a hug and started packing my bags to go back to California. I was going to take one semester off of college, try out stunt school, and see what happened. Though I'm sure my parents thought I would be back in school in a matter of months, I was confident that I had found my true calling in life.

A KILLER IN TRAINING

After making a lot of phone calls I found another old classmate of mine from Kwaj, Freddy Baca, who lived in California, in east L.A. He was fine with me staying with him, as long as we split the rent. I was going to have to pay a whopping $62.50 a month. It was East Los Angeles, after all, not the safest place in L.A., but it didn't matter. Sadly, without having a job and having spent most my savings getting out to L.A., I couldn't afford the measly sum. It didn't matter though; I took the first step and made it out there. I'd find a way to pay for the rent—at least I told myself that. We ended up always being broke and even resorted to things like adding water to the milk to make it last longer. Many nights it was peanut butter for dinner. No bread. Just peanut butter.

The morning after arriving, I woke up stiff from sleeping on a couch half my size, yet I was ready to go down to the school. I finally had a car at this point, so I made the long drive over to Santa Monica. I was so excited to join the school, I foolishly hadn't thought about how much it was going to cost. The fact that I couldn't come up with $60 to pay the rent should have given me the first clue that I wasn't going to be able to afford the classes.

Meeting the owner, I told him how much I wanted to join. He sat me down, showed me the prices, and I just clammed up. He must have seen the panic and determination in my face, because when I told him I couldn't afford that much, he scratched his nose, looked around and told me, "Listen, the

East Los Angeles Apartment

classes are on Monday, Wednesday, and Friday

The people who are in the classes train here on the off days as well. They pretty much practice every day. Why don't you join the gym? It's only a few bucks. That way, you can come on the off days and see what you can learn from them. Then, when you make some money, you can join the class officially."

Without even answering, I stood up and shook the man's hand. I had a few dollars hidden in my pocket from my roommate that I was saving to eat dinner with, but I didn't care. I whipped it out and paid for several weeks of the gym in advance.

The next day, I was standing outside of the gym doors an hour before they opened. I was so anxious to get in there and learn, I couldn't help but be early—that and I wanted to make a good impression on the "real" students in the class. When the doors opened, I hurried in and looked around. There was a boxing ring and a lot of boxing stuff, but also a large area of mats. Next to it was a large ladder and a foam pad. The idea of climbing up and falling down had me drooling. Of course you weren't supposed to touch some of the equipment without permission, so I headed to the mats and started to stretch out as I waited for the stunt people to show up. I didn't have to wait long.

Within a few minutes two men and a woman walked over to the mats and threw down some bags. I didn't even wait for them to start stretching, I introduced myself, told them I wanted to be in the school but couldn't afford it, and that I wanted to learn whatever they'd be so gracious to show me. Thankfully, they didn't tell me to get lost; in fact, they seemed rather enthusiastic about teaching someone what they already learned. Really, not being able to afford the class was almost better. Paul Stader, the guy who ran the school, was an old time stuntman, a legend really. He used to double Tarzan in all of the old movies. Being up in his years though, he didn't have the enthusiasm the students did. Getting taught how to do the stunts with people just as excited as I was helped me get a better grip on the craft.

The three students soon became good friends of mine: Tom Morga, Dennis Madalone, and Leslie Hoffman, all of whom went on to great careers. Dennis went on to do work on the *Star Trek* movies and *Pulp Fiction*, along with dozens of others. Oddly enough, Tom went on to play Jason Voorhees in *Friday the 13th Part V!* And Leslie went on to be a fantastic stuntwoman and coordinator, along with being the hall guard in *Nightmare on Elm Street.*

My Long Hair

Obviously, what we all learned at this school worked since we all still have very successful careers in the industry.

They started off teaching me small things—how to fall properly (from just standing up), how to throw and receive fake punches, do shoulder rolls, and other things that required only a mat. Having the desire and very little fear, I was able to pick up the moves rather quickly. We then progressed on to harder things like how to fall down the stairs. Being that the stairs were metal, this was much scarier than falling on the mats, especially since you always hear about people falling down stairs and breaking bones, or worse, their neck and dying. I learned how to tuck my head and roll just right so you hit non-vital, safer parts of your body. When I had finally worked my way up to falling from the top of the stairs, I wanted to keep doing it, even if it did make me a bit dizzy. Oddly enough, it turns out that the faster you roll down a flight of stairs, the less damage it does to your body.

The high falls, on the other hand, were not as scary for me—they were thrilling. There is just something about falling through the air, landing, and being able to get right back up…when normally, you'd be in the hospital or dead. To practice the high falls, there was a ladder we would climb up and then jump from into the foam pad. The pad itself was sort of small, only six feet by eight feet, meaning if you were just a bit off, you were going to crack a body part on the hard floor edge. They had me start off small—step on the first rung and fall. Work your way up to the second, and so on. They taught me the proper way to land to correctly absorb the impact. High falls are all about how you land, no matter how much padding you fall into. If you land wrong, you can be in for a whole world of hurt. After mastering, or so I thought, the proper ways to fall, I worked up to the sixth and seventh rungs of the ladder. I was comfortable doing them; in fact, I enjoyed it. I wanted to work my way up higher, but they made me do only two rungs a day, working my way up slowly.

Finally, I reached the top rung, the one right before the platform. Without hesitating, I did my fall and landed perfectly. It was now time to go to the top. I wasn't nervous; I was excited to finally conquer the highest jump. Standing on the platform above the ladder for the first time, it suddenly seemed all different to me. Even though I was only a foot higher than my last fall, it felt like a mile higher being off the ladder. For the first time, I was nervous. I was 30 feet above the pad, and just to put this into reference, most falls over 20 feet are deadly. Now, I'm pretty tall; the pit was only eight feet long, and that left only a foot and a half or so of leeway, meaning if I was off by a foot one way or the other, I would crack some body part. It could have been that thought or my nerves, but on that fall, I over-rotated just a bit too much, my chin jammed into my chest, putting way too much pressure on my neck.

There was a flash of light, pain, and worst of all… embarrassment. I could still move, which told me nothing was broken, but it wasn't good. Climbing off the pad I gave a sheepish look to the others; they all knew I landed wrong, but they didn't say anything. As I rolled my neck to stretch it out I gave them a light nod to show I was alright, but I was done for the day. Back in the apartment I iced my neck as it stiffened up. I was angry with myself for screwing up. The anger and pain made me one cranky fuck to deal with, especially since I didn't have health insurance and couldn't go to the doctor to get it checked out. The next day, getting out of bed was a chore. I was so stiff, and my neck hurt so much, I gave up on trying to sit up and stayed in bed an extra two hours. Regardless of the pain and stiffness, I forced myself to get up the day after and got my ass back in that gym. I might have taken things a bit easy, but I was there. Sadly, to this day I have some neck problems, but never having had another injury there, I can't help but think it was caused by that fall.

Slowly but surely I got a good grasp on the basic stunts I needed to know. When they couldn't teach me anymore, I felt I was ready to move on… to the industry.

BREAKING THROUGH
THE STEEL DOOR

With my new-found knowledge of stunts and a sore neck, I felt I was ready to try to break into the industry. Little did I know how hard it is to accomplish. To do stunts in a movie or a television show you have to be in the Screen Actors Guild (SAG). You cannot be in a production without being in SAG and at the same time, you can't get a SAG card unless you are in a production. A classic Catch 22. In the late '70s, the industry was run differently than it is today. Now, you can get "vouchers": work as an extra on certain films or have tiny bit parts, and you can get a voucher. You can even buy some vouchers. Get enough vouchers and you're in. Back then, it wasn't that simple. You pretty much had to get a role or know someone to get into SAG. Not being an actor, I couldn't just audition for a role. I had to prove my chops somehow… or make a connection.

Six months solid, I beat the pavement, meeting anyone and everyone I could in the industry, trying desperately to make the one contact that would get me in. If I wasn't out trying to meet people, I was making phone calls all day to every studio and producer I could find in the phone book. Still, nothing. I was too in love with the industry at this point to give up. Unfortunately, I was set to go back to school in a few weeks. Regardless if I made a contact or not before I had to go back, I knew I wasn't going back to school. Hollywood had sucked me in, and I wasn't going to give up. But I did need some money and I had to tell my parents that I wasn't going back to school, so I planned a trip to Sparks.

My parents were happy to see me home; unfortunately, I had to ruin the homecoming by telling them that I was giving up on college for good. I didn't want to beat around the bush, so I told them a mere five minutes after walking in the door. My father's face dropped a bit and he started to nod; my mother pouted her lips.

"It's a stupid decision. But you do what you have to. Just remember that you can always go back to school." With that, my father walked out of the room. All he ever wanted for me was to get a good education, since he had only an eighth-grade education. I felt like I was failing him, but at the same time it motivated me more to succeed, to show him I could make a living as a stuntman, even if I had yet to make a dime. My mother on the other hand, kissed me on the cheek, patted my hand, and sighed deeply. She didn't have anything to add to my father's statement. Later that night, I overheard them talking in their room, my father repeating to my mother, though I think more to himself, *It'll wear off, he'll go back to school, he'll go back... he'll go back.*

California was expensive for a 20-year-old jobless kid. While I was home, I worked my ass off to save up what I could so I didn't have to work while I was out there trying to break into the industry. During my short time in Hollywood, I met a few dozen people who moved out there to work in the industry, who ended up working several jobs just to get by. They worked so much just to pay the bills that they never had time to audition or go on interviews. Little by little, their lives slipped past, and they never made it in the industry. I didn't want that to happen to me, so I worked every second I could while I was in Sparks. My old friend, Tracy, would get me work at his step-father's flower warehouse whenever I needed it. It was hard work, sweeping floors, boxing flowers, and loading trucks. They were long sweat-filled hours, but I gave it all I had and worked every second I could—I *had* to make money. I wouldn't let myself become just another dreamer who never made it.

After a few weeks my mother saw how hard I was working. I think she realized how determined I was to get back to California, to get my SAG card, and start working because one day she offered some help.

"Kane, my old friend's son is the mayor of Burbank. Would that help at all? I don't know anything about the business, but any connections in the town would be helpful, no?" Most of the major studios were in Burbank, but I had no clue how active the mayor was with them, but it was worth a shot.

"That would be great, Mom, give her a call." She smiled, almost as if she was blushing, I could tell she was proud of being able to help me.

A few weeks and a lot of long days of working in the flower warehouse later, I was back in California, getting ready to meet the mayor of Burbank. Never underestimate the power of a mom. My mother made the call, and the mayor's mother *made* him meet with me. I'm sure the mayor of some big city didn't want to meet with some young punk who wanted to be a stuntman, but he did it; I'm sure, to make his mother happy. The mayor was Lee Ayers. Personally, not having been in the town long enough, I didn't know anything about him, but sure enough, he had pull *and* friends in the industry.

The meeting, if you would call it that, was less than three minutes. The entire time I was in his office, he had the phone in his hand and a pen in the other. He was busy to say the least. Though he was multitasking, I still felt that he was genuinely listening to everything I said. I told him that I wanted to break into stunts, that I was trained in the field, and that I knew I could do it. As I rambled, he stared at me, nodding, the phone in his hand inches away from his ear. Starting to ramble on about the stunts I knew how to do, he held up his pen to silence me.

"I'll see what I can do, shouldn't be too hard. Expect a phone call." With that I offered my hand to shake but he was already talking into the phone. I raced back to the apartment as if the phone call would come that quickly. While the call wouldn't come that day, I didn't have to wait too long for it.

Two days after our meeting, the phone rang. It was a producer named Neil Maffeo. He worked on the very popular series, *The Waltons*.

"I heard you want to do a Taft Hartley," he said in a light tone as if he was asking me if I wanted a loaf of bread. The question horrified me. I didn't know what a Taft Hartley was.

"Yes, sir. Yes I do. Anything I can do to get my SAG card, sir," I said, hoping to God that I wasn't agreeing to something odd.

"Great, I'll send over some contracts, hire you for a new show called *Hunter*, though you won't have to do any actual work on it; it'll just get you in. (This was not the popular Fred Dryer series; it was way before that, starring James Franciscus.) Welcome to the industry, kid." Before I could even say thank you, the phone disconnected. Hanging up, I screamed a guttural yell of joy. Somehow, my mother, a retired school cafeteria worker all the way in Sparks, Nevada, did what I couldn't do for months in the town I lived in. After calming down, I picked up the phone, called my mother, and thanked her over and over again.

A courier came a few days later with a contract from the studio for me to sign. Seeing the studio's name, my name, and the TV show *Hunter* on a piece of paper, I couldn't believe it. The courier, used to doing hundreds of these, gave me a look that said to get over the excitement and sign the damn thing already. With a quick signature, I was officially hired on to work on the show. Unfortunately, I wasn't going to get to *actually* work on the show. The deal was I wouldn't do a thing. I even ended up getting paid for "working" on the show even though I never left my apartment. Since I got paid for *working* on the show, I was able to receive my SAG card. I got into the union through a matter of favors, winks, and handshakes. I would have much rather earned my stripes, but it didn't matter—being in the union meant that I could now get work. And that was all that mattered.

The only hard part about getting into the union was paying the union fees. Six hundred dollars up front, another financial burden I wasn't expecting. Not being able to afford my $60-a-month rent, having to pay $600 was like asking for a million. There was no way I could come up with it on my own, so I had to swallow my pride and ask my parents. It killed me to do so, because they were both retired and didn't have much money to begin with, but they knew how much it meant to me, so they scraped it together and helped me out. With the $600 in my hand, I paid my dues, and became a member of the Screen Actors Guild. With my SAG card, there was no way I was going back to school. After borrowing the money from my parents, I think they expected it, but it didn't make it any easier telling them I was not going back to school…again. I was starting a new chapter in my life, and school was not part of it.

Though I actually never met Neil Maffeo, I called him on a regular basis and left messages telling him I was ready to work and how grateful I was for him helping me get my card. Then one day he actually called me back. There was a producer on the television show *Emergency!* who was looking for a stuntman to do a small stunt. Personally, I think Neil just wanted me off his back, so he asked the producer to take me on, but I didn't care how I got it, I had my first *real gig*.

EMERGENCY!

Over the phone I was given a quick rundown about the stunt I was supposed to do on *Emergency!* Basically, all it called for me to do was… lay down and not move. I was to be an oil rig worker who got caught in an explosion and knocked out, the twist being I was stuck on top of a tower with another worker. The bottom of the tower was on fire, so there was no way out for us. That's where the *Emergency!* cast came in. They were to be on another tower, throw a wire over, and hook up a Stokes Basket and pull it across. My character, being unconscious, was to be lifted onto the basket and pulled across to the other tower. Even though they explained the stunt to me, and that I knew I didn't really have to do anything, I spent the night before the shoot doing shoulder rolls, practice falls, and countless other small stunts, just in case…that and I wanted to be on the top of my game for my first real stunt job.

I had been watching *Emergency!* since I was a teen. For a solid six years, I would turn on NBC and watch all the different calls that John Gage and Roy DeSoto would go on, and now I was going to be one of them. Mom and Dad, also being big fans of the show, were thrilled about my casting in the show. I tried to reinforce the fact that it was all because of their help, my mom's call, and their help paying the SAG fees. They were proud, very proud, though I could still hear in my father's voice the fact that he'd rather have me in school.

Unconscious Scene from Emergency!

Stunt Scene from Emergency!

On the drive over to Carson, California, where they were filming, my stomach did flips. Part of it was nerves, because I didn't want to mess this up, but mostly, it was excitement. This was it; I was finally going to be in the industry! Following the directions, I pulled into a dirt lot near some old refinery. There were trailers all over the place, and I had no clue where to go. The cars I parked next to made the piece of shit I was driving stand out even more, but I didn't care. Leaving my car behind I didn't know what to do or where to go. Figuring it was my best bet, I walked towards the row of trailers. Each of the trailer doors had a thin piece of tape on it with a star's name written in black marker. My eyes lingered on each name. Randolph Mantooth...Kevin Tighe—I couldn't believe I was going to be working with them. As I made my way down the row I suddenly stopped in my tracks. *It couldn't have been.* Turning, I looked at the door again, and sure enough in black ink on the strip of tape was...Kane Hodder.

Looking around, I thought it was a joke. It couldn't be for me, could it? I mean, I was just supposed to play some guy who was knocked out. There was no one around, so I took a chance and knocked on the door, no one answered. My palms started to sweat a bit. *Was it really for me? Should I go in?* I tried the handle, and it was unlocked. Part of me expected something crazy to happen, that there would be dead hookers inside, the cops would come and blame me, I'd panic and then at the last minute, Allen Funt from *Candid Camera* would burst out and tell me it was all a joke. When I stepped inside, I didn't find any dead bodies or a guy dressed in a gorilla suit in the closet. All I found was a clean, well-stocked trailer. As I walked around, I couldn't believe it. The place was cleaner, bigger, and fancier than my apartment. There was even a microwave! (In the '70s, they were still a novelty that only rich people had.)

In the back of the trailer there was a small bedroom. On the bed was an outfit on a hanger in a plastic bag. A small tag had my name neatly printed on it. *My own costume.* After checking out every inch of the trailer, I sat on the couch in the living room and stared at the microwave. *I had made it… I had made it.* Little did I know, it would be my last job for a very, very long time.

After getting into my costume, I made my way to the set. Everything I saw, I took in, ate it up, and wanted more. The cameras, lights, craft services, hell, even chatting with the non-paid production assistants made me want to stay on the set. This was the world I was *meant* to work in. I was ushered to the make-up department and *ironically* had make-up applied to my neck and face to make it look like I was burned (I had a beard at the time so I didn't need much make-up on my face). Ready to go, I finally met the other stunt guy who was going to play my co-worker in the scene. His name was Charlie Picerni. I didn't know who he was at the time, but he was already on his way to becoming a legendary stuntman. Charlie would eventually work on such legendary projects as *Starsky & Hutch, Die Hard, Die Hard 2,* and over 300 other films and shows. I eventually went on to work with Charlie in *Lethal Weapon 3, The Last Boy Scout, Demolition Man,* and a few others. I also became good friends with his son, Chuck, and eventually worked with him on movies like *Enemy of the State, Se7en,* and *Most Wanted.* Both of them were great to me over the years. When I first met Charlie, he saw how green I was and gave me pointers on the set and about the industry and told me some trade secrets to succeed.

When it came time to actually film, it was hard for me to play an unconscious man; I was so excited I had to force myself to not smile. After the first few takes laying there on the cold hard steel grates 100 feet in the air, I got the hang of it. In fact I got into a sort of Zen moment of being still and calm as I listened to the chaos around me. This moment of calm came in handy, especially when it came time to do my stunt. Getting in a basket and pulling yourself across a wire, 100 feet in the air, is pretty nerve wracking, but at least you are in control of it and can hold on. If you fall, it will more likely than not be your fault. For my stunt, on the other hand, I had to pretend to be unconscious, which meant that I had to trust the other stunt guys to put me in the basket, get me over the railing, and then send me across. It was one hell of a way to get introduced to stunts.

Though my scene is only a few minutes long in the episode, we still filmed for two full days. It was heaven, two days on a television set, working next to people I watched every week, having my own trailer and... on top of it all, I got paid, $600! Though I never wanted it to end, I couldn't wait to get back to Sparks to tell everyone that I had my SAG card for only two weeks and already made money.

Disappointed, I did not immediately get work after *Emergency!* like I hoped I would. Instead, my money ran out rather quickly. Needing more dough, I headed back home to work for a while. Though I didn't tell anyone that, I used the premiere of the episode as my excuse to come home and if I was home...why not work? When I arrived, I felt like a celebrity. Friends who I hadn't talked to in ages were suddenly calling me, leaving messages with my parents, having heard I was now a "star." Word had gotten around about my role on the show. While I never cared about getting fame—hell, all I wanted was to be a stuntman—I have to admit, I did like all the attention.

In between lectures about going back to school, my father still found time to be excited when the episode aired. The whole family came over the night it was on. We all sat around the television, popcorn and drinks in our hands. The fact that my scene was in the last ten minutes of the show helped build up the tension. Everyone laughed and talked through the opening scene where some idiot got his hand stuck in a garage door. When the *Emergency!* crew had to save a woman who has a reaction to some chemicals while driving, everyone quieted a bit, but when the oil rig exploded, everyone shut up. Though cheesy by today's standards, everyone was riveted to the plot and when my face came on the screen, there were screams all around. Feeling the pats on the back and hearing the hoots and hollers was my first reward I received for all the hard work I put in to learning stunts. Afterwards, since it was only a few weeks after my birthday when the episode aired, we celebrated my birthday and then watched the scene over and over again on the Betamax recorder that my sister owned.

YESTERDAY'S TRAINING

After my one episode I had a hard time finding work, so I stayed in Reno and worked in the flower warehouse when I could. When I wasn't working, I would make calls to whomever I could in Hollywood to try and make connections, but none really seemed to work out. I did, however, meet some local Reno guys who did a Wild West stunt show called *Yesterday's Guns*. The show would perform at parks, parties, and different events. Hearing about my stunt background, they immediately offered me a role in the show. I didn't hesitate to say *yes*. I wasn't doing much at the time, and a chance to get some stunt practice in with a live audience was irresistible. I also couldn't help but love the fact that a live action Wild West show was what got me into the industry, so doing this show, somehow, felt right.

Even though we usually made no, or very little, money doing the shows, it didn't stop us from putting everything we had into the performances. Since we were always doing the show in different locations, we constantly had to change the stunts, which in the long run, ended up being the best training I ever had. One weekend we would be in a ballroom, trying to figure out how to do a high fall. The next week we would be at an outdoor park, seeing if we could use the stream to fall into. Each location forced us to use our creativity and minds to come up with something that would not only be exciting, but safe. I can't think of a better way to get trained than on the job like that.

At one point we got a long running gig in Virginia City doing a show for a steam train ride. The train would take tourists for a ride and then turn around at the end of the tracks, which took a few minutes. During those few minutes, we would pretend to try and rob the train car to entertain the passengers. Being the most daring of the group, I would always be the one doing the big falls or stunts. Where the train turned around were dozens of sandy dirt hills. During the show, I would hide up on one of the hills and then stand up and fire at the good guys. I wanted to make it realistic so I rigged up a small piece of wood on a rock. On one end I would put a pile of dirt, when the other guys fired at me, I'd hit the wood, sending up a cloud of dust as if the bullets hit the ground. Then I would stand up, get shot, and then roll all the way down the hill. It was always the closing stunt as it looked pretty dangerous and exciting.

During this time, I also had a stunt hero of sorts on TV. Chevy Chase was on *Saturday Night Live* and at the time, he would open each show with some kind of stunt pratfall. I loved watching him do those stunts. So much so, that I would make sure I was home by 11:30 every Saturday night so I could watch him work. No matter where I was, a club, bar, or whatever, I would make it home for his fall. (Years later I got a job where I would be working with him for a few weeks on a movie called *Nothing But Trouble*. I was extremely happy that I would be working with one of my idols. Unfortunately, without going into detail, it ended up being disappointing).

I worked for *Yesterday's Guns* for almost two years, loving and learning every minute. In our downtime between shows, I trained myself how to do a "burn" stunt by reading up on it and asking some friends back in Hollywood how they did them. Not being able to afford the proper equipment made it pretty difficult, but I ended up getting it down to where it looked very realistic without getting hurt. Each time, I got the burn to last a bit longer and look a bit cooler. Even though I didn't have the proper equipment, I had come up with a system that worked and kept me safe. It was right around this time, when a local Reno reporter called me and asked if she could do a story on the "local stuntman." Of course I agreed to do the interview…little did I know it would change my life forever.

FIGHT
INTERMISSION
I

FIVE ROUNDS

Some people can be a dick, and I'm one of them. I will go out of my way to make any of my fans happy, and I can be a nice fucking guy when I want to. At the same time, I don't put up with shit, and I say the things people really want to say but never would dream of really saying. At times, this makes me an asshole, at least in the eyes of some people. My no-shit attitude and non-sugarcoating ways at times gets me into trouble, especially when my attitude clashes with someone who has an attitude like mine. Over the years I have been in numerous fights. Some I started, some I didn't. I didn't win them all, but I never backed down from one… and I never will.

Interview with Rob Zombie

While fighting might seem like something a macho ass guy who has no brains might do, that's not the case with me. In fact, after one particular fight I got into (which is not mentioned here for legal reasons), I was so upset with myself for being as stupid as I was, that I set out to prove to myself how smart I am. Having dropped out of college to follow my stunt career, I never finished my formal education and it always bothered me, especially when I felt dumb. After that fight I needed to prove to myself that I wasn't an idiot. To do this, I went to the USC campus and took the test for MENSA. In case you don't know, only two percent of people in the world are smart enough to get into MENSA, which is basically a smart person's club. After taking the test I felt pretty good about it; it hadn't seemed that hard. When I got the results, I was surprised and disappointed at the same time. I hadn't made it in, but at the same time, I only missed it by one point, meaning I scored in the top three percent of the population.

I never told anyone about taking the test. I wasn't trying to show everyone that I was smart—I only needed to prove it to myself so that way the next time I made a stupid decision, I could tell myself just that. It was one mistake, and that I wasn't an idiot, and most likely a mistake made by impulse and rage, by not using my brains. The results of the test at least made me feel a bit better when I decided to do a college speaking tour. I may not have a degree, but I'm not stupid and had life experiences these kids could learn from. Together with my good stunt buddy, Alan Marcus, we lectured at over 90 schools around the country. It was a great time, even if Alan fell off the stage once and knocked himself out.

At this point in my life, I can still study a map for hours just for fun, but I do regret not getting my degree. On a personal level, it would have been another sense of accomplishment. Let's face it, if I had spent all that time devoted to making a career in stunts and it had not worked out, I would have been fucked. Thirty years old with no degree and no skills? What would I have done? I busted my ass to have this career, but I still got very lucky also in the process. Ninety-eight percent of the members of the Screen Actors Guild don't make enough money to live on. I'm obviously an example that it can be done, but the smart way to embark on this career is to also have a backup plan, like a degree. No more preaching, I'm just saying what I feel. This has been an unbelievably rewarding career for me, and I wouldn't change it for the world. However, there are rats and snakes everywhere, and you have to watch your back at all times. There have been people in my life whom I thought I could trust and believe in, and that they could never betray me, only to be backstabbed and shit on by those who were the closest to me. You know who you are!

Throughout the book are some situations where I didn't use my brains and used my fists instead. I could probably write an entire separate book on the stupid fights I have been in. Instead, I have decided to include four fights that were memorable in some way.

ROUND ONE

When I was in high school, there wasn't much for us to do on Kwaj; the place was tiny and we knew everyone. Therefore on Spring Breaks, we would sometimes take a 40-minute flight to a bigger island called Majuro. They had cars, hotels, bars, and a ton of other shit we didn't have where we lived. One particular break, my best friend, Steve, and our buddy, Freddy, and I flew over for a small break. We borrowed a car from a family friend on the island and stayed in a hotel. We partied, drank our asses off, and caused trouble wherever we went. The main thing we did, though, was drive. On Kwaj we took driving lessons, but after that we never got to drive, so getting to drive a car was exhilarating to us. On Majuro, we tooled all around the island, taking turns every few minutes. One particular day we decided to stop and take a break at this nice hotel since ours was a shit box (our room had no windows and five beds). We hung out in the open air lobby bullshitting. For some reason, as we sat there, I thought it was too bright in the lobby, and I started shutting off all the lights. The guy who ran the motel, a native to the island, didn't seem to like what I was doing and told me so. Not liking his attitude, I got in his face and we had a screaming match. As he looked like he was about to get into it with me, Steve and Freddy dragged me out of the place. The guy followed us out to the car. Steve jumped in behind the wheel and spun the tires, sending gravel shooting up at the man. We all laughed and drove away thinking nothing about it.

About ten minutes later, some jackass started to tailgate us as we were driving. I told Steve to let them pass, so he pulled over (in our one nice act that day). As we pulled over, the other car whipped around and skidded to a stop in front of us, boxing us in. It was the hotel manager and three other big ass natives. Before we could even process what was happening, they had the car surrounded. One guy opened Steve's door and kicked him in the face. The manager then grabbed Steve's leg and tried to break it against the door frame. Unfortunately, all the windows in the car were down, and while Steve was getting attacked, another guy reached in the back window, grabbed my hair (it was long at that time), and held my head back against the seat. Not being able to move my head, another guy came up to my window and started punching me in the face. I tried to defend myself, but it was pretty useless.

The Car We Got Beat Up In

Freddy in the back seat was pretty lucky; he was able to roll up one window and lock the door. He pushed himself against that door and kicked at the guy who opened the other back door and was trying to get him. As this was all going on, a crowd started to form. Out of nowhere, I heard someone yell *do you want a gun?* I had no clue if the comment was for us or for the natives; whomever it was for, the guys started to back off. They were probably afraid that the crowd would get involved or act as witnesses. When they left us, my nose was bleeding everywhere. Steve had a gash on his cheek and was bleeding too; Freddy was fine. During the entire incident, we didn't get one fucking punch in.

Amazingly, it wasn't traumatic like the beating I got when I was a kid, probably because I caused the whole situation and *knew* it was because of my big mouth. Steve and I laugh about this story nowadays, and he likes to say he saved our lives by taking a left out of the hotel rather than a right. If we had taken a right, we would have been in the middle of nowhere where a crowd wouldn't have showed up... if we were alone, I doubt those guys would have stopped beating us.

In fact, Steve has saved my ass more than once. On Kwaj, around the same time this fight happened, we were walking down a street by the post office. We happened to pass by this Filipino guy and for some reason I jokingly put my hand over his head as if I was going to grab him. The little bastard did some sort of ninja move and spun around and punched me in the chin. Before I could even brace myself, the guy pulled out a makeshift knife made out of a whittled comb, like some prison shiv, and hit me in the stomach with it. *I'll be right back, you fuck,* the guy screamed as he ran into an apartment that was above the post office. Of course I was pissed and barked back that I wasn't going to move. Steve, being the calmer one, told me that we better get the hell out of there because he could be getting a gun or friends. Realizing he was right, I reluctantly walked away. Thankfully, Steve acted as the rational side of my brain for me once again, saving my ass as always. Consider this round lost.

I'M AN ASSHOLE WHO
GETS AWAY WITH SHIT

Throughout my life, starting from my youngest memories, I was the troublemaker. I never picked on people; in fact, I stood up for them more than anything—it's just... I'm an asshole. I always fuck with people—make jokes, scare them, trip them, tie their shoelaces together, and any other thing I can think of. I can't really put my finger on why I'm like that, but I just am. It might be the attention I get from it. All of us actors and stunt people crave attention. Why else would we want to get in front of a camera? Or maybe it was just in my genes? Whatever the reason is, I have always been *that guy*.

Guess Which One Is Me

Hell, you could always tell who I was in pictures because I was the only one not smiling at the camera; I was the one with my finger in someone's ear. So let's just say that if you're a victim of a prank when I'm around…most likely it was me.

GO AHEAD, POKE ME IN THE CHEST

There is just something about the horror and wonder of death. The frailty of our own lives makes horror so enjoyable. We love watching horror because it makes us feel something: fear, adrenaline, and shock. A horror movie is no different than a roller coaster. They both make us feel alive, by showing us that we could die at any moment. For those who don't love horror, it's because they can't stomach the fact of dying or what could happen to them. The sense of life being short is too much to handle. For the rest of us, a good horror movie gives us a shot of adrenaline that makes us want to live life to the fullest.

As for me, killing people on film gets those demons out of my soul. Without the cathartic release, I would probably be in real trouble. I have gotten in enough fights and caused enough trouble, even with having that release. In fact, I have been arrested for letting those demons shine through just a tiny bit and getting in fights from people just pissing me off. I cannot imagine how much worse off I would be if I didn't have the ability to get my aggression out by killing on film.

The first time I was arrested, I was in Baltimore doing an event for a radio station. It was the late '80s and my fame was just starting as the Jason movies were propelling me. I was receiving offers to do things all over. At this particular event I was asked to help MC and pick a winner for a contest they were holding. They were raffling off an autographed guitar from some big hair band at the time. To win, the person had to be present. On the stage, the DJ held out a big bag of tickets for me to pull out a winner. As I went to reach in I noticed the guy was holding a ticket between his thumb and forefinger, moving it to get my attention. The asshole had rigged the contest; he wanted me to take the ticket in his hand. I'm not the most moral person in the world, but I try to be as good as I can. The fact that this guy wanted me to pick a friend of his over a few hundred people who waited hours to try and win the guitar—no fucking way.

Ignoring the outreached ticket, I stuck my hand way in the bottom and pulled one out. The douche bag read the number, looking angrily at me. The person wasn't there, so we had to draw another number. Again, as I went to stick my hand in the bag, the jerk held out the ticket, this time waving it frantically. Ignoring it, I dug even deeper in the bag, pulling out another ticket. I couldn't wait to see his face when the rightful winner got the guitar. And what happens... again, the person was not there. Back into the bag it was, only this time, the shit head didn't let me dig down, he pulled out his own hand and read the ticket as if he just found it. This time, the winner was there...what a shock.

I was fuming at this point. Don't ever fucking try to involve me in a scam, especially without talking to me first. What kind of bullshit is that? Backstage I confronted him about it, and he got all pissy with me, saying shit about me and that I was a dick for not helping him out. Then... he got close to me and poked me in my fucking chest. I don't know why, but poking me in the chest is like showing a bull the color red. It makes me snap. Maybe it's the lack of respect and forced authority it tries to show, or maybe I just don't like being touched without asking, but whatever it is, I instantly slammed my forearm into the guy's face. He is lucky I didn't deck him, though a simple forearm was enough to send him backwards. He tripped and nailed his head into the DJ booth. That one simple forearm to the face got me a trip to jail.

Sitting in a jail cell, I was pissed at myself for not being able to control my anger. One tiny thing sent me over the edge and landed me there. The worst part was I was supposed to leave that next morning to go do another appearance, and two days after that I had another. The whole ordeal left me stuck in the cell for a while before everything was dropped. I have no charges and no record from it, but it still fucked up my schedule and really pissed me off for a long time.

Another time I had a run-in with law enforcement; it was not due to my anger but because of a corrupt dick of a cop. I was in a southern state doing a convention. During some of my time off I was driving my rental car around the area to see what they had to do. I ended up getting pulled over for speeding, which I was, but not that much. The cop saw that I was from out of state and told me that he was going to write me a ticket. He also noticed that I was wearing a jersey from the music group called the Insane Clown Posse. I have been a big fan of theirs for a long time. I even shot a video with them for a song in my favorite ICP album, "The Amazing Jeckel Brothers". When he asked about the jersey, I could tell he hated ICP and since he did, I decided to talk about how much I liked them, just to fuck with him. He said he was going to be nice, though, and let me pay him right then instead of having to mail it in. I told him he had to be kidding. I wasn't going to let some little hick town cop shake me down so I told him to take me to jail because I was not going to pay him. I figured standing up to him would make him back off... I was wrong. He took me to jail. I couldn't believe it. In the jail there was no way for me to complain about what he did. There were only a handful of cops, and I'm sure they were going to back his ass.

Kane the Juggalo

They held me overnight and made me rake leaves on the town green the next day before letting me go. It was a bit insane, but at least I didn't get a record or have to pay a fine. I have a feeling I'm not the only juggalo to go to jail because of ICP.

The last time, I wasn't so much arrested as I was detained. I was in Atlanta and late for a flight. This was before

9/11 so the screening wasn't as tight, but for some reason, they felt I looked suspicious racing my ass through the checkpoint and asked me to come to the side to be searched. I was already pissed that I was cutting it close with my flight, and now they wanted to search me. Let's just say the anger was boiling. As the fat ass attendant took his sweet time checking me over, I started to curse him out. He had nowhere to go, so why not fuck with a big guy and feel all powerful. I guess my cursing got a bit loud, for he called over the supervisor. The boss, another fat ass, strolled over to me and said in an all-too-rude manner, I better calm down. I called him an asshole, and he got up in my face and did the one thing that always set me off... the fucking finger poke in the chest again.

It's like an uncontrollable instant reaction—the second the guy's finger hit my chest—wham. I pushed his ass back with both of my hands. A full-out shove. The guy went flying, but thankfully he didn't slam his head into anything. Within a few seconds, I had half a dozen TSA agents on top of me, trying to take me down. Realizing I was screwed, I fought the urge to fight them off and let them cuff me. They detained me in some small office, chained to a table for hours. I was asked a list of questions and they did a background check on me, then suddenly they decided to let me go. Honestly, I think they only let me go after watching the video and realizing the guy had touched me first. It might have only been a finger, but he touched me first and in court it would have been a good argument that he provoked it. I got in about ten hours later than I was supposed to, but at least, once again, I got away unscathed.

The anger and rage issues have gotten me in trouble from time to time, but I have always come out of situations just fine. After these scuffles, I always think back to the beating I took as a child. I believe, without a doubt, that the rage I have was from it. The second someone touches me, it's an instant reaction to defend myself. Then the defending turns into this rage of revenge, as if I'm seeking the revenge I never had all those years ago. It scares me to think about what I would do if I ever ran into the guys who did that to me. I'd probably end up killing them. At one point, when my kids were around the same age I was at the beating, I thought, *What if it happened to them?* There is no doubt in my mind I would end up in jail. I wouldn't touch the kids who beat them. I would never hit a kid, no matter how much of an ass they were, though I would seek out their fathers. If a kid is that messed up that they would beat a child younger than them for fun, their fathers would have to be assholes as well. I'd find each father and beat the shit out of them; it would probably be hard to stop myself from killing them, but I would do it and I wouldn't care if I went to jail. That isn't just big talk. I promise you I would do that. That is how much the incident scarred me—I would never let it happen again without punishment.

And for those of you jackasses reading this who think it would be funny to come up and poke me in the chest at a convention… just remember I snap and I have machetes on my table.

SCARED

Usually, I'm the one who does the scaring. Not much makes me jump or my heartbeat race. Even when I do a ghost hunt, I go to the one place that no one wants to go to, set up my night vision camera right on me, and just sit there... alone. I hate saying this because I sound like I'm trying to be some tough guy, but I honestly have no fears. Snakes, spiders, heights, and all the shit that scares normal people, doesn't bother me in the least. I have wracked my brain trying to figure out something... yet I come up with nothing every time. Of course I have worries and concerns in my life, but there is not one thing that I can say I'm scared of or that I fear. Most of it I attribute to the beating I received as a child, the unexpected one by the pool, the one I never found out who or why it happened. It was so horrible and frightening; I think it shut off the fear mechanism in my brain... as if I never wanted to feel that again.

The year after the beating, this big fucking kid, biggest in the school (who ended up to be 6'8" as an adult) starting messing with me. It was after gym class and I had my jock strap wrapped up in my towel. The bastard purposely knocked the towel out of my hand, sending my jock to the ground. The girls walking by all started to laugh. This pissed me off, but I wasn't going to do anything. I never fought back at that point of my life yet. As I tried to pick up my towel he started to push me, getting more of a laugh. All of a sudden this flash of hotness ran across my body, and I felt this adrenaline course through me. All I could think of was the day by the pool, and I was not going to let that happen again. Standing up straight, I turned and punched him straight in the nose. There was this look of shock on his face as he grabbed his nose and fell backwards. Everyone was silent and after he hit the ground, there was applause. It felt fucking amazing. Instead of getting the shit kicked out of me, I turned the tables around. I didn't realize it then, but looking back, I can say those two moments were the defining incidents in my mental toughness. Ever since that day, I never backed away from a fight.

Though nothing really scares me, there were some things in my youth that freaked me out. One of my earliest memories of being terrified was as a kid in Sparks... while watching a movie... a horror movie.

In its time, *The Birds* was a scary movie, it still is, but add to the fact that I was a kid and I was watching it late at night with my buddy, Joey Martinez, at his house by ourselves... it was a little terrifying. I lived right across the street, so my mom let me stay over there late on the weekends. Being little boys we tried being brave about watching it, and even when were terrified, gripping the couch cushions, we acted like it was nothing. Neither of us wanted to be the one to scream or run out of the room. We toughed it out and did our best to not piss our eight-year-old pants. When it was over, we both made lame comments about how it was stupid and not scary at all. *Birds? I mean come on, that is just stupid.* Seemed to be the common theme as I delayed my trip *outside*, where there were many trees that birds nested in and could attack me on my 30-second journey across the road.

Realizing I couldn't delay any more without Joey noticing I was scared to go home, I puffed up my chest and did my best to act like I was fine when I walked out the door. As the door shut behind me, I prayed he wasn't watching me as I ducked my head a bit and looked to the sky. It was less than 100 yards. I could make it across in seconds if I sprinted, yet my legs wouldn't move. My eyes shot from bushes to trees, looking for those winged bastards. I didn't see any, so I forced my legs to move, one at a time, they crept instead of ran like I begged them to do. Suddenly, a *chirp*, right behind me. My head snapped around with lightning speed, my eyes scanning like laser beams. There it was, slowly circling in the sky—a large black, ominous-looking thing. It was going to get me, I just knew it.

Keeping an eye on the enemy I started running, hoping I was heading in a straight path. Sure enough, I tripped, right in the middle of the road, scraping my knees. Taking my eyes off the bird, I knew this was going to be the moment he would sweep down and bite my ear off. Sensing it was right behind me, I rolled over and swatted at the air... at nothing. The bird was gone. I searched the sky for it, but it was nowhere to be seen. Taking this as an omen, I got up and sprinted to my house, burst through the door, and slammed it behind me.

That night in bed, I started to curse the movie. As much as I told myself it wasn't real, at that age... I believed it could and *would* happen. Eventually, even though it was the birds doing the killing, I ended up hating the star of the film, Tippi Hedren. There were too many birds to hate at once for making me scared, so I had it out for Tippi. Screw her for making me so scared! If I had been older and known what a director was, I would have hated Alfred Hitchcock. For weeks I was scared of every bird I saw; if it flapped its wings too fast or flew over me, I'd duck and, even at times, run inside a house to take cover. Each time I ducked, I cursed Tippi, wishing I could get even with her for making me so scared. Thirty years later, I got my wish.

In 2003, I did a small film called *Dark Wolf*. When I found out Tippi Hedren was going to be in it, it brought back those memories of being terrified of stupid birds. I couldn't wait to tell her how much she scared me. When I found out that I was going to kill her in the movie I couldn't contain my excitement. Here I was, getting to meet and kill the woman who haunted me as a child. Talk about the ultimate revenge.

Tippi was great, and a wonderfully nice woman. I wasn't on set with her too often, so we didn't get to talk much. It wasn't until a few years later when I was doing a convention did I really get the chance to talk to her. We were in Orlando at the Spooky Empire Convention and she just happened to have the table next to me. The little kid in me seemed to come out as it took me a while to build up the courage to tell her how much her movie scared me as a kid. When I told her, I loved her answer—she simply said… good. I was floored; it was the same answer I gave my fans when they told me the same thing. A lot of actors feel the need to apologize for scaring people. I always wondered why they did that when the whole point of a horror movie is to scare you! If it scared you, then it worked. The fact that this sweet old lady loved that she scared me as a kid… simply amazing.

The only other movie that freaked me out, along with the rest of America at the time, was *The Exorcist*. I was in college when I saw it. There was all sorts of hype for the movie; the news even reported how people were vomiting and passing out in the halls… of course, this helped build the tension. I loved horror movies and planned on seeing it, but hadn't had much time with classes and work. I made time to see the movie after a girl in one of my classes broke down in tears in the middle of the lecture and walked out. Her friend got up and explained to the professor that she had seen *The Exorcist* a few days before and hadn't been able to sleep since; she was exhausted and emotionally distraught. When the professor let us out, I skipped my next class and went straight to the theater.

Even though it was an earlier showing, the theater was still packed, mostly with rowdy students who were eager to see what all the hype was about. There was talking and joking going on, but once the movie started, you could hear a pin drop in the theater… with the exception of gasps and screams. Though I was deep into the movie, tense myself, I suddenly had a need to sit up and look around the theater. That's when I saw it for the first time, hundreds of faces, lightly illuminated with flickering blue light. Every eye in the theater was staring intently at the screen; lovers and friends clenched each other for support. Faces cringed and crunched up, fingers covered eyes and mouths fell open. Hearing a vomiting noise coming from the speakers I saw every head in the theater jerk with shock. It was amazing… these people were not in the theater anymore, *they were part of this story*, having the shit scared out of them right along with the priest in the film. Turning back around I smiled to myself as I imagined what it must be like to evoke such emotions from people. At that point in my life I didn't know I wanted to be in movies, but there was something about the feeling in my stomach that made me know that horror was going to be in my life for a long, long time.

PART II

BURN

IGNITION

For almost 30 years I have lied about how I got burned. I lied about it because I couldn't admit how fucking stupid I was. Well, there comes a time in everyone's life when they have to fess up to your mistakes, admit you were wrong, and take it like a man. That is why now, for the first time ever, I'm going to tell the true story, the whole story, behind the incident that left me scarred for life. No more bullshit about how I got burned on the set of a pilot for a new television show that never aired, which was the story I told most of my life. Only a few people know the real story. Now that I'm older and more mature, I can finally admit to *myself* what happened. It has never been easy talking about my burn, the aftermath, and the long-term effects it has caused me. Hopefully, telling the truth will be somewhat therapeutic for me and help heal some wounds.

The episode of *Emergency!* that I did aired in April and re-ran a few months later. It was the re-run and the fact that our *Yesterday's Guns* show was getting some good feedback that inspired Marilyn Newton, a local reporter, to contact me about doing an interview. After a quick phone interview, she asked if she could get a few pictures of me for the article. Of course I agreed, telling her I would do a stunt for the picture. We set up a date, July 12, 1977. We were to meet at a park and take pictures by Paradise Pond in Sparks. Having done fire stunts for the past few weeks, I felt comfortable doing them and figured it would look great in the newspaper.

Marilyn picked me up and drove to the park. We chatted some about my "budding career," and I told her about the stunt I was going to do for her. When we arrived at the park, I got out of the car and a wind gust hit me. Wind and fire do not mix, but we went about trying to get the shot anyway. At a picnic table, while Marilyn got her camera ready, I prepared for my stunt. Since I couldn't afford proper equipment, I used my own homemade method (if you try this at home you are an idiot— learn from my mistakes). First, I wrapped my arms and legs in towels and taped them to my skin. Next I wrapped those towels with sheets of tin foil and taped those down. Then I put my clothing over that. The next part, the key ingredient if you will, was rubber cement. Using the few cans I brought with me, I lathered the parts of my body with the smelly goo. Rubber cement is highly flammable, but it takes a few seconds to burn off, making it perfect for doing a fire burn. The last tool I had, which I used as a fire extinguisher, was a few wet towels. I know, really stupid. This is why it has taken me so long to admit how it really happened.

Yet, having followed this process several times without any injury, I was confident that it was going to work again. Wrap myself up, cover me in the cement, light it up, and then put myself out with the wet towels. Doing this usually enabled me to do a good ten to fifteen second burn which should be just long enough for her to snap off some good pictures. The only problem was the damn wind was so strong.

Marilyn placed me a few feet from the water's edge to get a good shot. When she was ready, I pulled out my lighter and cautiously flicked it. It ignited perfectly, like always. The problem was the wind was so strong that it blew the flames down and minimized the effect of the stunt. I did it again with the same result. I was on fire, but it didn't look dramatic enough. If only I hadn't been so much of a perfectionist. Finally, we gave up. The wind had picked up even more; there was no way we could get the shot. Back in the car we decided to try again the next day. Only we'd do it out in the desert where there would be less wind. The next day was the 13th.

Preparing For the Photo Shoot

That next morning we went through the same routine, only this time we drove out to a patch of desert at the edge of Reno. I was pretty excited because there was virtually no wind, *and* Marilyn volunteered to bring me some rubber cement from the newspaper office. I had run out the day before and being broke as shit, I jumped at the opportunity to save a few bucks. I had never used the brand she brought before, but I didn't think anything of it—rubber cement was rubber cement.

The spot we stopped at didn't have a picnic table, so I awkwardly rested on a large boulder, sweating in the sun as I prepared myself for the stunt. I wrapped my left arm, both thighs and part of my stomach. Just like the day before. Wrapped up and with my clothing back on, I set my wet towels off to the side of me in the dry dirt, out of the frame of the picture. Lastly, I opened up the cans of rubber cement. The smell was so strong it made me shake my head in surprise. Rubber cement always stinks, but this one was even stronger than normal. Of course, I thought nothing of it. Looking back, I kick myself for not testing it out on a small spot first.

The cans were smaller than what I was normally used to, so I used three of them, liberally lathering my left arm and legs. It was going to look great. Getting into place for the picture, I wasn't nervous at all. Instead, I was excited; we were going to get an amazing picture that all of my friends and family would see in the paper. I was already getting a reputation as a local celebrity, and an article would add to that image.

In hopes of getting a better picture, I sat on the ground. I was going to keep one hand up in the air, legs splayed in opposite ways, giving the effect that the fire was attacking me. As I pulled out my cheap gas station lighter, little did I know my life was about to change forever. I had the lighter in my right hand, away from my body, to be cautious like I always was. Normally once the lighter was lit, I would then bring it to the area I wanted to light and it would ignite. Usually it would make a small little puff and then spread out, quickly, but nothing shockingly fast. Well, this time, everything was different. Watching the lighter in my hand, waiting for the flame, my thumb hadn't even gotten to the base of the wheel when I saw a giant flame fly right at my face. A high pitch whining sound followed by a crackling noise whizzed into my ears. The burst of orange that headed for my eyes was all it took for me to realize that I had just exploded into flames...

Though it was less than a second, it was like a giant steaming hot, wet blanket was wrapping around my entire body, pinching and pulling at my skin. The haze from the heat blurred my eyes and forced me to shut them tightly and bring a hand over my face—instinct I guess. The same reason I didn't do the one thing you are told to do when you are on fire. Stop, drop, and roll is a good theory, and great for kids to know. But I'm sorry; your first and only instinct when you are suddenly on fire around your head is to run. Of course it's not the correct thing to do, but it's a reflex. Not a decision. If your body is the only thing on fire, you can have the presence of mind to stop, drop, and roll. When your head and face are on fire, everything is different. You hear your face burning. You hear your hair singeing. You are breathing in the flames. There are no words to describe how terrifying it is. Keeping one hand over my face I rolled onto my side and forced myself up and started to run. If this had happened the day before, I would have been hurt, but probably just minor burns, being that I was only six feet, *six fucking feet*, from a lake. A nice giant, cool body of water to jump in and put myself out. Instead, I was in the god damn desert, nowhere near *any* water.

Unfortunately, Marilyn had no clue that running around on fire was not part of the stunt. Though I couldn't see her, I could hear the snapping of the camera shutter as I ran by her. Oblivious that she was about to watch a man almost burn to death, she kept taking pictures. She wasn't my concern though; the fact that I was completely engulfed in flames was. Using both hands to cover my face, I kept running, peeking through tiny slits in my fingers, thinking of what to do. The high-pitched squealing, snapping, popping sound of hair burning was making my stomach nauseated. I had to think of something... The wet towels I brought would do nothing, especially since I would have to grab, unfold, and pat them on my body, it would take too long. If I had a fire extinguisher, I would have been fine, but I couldn't afford one. Just as I thought I was about to die, my foot slipped a bit. Stumbling, I slowed my run down and looked at the ground—mud. Not water, just slightly damp mud. After the wind we had the day before, it rained a little that night. Amazingly, in the rapidly drying desert, there was still one small mud hole left. Without hesitating, I dove in it and rolled.

You would think the mud would feel good against my skin that was just on fire, but honestly, I didn't feel anything different—there was no pain to be soothed. Spitting mud out of my mouth, I automatically stood up. Using the back of my hands, I wiped mud out of my eyes, and finally being able to see, I looked down at myself. My shirt and pants were gone; with it being summer and having plans of going swimming later, I had swim trunks on under my jeans, and they were intact but had mud and singe marks all over them. All that was left on my body were my sneakers and those swimming trunks. Everything else had burned off. When I saw my arm, I almost passed out. Trembling, I noticed my hands were just as bad. Ignoring how everything looked, I lifted my left hand and touched my right arm. As my fingers touched the black flesh, it peeled off, just like the burned crust on a toasted marshmallow. A large sloppy chunk slid off my bicep and fell. I watched my skin, the skin that was so tan and taut just a few minutes ago, fall into the mud. *Why wasn't I feeling any pain?* As I stared at the slop of my skin in the mud I could hear Marilyn screaming in the background. Her screams brought me back to reality. *I had to get to the hospital.* It was the only thing running through my mind when I saw Marilyn skid to a stop in front of me.

"I have to get to a hospital," I said, looking into the reporter's terrified face, with no emotion at all. It was surreal…here I was, my skin literally falling off of me, and I felt nothing. Looking at Marilyn, I saw the panic that I should have been going through. Her hands went out to me and then back to herself several times. She wanted to help me, but she knew if she touched me, she would just pull more of my skin off. With my arms out in front of me I walked like a zombie to her car. She opened the door for me and I got in…slowly. In the back of my mind I braced for a scream as I was about to make contact with the seat, but again, I still felt nothing…I was in shock and my nightmare was just beginning.

FEELING THE BURN

Marilyn was in almost as much shock as I was. She just watched a man almost die in front of her. Then suddenly she was stuffed in a hot car with the smell of burned flesh and skin surrounding her and a half-dead man in her passenger seat. Every few seconds, she'd glance over at me just in time to see a piece of flesh slide off me onto her upholstery.

"Where…where do we go?" she asked, her voice trembling. In that moment, I didn't want to look at my body, so I stared out the window straight ahead as I answered her.

"I don't know, anywhere." With that, the wheels kicked up dirt behind us, and we were heading into town. For a few moments I sat as still as I could in the silence of the car. Amazingly, in just a few minutes, we saw a fire station in the distance. What better place to go to with a burn victim? The sight of the station made me start to think that someone was watching out for me—a mud puddle in the desert and now the fire station only a mile away?

Marilyn skidded the car right up to the garage doors, jumped out, and started banging on them. Every few bangs she looked over her shoulder at me in the car, as if she thought I wouldn't make it a second longer. Five, six… twenty bangs later and no answer. With more panic in her eyes, she gave me a look that said to hold tight and ran to the main entrance. I was happy I could still see her at the door; the thought of being alone made my head feel light. I watched as both of her fists banged on the door, followed by the occasional kick. Part of me kept saying to myself that they were just busy in there, maybe taking a nap? When I saw Marilyn's shoulders slump, I knew, *no one was fucking there.* Maybe there *wasn't* anyone looking out for me.

Giving up, Marilyn came back to the car and opened my door. She instinctively held out a hand, but then pulled it back as she got a glimpse of my skin.

"There is a house over there. Let's go see if they'll let us call for help." As I grabbed the door handle to get up, I left behind slime, mud, and skin. Instead of thinking about my injuries, I was worried about making a mess in her car. I felt horrible at the thought of her having to clean it up later. Marilyn led the way as we shuffled over to the house, which was about 50 yards away. Still…I felt no pain. Before I could get onto the porch steps, Marilyn had jabbed the doorbell three times. There was a car outside, so we were hopeful that someone was home. Sure enough, within a minute the door opened. A pretty, 30-something housewife wearing a flowery apron opened the door with a big smile on her face. She was probably expecting a door-to-door salesman or the Avon lady; instead there was a burned monster on her front steps. Despite the sight, without hesitating, the woman opened her door more.

"Get in the shower and turn the cold water on, quickly. I'll call for help." With that she lead the way into the house, Marilyn stayed behind at the door, I think she was relieved to finally not be responsible for me. As I stepped through the entranceway, I hesitated as I saw new, clean white carpet in the living room. I was still dripping skin and mud, yet, the woman didn't hesitate in ushering me through the room.

"Hurry up, come on!" Reluctantly, I started to shuffle across the carpet and that is when I saw her… the sweetest little girl. She couldn't have been any more than four years old, playing with dolls on the carpet in front of the television. Holding one doll in each hand she looked up at me. There was a slight quiver in her lip as if she was about to burst into tears, but she didn't. I paused, wanting to tell her it was alright, that I just had an accident, but I couldn't. I couldn't even force a smile for her. As I felt a large slough of skin slide off my calf, I started to walk again.

The lady had the shower on. She was standing there holding the curtain back with a look on her face like a scolding mother.

"Get in and stay under the water until the ambulance arrives." I desperately wanted to tell her I was sorry for making a mess in her house, for ruining her afternoon of playing with her daughter, but nothing came out of my mouth. I did as she said, got into the shower, and closed the curtain. I waited for the spray to hurt, burn, sting, and make me scream with pain, but I still felt nothing. As the water beaded down my body, the few stubborn pieces of flesh that were holding on slid off and stuck in the drain. In a matter of seconds the tub was full of slimy chunks of what use to be my flesh. The water started to rise; I wanted to bend down and pull the chunks away so it could drain, but I couldn't fathom touching it. Instead, I pulled back the curtain and took a look in the mirror. It was the first time I saw myself. My beard was melted; it looked almost like melted brown plastic stuck to my face. I had no eyebrows, my hair was pretty much gone except for a few small tufts and my scalp looked like someone took a cheese grater to it. I couldn't understand how, but I *still* wasn't feeling any pain.

Back under the water I stood there, frozen, not thinking, not feeling. Every few seconds I would peek out from the curtain to look at the monster in the mirror. I couldn't believe it was me, that I was alive and that I felt nothing. Shock was in full effect. The water beating down on my crispy ears drowned out the world. I was in a bubble of no pain and no thoughts. If I could have stayed there forever ignoring my situation, I would have been happy. As I felt the water reach my calves, I had to kick the chunks of flesh blocking the drain with my foot several times to let it drain down a bit. As I took one last look in the mirror, I heard voices outside the door. Two paramedics, eerily similar looking to the two who saved my character in *Emergency!* where I played a burn victim only a few months before, came into the bathroom. The first one's eyes popped open and he jumped back a bit as he saw me. He mumbled something under his breath and looked at the other paramedic who swallowed hard and kept a straight face.

"Let's get you to the hospital, kid." As they ushered me out of the house I walked back over the mess I had created on the white carpet, now adding a liberal amount of water to the filth. The back of my brain was searching for the mother and for Marilyn to thank them for all of their help, but shuffling like a zombie, my mouth frozen in shock, I was rushed past them and placed in the back of the ambulance.

I never got a chance to thank that woman or to apologize for the mess I made in her house or the trauma that I might have caused her daughter. To this day, that is one of my biggest regrets. This woman, without hesitation, opened her door to a stranger and helped beyond what anyone would ever be expected to do. After helping me, she was left to clean up piles of mud and burned flesh off her clean carpet and out of her tub. She had to explain to her daughter that it wasn't a monster in their house, that it was just a hurt man. I can only imagine the nightmares I gave the poor little girl. The woman also had to live with the trauma of what she saw herself. Almost 35 years later, I
can't talk about that woman without tears welling up in my eyes.

Whoever you are, thank you from the bottom of my heart.

STILL BURNING

When I got into the ambulance, they had me sit on the bench next to the gurney so I wouldn't scrape my burns any more than necessary by lying down. Being the '70s, it was one of those station wagon ambulances, so I had to hunch over a bit more than I would have liked. One medic drove while the other sat next to me. He put a sheet on my shoulders and poured saline all over me to keep the wounds moist and cool. Over the sound of the siren we chatted as if we were on our way to go out to eat. I could tell he was trying to keep me talking to make sure I was lucid. In fact, I was so coherent that after I told him how I got burned, I started to tell him about *Yesterday's Guns*. After enthusiastically explaining the show there was a pause in our conversation. Looking down at my legs, I looked up at the medic; his face held a lot of the same panic Marilyn had.

"I'm fucked aren't I?" Breaking eye contact, he looked at his hands before answering.

"Yeah…you are." Taking a deep breath I wondered if this was all real. If it was, wouldn't I have felt the pain by then? Just at that moment, the ambulance sputtered and started to shake hard. The medic reached out to help steady me, but couldn't find a place to grab me that wouldn't be on an open wound.

"What the hell is going on?" he yelled to the front.

"Goddamn thing is dying on me!" the driver hollered over his shoulder as he started to pull over. As we came to a stop on the side of the road I could see the panic in the medic's eyes. Being stuck on the highway was not going to help my situation, especially since they were running out of saline to pour over me.

In the front of the ambulance I could hear the driver radio for another ambulance. The crackling voice on the other end said it was going to be a while. The driver got out, opened the hood, and cursed. The medic sitting with me tried to keep the conversation going, but I was starting to withdraw mentally. My mind was blank; I just kept staring at my burned arms sticking out in front of me. We waited for about twenty minutes in the breakdown lane at the center median of a four-lane highway. Finally, I got into the other ambulance and arrived at the hospital as I sunk deeper and deeper into shock.

Once inside the hospital, for some odd reason, before they did any work on me, they handed me a phone and told me to call my family. Standing in the emergency room, practically naked, skinless, I dialed my parents' number. Dad was a jovial man. I had never heard him answer the phone with a *Hi* or a *Hello*. It was always a loud, booming *Yooo!* That day it was no different. Dad answered with the same loud, humorous *Yooo!*

I took a deep breath, feeling a tickle of pain in my throat and chest for the first time, before answering.

"Dad… I'm in the hospital. I got burned; it's not good."

"Be right there." With that, the phone went dead. I noticed the calendar above the desk. That weekend I was supposed to go see a Mr. America bodybuilding competition with my buddy, Rick Bell. I was in very good shape at the time, always working out, and really into bodybuilding. I had been looking forward to going to that competition for weeks. Even though there was a very real possibility that I could die, all I could think was *Shit, I'm going to miss the show.*

By the time my parents arrived, the medical team had cut and peeled the shorts off me, stuck an IV in my arm, and put me in a bed. Though I didn't learn it until later, the hospital did not have a burn unit, meaning they didn't really have the right equipment or knowledge of how to treat me properly. I should have been quarantined in a sterile room right away, had the dead skin removed, been rubbed with antibacterial ointment, and finally wrapped in gauze. Instead, I was lying in a bed, in a normal room with nothing being done to my wounds as I waited for my parents to arrive. A nurse said the doctor wanted me to see them before I went into surgery. It wasn't a comforting thought. Why did he want me to see them…could I die?

Staring at the IV drip waiting for my parents, the shock started to wear off and tiny pricks of pain eased into my body. They felt like little electrostatic shocks followed by heat. They were not bad; I thought I could live with it. Sadly, it wasn't even the sprinkle before the hurricane of pain was to arrive. As more and more pricks of pain started to work their way into my body, my mother rounded the corner of my room. She had her purse clutched to her chest, my father's hand on her shoulder.

"Kane…oh baby…" she said with tears in her eyes as she rushed over to my bedside. I hadn't realized that my right arm was hanging out from under the sheet; it was one of the worst burns, and my mother's eyes went to it immediately. There was no flesh left—it was just raw, singed meat. I will never forget the look of terror and sadness she had when she first saw the extent of the burns. The color suddenly flashed out of her face, leaving her looking sickly white. Her hand went to her mouth as if she was trying not to throw up. Turning away, my father stepped up and took her place. His face was tight and stern. Reaching out he went to pat my leg, to give me assurance, but he quickly pulled it back realizing how much it would hurt. It was becoming a trend, people being scared to touch me. I was never that much of a touchy feely guy, but in that moment, I wanted nothing more than for someone to touch me... but it wasn't possible.

"You are going to be alright, Son," was all my dad could manage to get out. After holding my gaze for a few seconds, he started to look around the room.

"I got to talk to the goddamn doctors, see when they are going to treat you, for crying out loud." With that he turned and left the room, booming out with big steps of authority. My mother had regained her composure and made her way back to the bed. After a long blink, she forced a smile and reached out to my face. With the back of her fingers she touched my cheek. It was the touch I wanted, my mother's touch, telling me I was going to be alright. The tears finally came. A slow, steady flow of tears ran down my cheeks, stinging as they reached the burned flesh of my ear and neck.

"At least you still have your beautiful face, Son," she said, again lightly touching my cheek. It wasn't until I became a father of two beautiful sons that I fully realized how incredibly hard it must have been for my parents to see their son in that condition. I'm not a very religious man, but I pray that I never have to see one of my sons in that type of situation.

"The nurse said if I didn't have a beard, my face would be just as bad as my neck. That and the fact that I covered it as much as I could." As I spoke, I felt my throat drying out and starting to hurt. A slight cough followed my sentences, and my mother shushed me and got me a cup of water. She held it to my crispy lips, and I drank from it greedily. I hadn't realized how thirsty I was, that I hadn't drank anything since the burn hours before. After a few more sips and touches on the cheek, my dad returned with a furious look on his face and a doctor following him.

"Kane, this is the doctor who is going to be taking care of you. He wants to get you to surgery right away to do some skin grafts," my dad said, taking charge. The doctor didn't introduce himself or even look at my face once; he lifted the sheet a few times and talked directly to my father.

"They are prepping the operating room now. We'll have him into surgery in about a half hour. Don't worry, I'll get your son fixed up." With a pat on my dad's shoulder, the doctor left the room. I don't know if it was the fact that he ignored me or treated me like a car that he was about to fix, but the man gave me the creeps.

Though the doctor seemed confident in the fact that he was going to take care of me, my parents still said goodbye to me as if I could die in the operating room. Mom lightly kissed the tiny square of good skin on my cheek, while my father nodded and told me he loved me. Their goodbyes made my stomach tighten for what I was about to go through.

LET THE HEALING *NOT* BEGIN

During the first skin graft surgery I was unconscious. Getting rolled in and prepped for the surgery is a foggy memory of lights passing on the ceiling and white lab coats leaning over me. Waking up, on the other hand, was different. As the anesthesia wore off, I had forgotten where I was or what happened. The bright lights above me were not the dim bulbs in my bedroom that I was used to. Blinking over and over again, my eyes stinging, I tried to sit up, only to feel pain wash over me. *What the fuck?* I had to be dreaming, so I tried to rub my eyes to wake up, only…I couldn't move my arms. Not one inch. I started fighting to move, to move something, to wake up from this nightmare when, finally, a nurse came over and looked down at me. Seeing her little white cap and collar made me remember everything. I would have rather stayed in my nightmare than to wake up and realize it was all real.

The nurse gave me a few ice chips, which I voraciously sucked on, not realizing how dry and itchy my throat was. She then went on to explain that I had two skin grafts under my arms and the doctor had put both of my arms in splints because when you graft skin, it can tighten and tear if it doesn't heal properly. He wanted to let the skin have time to heal, so he locked my arms straight out, like Jesus on the cross. The idea of not being able to rub my eyes or scratch an itch put me into a small panic. The nurse saw this and adjusted a tube that came out of the IV above my bed; I started to calm down.

After a few hours in recovery, they decided I was ready to be moved to a regular room. They wheeled me down the hall, the lights on the ceiling zipping by my vision. Not being able to sit up and see where I was going drove me nuts, but I did my best to stay calm. If it wasn't for the morphine and the fact that I was still in shock, I would have been tearing the splints off and fighting to get out of that bed.

If my hospital stay was not a true story, if it were made into some Hollywood movie, it would end up being a comedy of errors. From the point of arriving at my room until I left the first hospital four months later, everything went wrong. The mistakes and the accidents were so stupid that it would almost have to play as a comedy, because no one would believe that people could screw up that much. But they did. And if I wasn't in so much pain, if my life wasn't in danger on a daily basis, it would have been almost funny how horribly wrong everything went. Sadly, the fact that everything did go wrong fucked up my life. And it all started with them getting me into my hospital room.

Somehow, no one realized that if you splinted a man's arms straight out, you couldn't fit him through a doorway. As they tried to wheel me into the room, this realization suddenly came about. All I could see was the ceiling and glimpses of the orderlies' faces as they leaned over and tried pushing the bed through the door. As I watched the top of the doorframe come close to my face, I cringed, knowing that my arms would hit the walls. Luckily they realized this just in time to pull me back to try another angle. Again and again they tried different ways to "angle" me into the room. One of them leaned over to me and told me to hang on while they got some help. Thankfully my brain was still swimming in a haze of shock; otherwise I would have exploded at the morons for trying to get me through the door. Their efforts were about as useful as trying to get a square peg into a round hole; it was impossible.

Some minutes later, still in the hallway, I could hear voices around me talking, whispering as if they didn't want me to understand what they were saying. Then finally, someone, who I guess was the doctor on duty, gave me a quick once over and said, "He'll be fine to get up. Just get him up and walk him into the room."

I wanted to tell the woman she was insane and to wheel me back into the recovery room, but at the same time I wanted nothing more than to have this over with, so I did as I was told. They wheeled the bed back; the two orderlies grabbed my splinted arms and *pulled* me up. The sudden tearing pain in my body caused the first of countless screams to be released from my mouth. Sitting up, they then grabbed my gauze-covered legs with their bare hands, squeezed them, and pulled them over the edge of the bed for me to stand. This time I let out a low moan as they put way too much pressure on my open wounds. With my feet dangling above the ground, they told me to stand up. Needing to get it over with, I did as I was told.

There I was, only a few hours after suffering third degree burns over most of my body, only minutes after waking up from major surgery, being forced to stand up and *walk* into my room...all because they were too stupid to think ahead and realize I would not fit through the door. As I waddled in, every step sent a shock wave of pain over all of my burns. My arms resting on their splints felt like a thousand pounds of pressure pushing down on my open wounds. As they set me down in the bed, the pain was even worse. Laying down, pulling and pushing me into place, it should have never happened. As they adjusted me, I could feel skin twist, tear, and stretch. Crying to myself, I thought that it would be all over in a few seconds and it was... only the pain didn't stop.

"Are you comfortable?" one of the orderlies asked when they finished getting me into the bed. Gritting my teeth, I did everything I could to give him the finger, but I couldn't even move one of them. As they left the room I heard footsteps approaching my bed, and not being able to see the door drove me nuts. Looking towards the noise the best I could, I saw my father come into view. His face was slackened; I could tell he had seen everything I just went through. And though he wasn't the one injured, I could see he was feeling the pain of the ordeal as well. Standing next to the bed, he looked at me with sad eyes. As he was about to speak his face suddenly contorted, his skin went a bit green, his eyes squinted, and he darted out of the room. I called his name out, but my burned throat wouldn't let me go above a whisper. Over the hospital sounds, I could hear retching in the hall way... my dad was throwing up.

It wasn't until much later I found out that my father had smelled my burned flesh when he was standing above me. For some reason, when he saw me in the ER before the surgery, he hadn't gotten a whiff of the awful smell. At that moment though, just a few minutes after surgery, the smell was strong, and he inhaled it fully. The stench would bother any normal person, but my father had also been in the Korean War. He saw his friends and colleagues burned and blown up a few too many times. The smell that day brought back those memories, only it was worse because this time it was his son. That first visit really fucked my father up. As any father knows, seeing your kid with even a scraped knee stabs your heart. Seeing your son burned beyond recognition, not knowing if he is going to die or not... I can't imagine.

EGOTISTICAL FUCKING DOCTOR

Over the years, I have become a sort of expert on burns and care for victims. It's sort of inevitable once you suffer a severe burn. At the time of the incident though, I didn't know shit about burns, and neither did my parents. It was the late 1970's when people still thought that putting butter on a burn would make it better. None of us knew anything about what you should or shouldn't do in this situation. It wasn't like modern times where you can pull out a cell phone and look up the proper methods for treating an injury. The three of us were oblivious of what to do; therefore, we trusted the doctor. He was the authority after all, so why wouldn't we trust him? The only problem was the doctor was an egotistical fuck, who didn't know shit about how to deal with burns. Instead of admitting this and sending me to a hospital that actually had a burn unit, he kept me in his hospital so he could prove to the staff, and to himself, that he could heal my injuries. Let's call him Dr. A, for Dr. Asshole.

These statements are not an assumption; these words came out of his mouth years later. Several years after my burns, I was so angry with my treatment that I went to confront the doctor. I was angry because if I had been treated properly, if I was immediately put in a burn unit and cared for, my injuries and scars would not have been a quarter as bad as they were. That day I went down to his office, I honestly didn't know if I was going to kill him or not. The years of trauma and rage over what I experienced had built up in a hatred for this man. The burn might have been my fault, but my fucked-up recovery was his.

Unannounced, I burst into Dr. A's office. I rushed his desk like a bull, I was seeing red, and I wanted nothing more than to jump over the desk and stick his fucking stethoscope down his throat and pull it out his ass. For some reason, and I don't know how, I didn't. Instead, boiling with rage, I accused him, told him he fucked up my life and to admit it. Though he could see in my eyes the fact that one wrong word might make me kill him, he did not seem nervous. Instead, he looked sad, defeated almost. Rubbing his face he started to talk and to apologize for my treatment. He admitted to being a young doctor who was determined to prove he could heal burns.

"I was wrong. I didn't know what I was doing, but I honestly thought I could help you. I wanted to heal you, I wanted to show everyone I could do it, but I screwed up." Though my rage was still bubbling, I no longer wanted to kill him, maybe because I never expected him to admit the truth? Though hearing him didn't change anything, it somehow made me feel a bit relieved. He went on to tell me more about how he fucked up. As he went on I looked around his office, looking for something to break over his head. When he finished his apology, amazingly, I did nothing. I turned around and walked out the door.

My life could have changed that day. I honestly thought I was going to kill him or, at least, beat the shit out of him. I would have gone to jail, life would have taken me down a different path, but something forced me out of the office. Part of me still wished I did get some sort of revenge. Though in a way, I like to think that my success in my career has been my revenge, because I didn't let his mistakes ruin my life. Regardless, I still want to go piss on his grave someday.

A STUD'S ROUTINE

With burns, the proper treatment should be immediately given. First off, a victim should be brought to a burn unit right away. Burn units specialize in treating the injuries and staff medical experts. Patients should be placed in a sterile environment and given pain injections, be debrided, and have expert skin grafts done. While Dr. A tried to do some of these things, the few he did do, he fucked up royally. He was so concerned about my being dehydrated he stuck an IV in me and pumped me with way, way too much fluid. In the first five days of my stay, I gained 25 pounds of weight, all of which was from fluid retention.

Saying you have big balls is usually a manly statement, but in my case during those first few days, my balls were bigger than big. They swelled to the size of grapefruits, and that is not an exaggeration. They got so big, I could not piss. The rest of my body started to swell as well. My feet looked like some ballooned cartoon character version of myself. Of course, this hydration process became counterproductive to my healing as they were stretching the skin that needed to be healed. They were also fucking up my organs by making them over-process fluids. It took them a few days to realize that they were slowly killing me with overhydration. When they finally figured this out, they cut down the IVs, and my weight dropped instantly. Over the next four days I lost the 25 pounds I had gained in the first five days. I may have shriveled back down to my normal size, but my problems were far from over.

At the time of my accident, I couldn't help it, but I thought I was a hot shit. I was 22 years old, dating three different girls, and thinking I was a Hollywood stuntman. I didn't think life could get any better. I might have needed some money, but other than that, everything was amazing. Then suddenly, I was in the hospital, disfigured, and on the edge of death. Lying in bed that first night, I was too angry to cry. I was furious at myself for fucking up the way I did. I kept going over every little detail. *Why did it have to be windy the day before? Why didn't we go back to the lake where I could have jumped in? Why was that rubber cement so strong? I should have tested it.* Over and over again I tried to figure out what I could have changed to not be in the situation I was in. A useless task, but it kept my mind busy.

The real humiliation came when I had to take a piss for the first time. There I was, lying in a bed not being able to move, which meant that if I had to piss, I had to call for help. Being that I couldn't yell with my burned throat, they put the call button for the nurse at my feet. It took a lot of work and pain to push it with my toe, but I really had to piss, so I hit it. The image of some hairy, old lady nurse flashed in my eyes and grossed me out—I didn't want her to touch me. Then when I saw the actual nurse come in, I wished the hairy old hag would have been there, for the nurse had to be about my age and cute as hell.

"What can I help you with, my dear?" Although my face had a constant slight burning feeling, when I saw her, it burned red hot. I contemplated telling her I accidentally pushed the button. I had to piss so bad though (from the excessive amount of fluids being pumped into me), that I couldn't. With a smile plastered on her face she reached under the end table and pulled out a piss bottle. I started to get nervous and sweat. Without hesitating or asking me if I was ready, the girl pulled down my sheets, pulled up the gown I had on, and grabbed my dick, and placed it in the bottle.

"Go ahead," she said in almost a whisper. I wanted to cry I was so fucking humiliated. It was the first time I had ever been touched in a non-intimate way, and it was strange as hell. Thankfully I had to go so badly there was no holding it in. I pissed, nearly filling the bottle. The woman gently covered me back up and went into the bathroom to pour it out. When she asked if I needed anything else, I just shook my head, too frustrated to say a word. When she left the room I laid there crying as quietly as I could.

Though it was mortifying, I got used to pushing that damn button with my toe. Those first few weeks I had hacking fits every few minutes. I'd cough over and over again until my mouth was filled with black phlegm from my burned lungs and throat shedding dead cells. Each cough sent a shock of pain through my body, but worst of all, I had to hold the nasty phlegm in my mouth until a nurse came in with a bucket for me to spit in. The gobs were thick and tasted of soot and bile. Sometimes I'd have to hold it in my mouth for five or ten minutes as I waited for them. Then, after a few days, the nurses stopped coming when I pushed the button. With the amount of fluids they had pumping into me, I had to piss literally every five minutes. They got so tired of waiting on me, they wouldn't come for an hour at a time. Though it disgusted me, I started spitting these mouthfuls of gunk at the wall. I would turn my head and just spit as far as I could so it wouldn't land on me. It was horrible, but there was nothing I could do. It was either hold it in my mouth for an hour and almost choke, or spit it. This added to my humiliation and annoyed the nurses more as they had to clean up my globs of spit.

During this period I had no appetite. The food caused a burning sensation on its way down my throat and left me not wanting to eat anything, especially since I had to be fed every single bite like a damned baby. Sometimes my parents would feed me, which I didn't mind much, but half of the time the nurses, who really didn't want to be there, fed me as if it was a race they were trying to win. After a while, I started to actually act like a baby and hold my lips tight when I didn't want any more. They supplemented my eating by pouring liquid nutrition down a feeding tube that was in my nose. Getting fed that way was an unnatural, horrible feeling. Eating so little thankfully meant that I didn't have to shit too much, though it still had to happen every now and then. Those moments... were the most mortifying in my life. Not being able to move my arms and laying down to take a dump while someone holds a pan under your ass, and then having to have them wipe you... I hate even remembering it.

By the third day the pain really started to kick in. The drugs they were giving me didn't do shit. Every inch of my body screamed with pain at the slightest vibration. If you have ever had a burn on your hand and accidentally hit it against something, it hurts like hell. Now times that by a million and over your entire body. The slightest touches made me scream. In fact, those first few days they hardly took me out of bed as if they were scared to touch me. One of the only times they did was to weigh me. The process of getting me to stand up was so painful I actually passed out on two different occasions. Even to this day, those were the only times I have ever passed out.

With the trauma of the injury, I had trouble sleeping. Every time I would start to fall asleep I would suddenly jerk awake. I'm not sure if it was from fear or just that my nervous system was all screwed up. Moving my body so suddenly would cause me to lift my arms, half sit up, and twist a bit in my bed. Since the touch of a feather would make me scream, the pain caused by these sudden movements was overwhelming. My body would ache so badly that it would take almost a full hour for the pain to subside. When it finally did and I started to fall asleep... it would happen all over again. It was a sickening routine.

Mom and Dad sat with me every day, and I was thankful for that. Only problem was my mom had tunnel vision. It's a disease called retinitis pigmentosa, something she suffered with for many years. Tunnel vision means you have no peripheral vision; you see small circles of vision and nothing outside the circle. When I was a kid I used to get so mad at her because I didn't understand it. I would work for hours on building a toy castle, and my mom would walk right through the living room and knock it down because she didn't see it. The same thing happened in the hospital. Time after time she would bump into my bed, making me scream my head off. It wasn't her fault; she couldn't see it, but it still pissed me off.

My poor mother was also hard of hearing. Those first few weeks, I could hardly speak because of the burns in my throat. Besides my sudden, painful screams, I could only whisper. She could hardly hear me so I'd have to repeat myself over and over again, hurting my throat and frustrating both of us. I was fucking miserable. Day in and day out I would lie in the bed, watch TV, have people force feed me, wipe my ass, and all I could do was feel sorry for myself. It was torture beyond anything that another human could cause. Looking back now I can't imagine living through one day in that bed, let alone six months.

DEBRIDEMENT

Debridement is a medical technique used to help burn victims' skin heal. Basically, it's the removal of the dead tissue that forms over the burns so the healthy skin can have a chance to grow. Serious burns need to be debrided on a daily basis. The way they remove the skin is…unsavory. At least it was in the '70s. The doctor would take the dull side of a surgical blade and scrape the burns until the dead skin was peeled off.

The first time the doctor mentioned this process, I had no clue what he was talking about. He didn't even explain it. Dr. A merely said, "We are going to take you downstairs to debride your burns."

I asked my parents what he meant, but they didn't know either. They gave me a small pill for the pain and then put me in a wheelchair. The process of getting into the wheelchair was painful enough to have me feeling like I was going to vomit. After a quick elevator ride, they brought me down a dimly lit hallway. Looking at the doors, I realized that this hall did not house patients. They pushed me into a small windowless room that had nothing more than a counter, a steel tub in the middle of the room and a large light above the tub. The room would work perfectly in any of the horror movies I would later star in.

"What are they going to do?" I whispered. The orderly ignored my question and helped me get up. Quietly removed my clothing and placed me into the tub that was already filled with warm water. The man's rough hands, the pressure on my burns, and the sudden feel of the water exhausted me. I wanted nothing more than to be back in my bed, where at least I could lay still enough to make the pain a little more tolerable. After several minutes of sitting alone in the tub, my arms out to my sides, I heard the door behind me open and close. Dr. A went to the counter without saying anything, opened a drawer, took something out, and walked over to me. I felt awkward enough as I was sitting naked in the tub, not being able to cover myself up, but then the doctor stood above me and stared down as if he was examining how to best attack me.

I kept my mouth shut, not wanting to show him how nervous and scared I was for whatever the hell he was about to do. Then, he pulled over a small wheeled stool and took a seat next to the tub. As he focused the light on me I noticed the blade in his hands. *Jesus Christ.*

"This is going to hurt, but do your best not to move." With that he grabbed my arm, flipped the blade to the flat side and scraped it along my arm. The pain was worse than getting the burns, worse than the rough orderly's hands squeezing them, worse than anything I had ever felt or could ever imagine... it was beyond description. I tried my best to jerk away from him, but he kept a firm grip on my wrist which made everything hurt all the more as I pulled away. By the second scrape, I was screaming my head off.

If Satan exists and tortures people in Hell, I do not doubt that debridement is his main torture method. Dr. A spent an eternity scraping the skin off of every inch of my burns. He rinsed the knife in the tub until the entire surface was covered in a thick foamy layer of my dead skin. By the time he reached my legs, my screams had turned into moaning sobs. When he was done, my skin did not stop burning and aching. Every inch of the burns had ached since I had been in the hospital, but not nearly as much as after the debridement. Now they screamed with pain. And this was to be a daily thing.

From that day on, every time they came in to take me down for the "treatment" as they started to call it, I would do everything I could to avoid it or at least delay it. There were times I would pretend to faint when they stood me up. That way they would put me back in the bed for an hour. I'd act like I had to throw up or that I had something wrong, anything, anything, to get out of that torture. It was simply the harshest, most indescribable pain that no one could ever understand unless they went through it themselves.

What made all of this worse, my entire experience worse, was something I didn't learn about until after I was out of the hospital. My father, having seen a lot of his wartime buddies become junkies after getting out of the hospital, didn't want that happening to his son. He was so scared of the idea of me becoming addicted to painkillers, that he pulled aside the doctor and asked him to stop giving them to me. Of course, Dr. A didn't try to fight my father; he simply agreed and took me off the painkillers without telling me. Meaning, almost the entire time that I was in the hospital, suffering in excruciating pain, I was on *no* painkillers. The only one they gave me was Tylenol 3®, which is just Tylenol® with a minuscule dose of codeine. In the pain I was in, it did shit.

Years later, when I first found out what my father did, I was furious. The realization that the pain I went through could have been numbed, it made me blow my top. Then, I thought about it from his point of view. He had to suffer for years seeing his friends deteriorate and become homeless, hopeless bums on the street, all because they got hooked on pain pills and other drugs. Whether it was that idea or the fact that I just loved him, I forgave him without ever mentioning to him the fact that I knew. There was just no way I could be angry with my father. Even if my suffering was worsened, he was just trying to help me.

WORSE

Everyday my parents came to visit me, and every single day they saw me get worse. With burns, you usually get a little better with each day. Some type of improvement. I, on the other hand, seemed to be going downhill. After several weeks of getting progressively worse, Dr. A finally decided that I needed to be in a sterile environment. Since I had been in the hospital, I had been in a regular room with regular "sick" patients. People were walking in and out all day long with no masks, gloves, or protective wear on. The roommates I had came and went and coughed and hacked their germs into the air, the same air that was landing on my open wounds.

The hospital did not have a sterile room, so Dr. A asked the maintenance guy to come and put up plastic in my room. One day, as I lay miserable as always, the maintenance guy, filthy as all hell, came in to do the job. He nodded at me, set up a ladder, and set down a toolbox on the foot of my bed. The movement made me yelp; he ignored it as he left to get the rest of his materials. The next two hours were filled with hammering, ceiling tile dust falling all over me, and sheets of plastic being draped over the walls, floor, and ceiling. The last piece he put in place was over the door. He cut a strip down the middle so people could get in and out. How regular, un-sanitized sheets of plastic he carried under his sweaty armpits made my room sanitary, I do not know.

The theory was to have everyone who entered the room gown up and sanitize themselves before they entered my new "sterile" environment. The nurses found this even more annoying and started attending to my needs less and less as they hated having to gown up all the time. Everyone realized how serious my situation was and followed the rule of putting on gowns and masks, even the people who brought me my food. Everyone that is, except for one person... Dr. A. For some unknown reason, the jackass doctor, who issued the order, felt he was above it. As if he could not possibly carry any germs, even after he just checked on ten sick patients. One particular day, he came in dressed in his street clothes as he was about to go play tennis. He just pushed aside the curtain and strolled in wearing sneakers and shorts. He looked me over, lifted my bandages without gloves on, and nodded as if he thought I was getting better.

It was like I was the boy in the bubble, only my fucking bubble had a giant hole in it and was useless industrial plastic wrap. Basically, Dr. A read in some journal of medicine that I should be in a sanitary environment and having the maintenance guy stick up the sheets was the best he could come up with to achieve that environment. He didn't even bother having them try to filter the air, it was pointless, and it just became a hassle more than anything.

During this "sanitized" period, I went through numerous skin grafts—another horribly painful procedure. They would have to put me out and then peel a thin layer of skin from one healthy part of my body and put it on one of the burned parts, hoping that it would take and heal over the skin. One after another, Dr. A would schedule and give me a skin graft operation. And every single one of them wouldn't take. The skin he grafted would die and slough off. He became more and more frustrated with the fact that the grafts were not working. I, on the other hand, was in more pain every day as each time they did a graft, I had a new wound to heal from where they peeled the skin off. Most of the skin he was taking was from my legs, and to this day I have scars all over them just from the donor sites. There was even a point when he started taking skin from my lower stomach, right above my groin. If he knew what he was doing, he would have known that you should never take skin from there.

I ended up having so many procedures and shots that my veins collapsed and hardened in my arms. They could no longer take blood or give me needles in countless places on my body; even my ass cheeks had become hard as rocks. They ended up having to take blood from the femoral artery in my groin. A needle there is no picnic, to say the least. As each one of these needles pierced my body, I got sicker and sicker. My body got weaker, I was losing weight, and I looked worse on a daily basis. Every time my parents would ask about this, Dr. A would make up some sort of an excuse and say it was all part of the process. It was bullshit, but again, we didn't know better and trusted him.

Frustrated that the skin under my arms wouldn't take the grafts, Dr. A came up with a new idea—locking my arms in place. That way the skin wouldn't be moved and could heal. Keeping them at a 90-degree angle should do the trick. Only he wasn't satisfied just putting them into a sling this time. No, instead, he drilled holes right through my elbows and put pins through my bones. Then he put me in skeletal traction so that I would lie flat on my back and my arms would be held up by the pins in my elbows so I couldn't move at all. The doctor then put me on bed rest and made sure no one took me out of that bed for any reason at all...

Thirty-one days, thirty-one fucking days I did not get out of that bed. Not once. Every meal, every shit and piss, every bath, all done from my bed. I saw nothing more than the plastic walls of my room, the TV, and my parents, all while not being able to move my arms. Near the end of the month I started to form massive bedsores. Bedsores are created from slow constant pressure on one spot. Not moving for that long caused these sores all over my back, ass, and legs. They were so horrible that when they tried to finally move me, my skin stuck to the bed. The fucking idiots did not move or rotate me the entire month. In nursing homes, the patients get bedsores for one reason—neglect. It was no different for me.

Over my entire stay in the hospital, I had bedsores. I couldn't lie in *any* other position but on my back. I couldn't lean on my side, not even for a second. Imagine six months straight, lying on your back and *never* being able to change positions. During eight hours of sleep the average person changes positions dozens of times. Always having to be on your back, no matter what, I can't even explain the torture it was.

For that entire month I did nothing but cry and get angry. Imagine not being able to move your arms at all. That itch on your nose, you can't scratch it. Have to take a dump, someone has to help you. Eating, need help. Then, add on massive amounts of pain and the fact that you can't get out of bed. Go ahead, try it; sit in bed for an hour with your arms above your head; see how well you do. Then just imagine it for a month straight. There is no way Hell could be any worse. The only fucking thing I could do was change the television channel with my toe. I couldn't even read a book. Pure and utter torture.

After thirty-one days, they finally decided it was safe to take the pins out of my elbows and lower my arms. Dr. A actually showed up for this, as if he wanted to show off the amazing work he did giving me new skin. They quickly removed the pins, bandaged up the wounds on my elbows, and stepped back.

"Alright, Kane, lower your arms," Dr. A said as if he was a magician about to pull the sheet off a box to show that his assistant was gone. When I tried to lower them, I quickly realized that I wasn't holding my arms up, they were stuck; I couldn't put them down.

"I...I can't." The doctor laughed as if not believing me. Grabbing my arms he gently tried to lower them as if showing me how easy it was. They wouldn't move. They had healed into place. Embarrassed, the doctor muttered that they would come down in time and that it had all been worth it, before rushing out of the room. It took a full week of therapy just to get me to be able to straighten out my arms. Dr. A, all along, said it was going to be worth it as I was going to have good healthy skin under my arms now. After all of that... the grafts did not take. To add to the already incredible amount of humiliation that I had already endured, I had another emotional setback. I always needed to sign my name for legal documents for various reasons. I couldn't use my hands at all, so for a period of a couple of months I signed my name with an *X*. That's right. They would jam the pen into my bandaged hand and I would make an *X* in the signature line. It was legal as long as there was a witness who signed it as well. Talk about feeling useless and utterly helpless.

TIME SLIPS BY AND I GET WORSE

Four months, graft after graft, horror after horror I sat in that bed. If I had normal, good treatments, I should have been up and moving and doing pretty well at that point. Instead, I felt worse at the four-month point than I did that first week they brought me in. Nothing was healing; my burns were *still* open wounds. They gave me seven major grafts during those months. Hardly any took and the area they covered was less than 15 percent of what it needed to cover. Worst of all, I started to feel horribly sick on top of the pain of my burns. I was getting so sick, that Dr. A called my parents in for a meeting.

The doctor did not want to talk to my parents in front of me, but my father was adamant that if it was about me, then I deserved to hear it as well. I was happy that my dad was sticking up for me, but at the same time, when I heard the news, I wished they had talked in the other room.

"As you know, Kane has been getting worse. We did some tests and we found out that the reason his grafts are not taking and why he is getting sicker is because he has a staph infection. It's rather serious and to be honest… I don't think he is going to make it." Hearing this I wanted to kick and punch anything and everything I could, but moving was still too painful. All I could do was clench my teeth and shut my eyes tightly as I cursed the world in my head. As I heard my mother sob and my father stand up and argue, I pretended in my head that I was doing a high fall. There was always something magical about the moment you start to fall through the air. The feeling of having no pressure anywhere on your body. The soothing sound of the wind whipping by your ears. The sensation of tumbling, twisting through the air. Having no pressure on my body and the wind soothing my wounds would have felt so wonderful in that moment, but as hard as I tried, the words of the doctor pulled me out of my daydream.

"There is not much more we can do for him here. We are going to transfer him to a burn unit in San Francisco. They will be able to treat him better there; they are specially equipped to treat burn patients." *What? A fucking burn unit? Why haven't I been there all along?* I screamed in my head. My father was obviously thinking along the same lines.

"Why didn't you send him there in the first place?" There was anger in my father's voice I had never heard before. As the doctor started to answer his question, he stood up and backed towards the door as if he was retreating.

"Well, we tried for months to get him in, but it's a small unit, and it has been full. A bed finally came open this week, and that's why we can now send him. We are going to transfer him by plane tomorrow. I have to go finish the paperwork." With that he left the three of us too dumfounded to talk.

Though none of us believed that a bed had "miraculously" just opened when I was on death's door, we didn't bother discussing it. There was no point in arguing the fact that the doctor tried to prove he could heal me, but when he couldn't he decided to ship me off before I died so it wouldn't be on his watch. It was done and over with, and I was to be sent to a new place, hopefully, a better one.

Before the burn, I was in excellent shape. I worked out every day and practiced my stunts any chance I got. I went from being a scrawny 140-pound teen to being a ripped 190 pounds.

It took me years to build up my body and get into the shape I was. It was a constant fight to get into that shape, and by the time I left the hospital in Reno, I was back down to less than 140 pounds. Having almost never left the bed, my muscles shrunk down to practically nothing. They were used so little that my legs had atrophied to the point where I couldn't walk, or even stand. The doctors said the only reason I lived was because of the shape I was in and the fact that I was young enough to handle the trauma.

The day I was to leave the hospital, my parents and I were ecstatic that I could finally get some *real* help. The only problem was that instead of being able to drive home every night after visiting me, they were now going to drive over four hours and have to stay in a hotel, all of which was going to cost them money they didn't have. I felt horrible about it and even told them they didn't have to come down to visit me, but I was told to stop being ridiculous. As I was prepped to leave, they both said goodbye to me and said they would see me in San Francisco. The looks they gave me were the same as the first time I went into surgery, as if they didn't think I was going to make it.

When they strapped me into the gurney they winched me in a bit too tightly. The straps cut into my burns, stinging. Just breathing caused great pain as each breath forced my burns into the straps. I asked them to loosen them, but they said I had a long, bumpy ride and had to be in nice and tight. I struggled a bit trying to loosen them, but it just caused more irritation. The first moment I went outside for the first time in four months, the sun was so bright my eyes killed me; I could hardly open them. You'd think someone could have foreseen that problem, but of course they didn't. I truly think I damaged my eyes for good on that day. They transported me by ambulance to the airport, and thankfully this one didn't break down, though of course, things still went wrong. Once again, they did not plan things out ahead of time. The plan was to use a small charter plane to transfer me. No one had the foresight to measure the door, meaning the gurney…I did not fit.

There I was, the sun beating down on my burns, the straps cutting into me, laying on a gurney in the middle of a runway as they tried to figure out how to get me on the plane. Since I couldn't walk, their genius idea was to *tilt* the gurney to get it in. Without warning, they tightened the straps even more and tipped me to the left. I let out a scream as I thought I was about to fall. When I slid tight against the straps, my new still-healing skin started splitting open. They jostled the gurney, bumped it into the doorframe over and over again until they got me safely inside. Though I physically hadn't moved, it was exhausting.

The flight wasn't much better. Every pocket of turbulence we hit caused a wave of horrible pain. The nurse, who was stationed to sit next to me and monitor my vital signs, fell asleep twice during the one-hour flight, letting my IV drip stop. I had to scream over the engine (we were near the engines strapped into a cargo holding area) to get her attention, but even then she didn't wake up. I gave up and figured, or more so hoped, that I would be fine without the shit they were pumping into me.

As we flew, I swore to myself that I would never set foot into that godforsaken hospital again. Unfortunately, many years later my nephew Danny got into a serious car accident and was in a coma. The only way to visit him was to go into that hellhole, to the same floor where I was tortured for months. It took everything I had in the world to walk through those doors. When I walked down the hall, I couldn't help but look at the lights. They were the same piece of shit fluorescent ones I stared at when they wheeled me back and forth down the hall for my treatments. It made me feel nauseated just being there, but I had to do it for my nephew. Sadly, it never got easier; every time I went to visit him, I had to go through the same physical and mental anguish.

After the short flight, which felt like a cross-Atlantic journey, we landed with a bumpy touchdown that made it feel like I was in a vibrating bed. When they pulled me out, I had to suffer one last time through the tipping of the gurney, but after that, I had arrived in a legitimate burn unit...and things started to change.

THE HEALING BEGINS

The second I was wheeled into the burn unit at St. Francis Hospital in San Francisco, I could tell everything was going to be different. First off, the entire ward was set up so the patients could be observed. Unlike the dark, dank room covered in sheets of plastic, these rooms had glass walls and sealed doors with proper ventilation to make them sterilized. There was a nurse's station outside of the rooms so they could constantly monitor the patients. Immediately upon entering they sanitized, debrided, and shot me up full of antibiotics. In a matter of a few days, I was looking and feeling a slight bit better. My parents looked happier than they had the entire time they had been visiting me. I was in a better mood than I had been since the burn, and everything was on the right path... finally. It was about this time that my dad realized that I couldn't heal fully without proper pain medication. As they slowly worked it into my system, it helped a lot.

It took a mere six days for my staph infection to be cleared up. *Six days.* In Reno I had the infection for months, to the point where the doctor was declaring that I was going to die. Before they arrived I had been put under so many times that they could no longer use the normal chemicals to knock me out. They ended up having to use Ketamine, or as it's known on the streets, Special K. The shot would paralyze me, but I would still be awake for the surgeries, which I never was beforehand. I couldn't feel anything, but I could see and hear everything. The worst part was that I couldn't move a muscle or even talk. Hands down, it was the fucking freakiest thing I ever had to live through. It was just like the countless horror movies you've seen where the main character is on the table, trying to scream in their head as the knife approaches, but they can't do anything about it. It was terrifying... but I just kept telling myself that it was going to make me better.

The first roommate I had in the burn unit, Paul, made me feel comfortable for the first time, for he *knew* what I was going through. Having someone else to talk to, who understood what I was going through, was a huge relief. Paul was actually in much worse shape than I was. He was a pipeline worker—a pipe exploded and he got burned over 85 percent of his body. I thought I had it bad being burned over 50 percent of my body. The sad part, for me at least, was that after only six weeks, he was up and walking, in better shape than I was at four months—four months! That simple fact made me so furious over how I was treated. It was then that it all really sunk in, how much Dr. A fucked up my treatment and almost killed me. The fact that the doctors in the burn unit were able to clear up my life-threatening staph infection in a week alone, really showed me just how horribly I was treated in Reno. In addition to my pain, there was now a layer of anger over my mood.

As I started to feel better, my mind started to work in a clearer fashion. This clear thought process got me thinking more and more about stunts. All I could think of was getting out and getting back to doing what I loved. Though I could hardly move, in my mind I went through every stunt, step-by-step, so I would be ready to perform them when I got out. The burn sidetracked my career, but I was not going to let it stop me. I was revving and ready to go.

My parents couldn't understand my enthusiasm. Dad even barked at me, "You are in stunts for six months and you almost die and you want to go back to it? Really?"

I had never seen my father's face show such confusion as when I answered, "Of course, why wouldn't I?" I honestly meant it, too. Regardless of what happened, I wanted to get back to the one thing I truly loved. And just when I thought I was getting better, when I would be back doing stunts soon…that's when the depression hit me.

THE MAN IN THE HALLWAY

I'm a fucking freak... what girl will ever look at me again? The better I got, the worse my thoughts became. Most burn victims suffer clinical depression at some point in their recovery. In fact, two of the people I was in the unit with killed themselves later over their burns. While those thoughts slipped in and out of my head, it was mostly thoughts about how no one would ever look at me the same way again, that I would be the grotesque freak that kids were scared of for the rest of my life. I lost all my muscles I worked so hard for, could barely lift my arms, and walking was impossible. I might have been getting better, but how could I ever *get better*? The damage was done and it felt permanent.

As I lay in the bed day after day, getting a bit stronger and physically feeling better, I got angrier. My parents would still visit pretty much every day, and every time they walked in, my mother would make a big show about how good I looked. Dad, who always grabbed a doctor to talk to before he came into my room, would boom about how the doctors said I was getting so much better. Even with all their smiles and praise, I slipped deeper into a dark place in my mind. All I could think about were stunts and the fact that I would never be able to do them again. How could I? I still couldn't stand on my own and who would want to hire a guy with burns all over his body? There was no way I could double someone without burns, and what if they thought I was too accident-prone?

Everything was fucking useless. Why waste everyone's time, the poor nurses and doctors spent countless hours a day taking care of me when they could be helping someone who wanted or needed them more? I was taking up a valuable bed in the burn ward. I was a waste of a life. The horrible part was that I knew I couldn't kill myself. I wasn't strong enough to do anything that would be detrimental. I knew I wouldn't really kill myself, but the thought that if I wanted to, I physically couldn't, and that pissed me off all that much more. This depression lasted for weeks. The longer I was depressed, the angrier and darker my mood became. I started to think about how my mood in the other hellhole was fine and here I was in a good place and now I was pissed? Just more fuel on the fire. Then, one day, in less than a five-minute time span, everything changed.

I was lying in bed, staring at the wall, ignoring the buzzing television above me. There was too much anger and self-pity floating around in my head for me to concentrate on whatever crap was playing. With one wall being completely made of glass, I spent a lot of time looking out at the people, the *normal people*, walking around and working, watching over freaks like me. Getting tired of staring at the wall, I took a sigh and focused my attention and anger at the nurses. There were several nurses I recognized standing at the desk. They were all talking to some man, a tall skinny man who was all gowned up (which you had to do to enter the unit). He was gesturing and waving his arms around telling some sort of big story. The nurses were laughing hysterically; the man was almost in tears as he smiled and laughed at whatever the hell he was saying. At first, I got pissed, *look at these assholes having fun out there.* Then the guy started to roll up his sleeves…

Burns, ugly, deeply scarred burns were all over this man's arms. Seeing this, I tried to sit up. Every thought of self-pity and anger in my head suddenly froze. The man slapped the desk he was laughing so hard. *He was happy.* I couldn't understand it—he was burned worse than me and yet, he was happy. Hell, he was downright enjoying his life. Whatever the story was, they all thought it was a riot. As the man went on and on, my eyes went from his arms to his huge smile. I just couldn't believe or, more so, understand it. My face started to get flushed as this odd sensation came over me. I hadn't felt it in a while, but it was a familiar feeling, *hope*.

How the man could live a normal life with burns like that, I couldn't really understand, yet at the same time, I didn't care. All that mattered was that the man *could* be happy, even looking like that. His burns looked so much worse than mine; if he could be happy, why the fuck couldn't I? It might have seemed simple, but that was all I needed to turn myself around mentally. Simply seeing someone else like me, living their life and enjoying it…was enough to let me realize that I could as well.

That day I did not get to meet that man or find out his name, though I did learn that he spent time in the unit himself and that he came back to talk to other burn patients, to give them hope. He never even made it into my room, yet he saved my life. To this day I can't think about that man or that moment without tearing up. Every time I tell that story, I cry and I'm not ashamed of it, because I know if it wasn't for him, I might not be here today. I may never know who that man was, but even if I did, there would be no way for me to thank him for what he did. It just amazes me that he never even knew that his silly conversation with some nurses changed someone's life.

After that day my mood was much better. I started talking more, taking a more active role in my rehabilitation and actually caring about getting better and getting out of the hospital. Of course I still had down times, but I did my best to think of the man during those moments and fight to find a smile in me. I might be scarred for life, but I was alive, and I was sure as hell going to live it to the fullest. Nothing was going to stop me anymore. No matter how hard I had to fight to get my life back, I was going to do it.

HOME FOR THE HOLIDAYS

The days and weeks slipped by, and I slowly healed up. My mood improved with each passing week, and I became more motivated as my wounds started to mend. By mid-December I was getting anxious to get out of the hospital—it had been almost six months straight, cooped up in stuffy rooms with nothing to do but watch television. Though I was eager to get out, I still wasn't healed up enough. That didn't stop my parents though; they wanted me home for Christmas and that was that. After numerous talks with the doctor, he finally agreed that I had made enough progress to go home for the holidays, as long as my mother learned how to clean and bandage the still-open wounds on my body.

Several days before my trip home, my mother stayed by my bed and took notes about every little detail the nurses did. She asked a hundred questions, and they even let her practice wrapping and sanitizing some of the still-healing wounds. I really didn't like having my mother touch me and take care of me in such an intimate way, but if it got me out of the hospital, then I was just fine with it. When the doctor approved of my mother's caregiving, he gave me the okay to head home. With a long list of instructions, a few medications, and explicit instructions to bring me back to the hospital if anything seemed to get worse, he gave me my walking papers. At first I thought it would be sad to say goodbye to all the people who took care of me and the roommates with whom I spent so much time, but I associated pain with them…I was fine leaving. As I sat in my hospital room alone waiting for the wheelchair to take me downstairs for the last time, I found myself reflecting on what I had just been through. I had survived 164 days, that's almost 24 weeks or 5½ months of torture, horror, terror beyond belief, and constant indescribable pain. I was still fucking here! I felt pretty damned proud. But now I realized something else. Most of the pain was gone, but now the really hard work was about to begin.

I flew back home from San Francisco on a commercial flight, and I don't really remember it. The only memory I have of that flight is when I stepped off the plane, I tried to wave to my friends and family and I could only raise my hand as high as my chest because the scars had tightened my whole body up beyond belief. The only clothing I could get on my body, since I could barely move at this point, was an athletic warm-up suit. I can't remember anything at all about the flight itself, but I distinctly remember the warm-up suit being baby blue. Weird. For almost six months the outside world was nothing more than an illusion to me. Feeling the fresh air on my face, to see the world zip by the windows, I was in heaven for the first time in ages. I hadn't realized how much I had missed the simplest things such as taking a drive, watching a cloud, or seeing the sun. On the ride home I vowed to myself to never take the small things in life for granted again. The million things we all do every day, we don't realize how wonderful they are until you can't do them, until you can't do anything but stare at a ceiling and scream in pain. I was thankful alright, and I was going home.

The homecoming was met with trepidation on my part. I had been bull-headed in the hospital, refusing to see *any* visitors except for my mother, father, and two half-sisters. Besides them, the only visitor I allowed in was a man I did not know.

Chuck Couch was a veteran stuntman, and at the time the stunt coordinator for *Hawaii Five-O*. He was in Reno on vacation when he saw an article in the paper about a local stuntman who got burned. The guy didn't know me at all, but he went out of his way to come and visit a fellow stuntman in the hospital. When the nurse told me I had a visitor, I told them to leave, but she gave me a look and said this one I might want to see. At the time, I had heard of his name as he was working on several shows doing stunts. When he came into my room I realized how fucking embarrassing it was going to be meeting him. Here I was some kid calling himself a stuntman, and I burn my own ass by mistake. He was going to think I was a fool, and he'd tell everyone in Hollywood to not hire that idiot. There was nothing I could do to stop him from coming in—at that point I still couldn't even move—it wasn't like I could jump up and shut my door.

When he did walk in, he had his hands in his pockets, he walked over to the bed, puckered his lips, and shook his head.

"God damn shame, kid. Burns hurt like shit, I can't imagine..." With that he pulled up a chair and sat next to me. He introduced himself, thankfully, without offering a hand to shake. We started some small talk about stunts and the training I had, but he never once steered the conversation to how I got burned. It was as if he knew I had fucked up and didn't want to rub it in my face. After a few minutes, I started to feel comfortable with him and actually enjoyed the company. We talked about some of the stunts he had done on certain shows and movies, and I told him how eager I was to get back into the industry.

"Don't worry, you are young, you have time. All you have to do is heal up and before you know it, you and I will be doing some stunts together." When he said that to me, for some reason I believed him beyond a doubt. After about a half hour, we said our goodbyes and he left his contact information with one of the nurses for me to have when I got out. Our conversation made me forget I was burned, even if for only a few minutes. It meant so much to me that he took time out of his vacation to come talk to some idiot kid who burned himself. The amazing part is that he was right. A few years later Chuck hired me on a little known TV show called *Time Express*, which starred Vincent Price. I only had a small stunt in the show, which required me to fall off a bike, but it was still one of my proudest moments being able to work with my childhood idol, Vincent Price, and with Chuck, whose compassion helped me get through my ordeal.

Besides that visit from Chuck, I had no other visitors, so my homecoming had made me nervous. I was about to see all the people I pushed away, whom I wouldn't let in to see me. It was also going to be the first time anyone saw how disfigured I was. We arrived home two days before Christmas to a small gathering of my family and a few family friends. I did my best to be polite and talk to everyone, but inside I became furious. I had to be in a wheelchair a lot of the time since all of my muscles were still in atrophy. I couldn't walk or even hold on to anything, therefore, everyone bent over and talked to me like I was a small child. Some of them even used soothing tones as if I couldn't understand what the fuck they were saying. It wasn't their fault though; they just didn't know how to deal with me. My mother wanted the party, she wanted me back in the family so I bit my tongue and put on a smile for as long as I could. After only an hour, I asked my mother to put me into bed because I was exhausted. She agreed and I left the party.

For weeks I had dreamed about being back in my own bed in my parents' house. The idea of home was just so soothing... those weeks of anticipation were over nothing. Yes, it was nice being in my room, but almost instantly I realized how ill-equipped it was for someone in my condition. The bed had no railings, it didn't move up and down with the push of a button, and it didn't have a nice tray that could be pushed over my lap to put a drink on. Things were going to be harder than I realized. Not being strong enough to move myself, I would have to scream for my mother to come into my room in the middle of the night to roll me over if I got too uncomfortable. I hated having to wake her up all the time. At least in the hospital the nurses were awake and were getting paid to do that shit. It was going to be rough, but at least I was out.

Just when a burn survivor thinks that things are starting to get easier, yet another ordeal presents itself during recovery. When your burned tissue finally starts healing, the scar tissue develops; it tightens up beyond belief. My right arm was contracted towards my body and my neck had tightened to the point where I could not straighten my head up as it was tilted to the right and locked into place. I couldn't even begin to raise my arms at all. The doctors said I would need surgery to get my skin back to where I could have any kind of normal movement. Limited as it would be, even at best—the thought of going back in the hospital and having more surgeries terrified me. I never wanted to drive by a hospital again, let alone go back in for more work. The fear of going back motivated me to make sure I didn't have to.

Every day, my mother would come into my room, help me go to the bathroom, (which was humiliating as all hell), feed me breakfast, and then stretch me. The stretching took a few hours a day. She would gently take my arms and push them the way they hadn't wanted to go for months. Using slow, steady pressure, she'd sit there and force the arm to stretch out. When the pain got to be too much, she'd ease off and move onto another area. She had the patience of a saint. Day after day, she fed and bathed me and spent hours giving me the therapy I so desperately needed. She hardly had time to even cook dinner because she spent so much time working on me.

After a few weeks of this routine, I started patient rehab; thankfully, I didn't have to go into the hospital for it. They helped me gain a little more movement, but I couldn't help but feel that my mom did a much better job than they did. Unlike the therapists I had, she was dedicated to me emotionally. There was much more at stake for her than there was from the guy who just finished college and was looking to "make some money." Though it exhausted me on a daily basis, the two therapies got me moving again. I could walk on my own, though not for long periods of time, and wonderfully, I could start to feed myself, roll over in bed alone and most importantly, take a shit without help. Things were tolerable and for the first time, I saw the light at the end of the tunnel. I started sleeping a little better but there was yet another odd phenomenon that would be something to overcome. Every so often, a few times a day, I would suddenly get a sharp, stabbing pain somewhere in my scars. It was an intense pain that was localized in one small area, always a different place in the scars. It felt just like I was being stabbed with a knife. A quick, sharp pain, and then gone. It was very strange. It would actually make me yelp sometimes. I didn't know at the time, but this would go on for years. I guess it was damaged nerves regenerating themselves or something.

When my flexibility started to improve and I could lift my arms above my head, I started to grab the doorframe and hang from it. The pain was excruciating. I would scream and spit to the point that the scar tissue in my armpits tore open. Horrible pain suffered at home would be a hundred times better than tiny bits of pain suffered in the hospital. Even though my skin ripped open, I would go back and do it the next day, tearing it again and again. Each night my mom would bandage the wounds after applying a cream the doctor prescribed. It was a painful routine, but I knew stretching myself out was a lot more important than a few rips in my skin. Little by little the tissue started to heal enough to where I could hang on the door without the skin tearing... my hard work was finally paying off.

Six solid months of the outpatient and "Mom" therapy and I was finally able to move my arms fully. Most of my burns were healed as well, but I was still a long way from being back to normal. When July rolled around, and the one year anniversary came about, I felt anxious. It was this odd feeling of unease, like I should be further along in the healing process or that I should have been back in stunts by then. Though I might have thought and felt this in my mind, I knew it was impossible. I was still too frail, and I had almost no muscle. Realizing it was time to get back into shape, I decided to measure my arms, so I could track my progress. When I saw the numbers, I almost died. My upper arms were nine inches, nine damn inches. That is smaller than a child's arm. Before the burn I was solid and double that in size. It was time to get back to working out.

In our backyard I had some old weights. The first day that I felt well enough, I went out there ready to tear through a major workout, just like the few hour sessions I used to do. I knew that I would be weaker; I just didn't realize *how* weak I was going to be. There was a 20-pound dumbbell sitting on the ground which hadn't been moved since my last workout a year before. I used to use the 20's to warm up with. When I tried to lift it, for some reason, it wouldn't budge. I might as well have been trying to lift a boulder. Slowly, but surely I worked my way down, trying each weight. In the end, I could only lift three pounds, *three*. It was all I could curl and even then it was damn hard. By the sixth or seventh rep, I was sweating and struggling as if it was a 50-pound weight. I was embarrassed by this and felt the crushing weight of defeat pounding down on my shoulders. It would have defeated me too, if it wasn't for my gear.

We had a small shed that my father use to let me keep my stunt stuff in. Just when I was about to give up on my workout and head inside, I had a strange feeling that I *needed* to check out my old gear. Sliding the old tin door aside, a musty smell came out. It smelled like a mix of mildew and old sweat. It made me smile. Off to the side of the shed were cardboard boxes that I collected to do high falls with, blankets that I would put on top of them, pads, rigging gear, and other things I had collected during my training. As I went through each item, checking them for damage from the neglect, I started to feel that tingly sensation of pure excitement and adrenaline coursing down my spine. Though my arms were already aching, I went back to the weights and forced myself to do more. This time I tried to do a bench press. The bar, at a mere 40 pounds was like lifting 300. Not only that, my skin was so tight, I couldn't bring the bar all the way down to my chest. The closest I got it was a good eight inches above. It was frustrating, but it was what I *had* to do to get back to stunts. No matter how hard it was going to be, I would be ready soon.

On the one year anniversary of my burn, I wasn't really strong enough to drive a car, but since I wanted to return to some state of normalcy, I decided to get in my van that had been sitting idle for a year and take a drive. I felt like I had to visit the site of the burn, to see where it happened and take it in. There was this sense that if I went there, I would have some sort of closure. Driving was painful, having to use too many muscles in my legs and arms, but I managed to brake in time and make all the turns I needed to. There was no air conditioning in the car, and being a hot summer day, I was sweating like hell under my Jobst body suit. Though I had gotten used to the sweaty second skin, it still drove me nuts on hot days. When the doctor first showed me the full body suit, I thought he was joking. It looked like a wet suit that a diver would wear…why would I need that? Come to find out, wearing it greatly reduced scarring in burn patients, which is why I had to wear it 24 hours a day since the open wounds had healed. It didn't feel like it did anything but make me sweat and smell, but even if it were a one in a million chance to give me less scars, I would have tried anything. Later, I realized that the Jobst garments had a second benefit. It was an easier way to get used to being back in public. People stared, but it was because of the Jobst. Not because they saw a shit-load of burn scars. Psychologically, it was a slow way to get used to people staring at me. Something that would follow me until this very day. You never fully get used to the stares.

A few miles from the spot in the desert where my life changed forever, I suddenly pulled over the car and jumped out. There was this pressure in my chest that was making it hard to breathe. I tried loosening the Jobst, but that was pretty much impossible without stripping down. Putting my hands on my knees I tried to calm down and breathe normally. *What the fuck was wrong?* After a few minutes of hanging my head, trembling, and sucking in the hot dry air, I was able to catch my breath and stand up. I tried telling myself that I was just exhausted and that the heat was getting to me. When I got back in the car and started driving towards the site again, I knew that wasn't the reason.

Another half a mile later I pulled over and caught my breath again, this time in the car. Flashes of the fire started to race in my head, bouncing back and forth like bullets, taking chunks out of my mental stability. The smell of my skin melting, the sound of my beard and hair shriveling up and singeing my flesh, the heat in my lungs, it was all coming back too fast and too hard for me to even open my eyes. In the year after the accident, I had cried countless times, mostly out of anger or pain, but this time, the tears were different. I started to sob, my arms shaking, I looked at my hands. They looked like an old man's, like dried cracked leather, yet with the pinkish hue of a baby's cheeks. The sight of them made me so upset that my vision started to blur with more tears. *What had I done to myself?*

An hour, maybe longer, went by before I was calm and feeling like I could drive again. Though I had just cried harder than I ever had, I felt better emotionally than I had in the past year. It was as if I had gotten all the "feeling sorry for myself" out of my system. With it gone, I could now look towards the future and take back my life. As I stared at the sun setting in the distance, right behind the location of the burn, I knew I didn't have to go there. It was behind me, I had to move on. It wasn't going to be an easy road, but I wasn't going to let my burns or anything stop me from living the life I wanted to live.

*Note: When I decided to write this book, I was afraid that the pain and suffering I endured during my burns would not come across. While I think they are depicted well, I realized there is no fucking way to put what I went through into words. I don't think there will ever be a way for me to express how much I suffered. Even burn survivors who had burns worse than mine don't know the pain that *I* went through. While burns are the worst pain possible, the treatment I received made it all that much worse. I'm not looking for pity or sympathy here. I just want people to understand what I went through. For as harsh as what is written in these pages sounds, the real pain was a thousand times worse.

CLIMBING BACK

With my mind straight and my body healing every day, I got back on the road to health. Within several months I was starting to gain muscle, and my movements were finally becoming more normal. The doctors agreed that I did not need any more surgeries and cleared me from having to come back anymore, which was pretty amazing considering they originally wanted to do four more surgeries. I was feeling good, and it was time to get back into stunts. My parents tried several times to talk me into going back to college and to give up this dream that almost killed me, but when they saw my enthusiasm, they stopped pushing.

Pratfalls were one of the first stunts I started to warm up with. Rolling on the ground, feeling the earth below me, and getting back up over and over again really got my body used to moving again. After a while I started to do fight scenes alone in my backyard—in a way, my own version of shadow boxing. Feeling comfortable with those, I moved on to more difficult stunts, including small high falls. Though it was extremely unsafe to do at home, I knew how to do it and needed the practice, so I would jump from our roof. I had to beg the local grocery store to keep all of their cardboard boxes for me. When I saved up enough, I would stack them up in the backyard in just the right order, and then lay a blanket over the top. Climbing up the ladder, I would carefully walk across the roof, get in position, and fall off. The only problem with using cardboard boxes was that I could only use them once. So I always made sure that I took advantage of each fall. Slowly but surely, I was fighting my way back to the business I loved.

About a full year and a half after the burn, I was back in decent enough shape and ready to try to work again. My movement was okay, but I had some tightness in my shoulders and arms caused by the scars, but I adapted to it rather quickly. Feeling good, I was ready to get back on the horse and try my hand in stunts once again. As I saved up money at home working some odd jobs for the first time, I started making phone calls again. I hit up every single contact I had. A lot of people had heard about my burn, but instead of it damaging my reputation, it somehow seemed that people respected it, especially the fact that I wanted to get back into stunts.

After the episode of *Emergency!*, I didn't get any work and then my burn happened. Amazingly, when I started putting out phone calls, I got my first gig rather quickly. The job was an episode of *Wonder Woman*, which I was more than happy about; it was a hot show at the time. The stunt coordinator was Ron Stein, and he was the first guy to believe in me again. Still being in Sparks, I had to get my ass back to L.A. quickly. I packed up, kissed my parents goodbye, and headed out for the long drive. On the way out of town, I drove by the road that led to the burn site, but I didn't let it phase me, I was back to the man I was before, scarred emotionally and physically, but I was back.

After a year and a half of suffering, walking through the gates at the studio to work on the episode was like walking through the gates of heaven. It had been almost two years since I had been on a set, and it felt so good to be back on one. Even though I was nervous about people noticing my Jobst (in fact, in the episode you can see I'm wearing it), I was happy as hell, even if all I had to do was get knocked over or be a character running through a convention. It was one of the easiest stunts you could do, but it didn't matter, I was back and ready to make a name for myself.

THE COST OF FIRE

Just when I was getting back on track with life, I got the hospital bill for the burn. It had been six months in two different hospitals and almost another year of physical therapy. The kicker was I had NO insurance, meaning I was expected to pay the entire bill myself. When I saw the small line that said *Total Due: $120,000*, I nearly fainted. A hundred-and-twenty grand is a huge sum to begin with, but if you inflate it to what it would be today, it would be just shy of half a million dollars. Before the burn I couldn't even afford the sixty dollars to pay my rent, needless to say, I was not going to be able to pay this off.

There was a slight panic that set in when I first received the bill. I just got my first gig back, made a few hundred bucks, and was able to finally get an apartment in Hollywood. If I had to start paying the bill off, I would have to quit everything and get a *real* full time job just to pay the minimum. After a half a dozen phone calls with people who did not seem to care, I finally was able to get an appointment with a caseworker. I thought about going out and getting a suit to look professional for the meeting, but I realized looking like I had money would not help my case. Wearing my normal jeans and work boots, I showed up to the office, faking a limp, going for the pity angle. Right outside of the door, I even loosened my Jobst to show my burns, something I had been hiding as much as I could.

When I got called in, I feared being sat in front of a big panel of people having to plead my case. Instead, I was ushered into a tiny cubical with a frumpy-looking woman who hadn't combed her hair in weeks. Looking through papers, she didn't even glance up at me.

"Welfare will pay forty-thousand. Your final bill will be eighty grand; your paperwork has been approved, so your monthly payment will only be fifty dollars a month. Can you afford that Mr. Hodder?" There was no way I could afford the $50 on top of trying to live in L.A., but I didn't care; it was hundreds less than I thought it would be, so without hesitating I said *Yes* and offered my hand to seal the deal, which she ignored. She made a few X's on the sheet and had me sign in several places. Two minutes later, I was standing outside on the street, not even sure what had just happened.

Several weeks later the first bill arrived. I had started to get small jobs here and there and had just enough to pay it—that is if I didn't really eat for a few weeks. The thing I hated most about the monthly payment wasn't the fact that I couldn't afford it. Writing that check every month was a constant reminder of the accident. That is what bothered me. Not only did I have to look at my burns every day in the mirror, I now had to sit down once a month and write a check out to pay for my own mistake. Every time I'd write that damn check, I would curse at the air, get angry at myself, and want to rip it up.

Theoretically, it would have taken me 133 years to pay off my hospital bill, something that would never happen. Years after the accident, I happened to mention the bill to a friend over dinner. They said they heard about how you can make a "good faith payment" and settle your bill. Intrigued I did some research and found out that knowing they would never get the full sum, they would close your account if you offered them a chunk of money at one time. I wrote up a letter and made a one-time offer of 3,000 dollars. At the time my career was doing well, and I could afford (barely) to pay that much. Amazingly, they accepted the offer and I got to pay it off in full, leaving the frustrating, haunting monthly check behind me forever.

WHAT BURNS?

When I was fully healed physically, the self-consciousness set in. In the morning, you get up and look in the mirror. Maybe wash your face, shave, comb your hair, and take care of any blemishes. If for some reason you have a pimple on your face, you get self-conscious about it. People are going to look at it all day; they are going to notice and stare at it. If you have more than one, it can ruin your whole day, and you might not even want to leave the house. Now imagine instead of a spot the size of a pea, that half of your body is covered in a blemish that will never go away. You have to worry about people staring at you, pointing and whispering behind your back, calling you a freak, and making up stories about what *must* have happened to you. Those first few months after the burn, all I could think about every day was hiding my scars.

When I was finally able to stop wearing the Jobst after a year and a half, I started to wear a dickey to cover the scars on my neck. In Los Angeles, a turtleneck is not the most common attire, yet I thought it would be less obvious than my scars. In 100-degree heat, I would be wearing a long sleeve shirt and a dickey. I'd keep my hands in my pockets and pretend that there was nothing wrong with me. It was tortuous being scared to show the world my true self. I hate to admit it, but when I was younger, there were times in my life when I saw someone that looked "different," and I would nudge my buddies and point out the person. Sometimes we'd snicker and laugh at their deformity, or we'd just stare in awe. After the burn, I was the freak whom everyone was going to point and stare at. I was terrified of that, so I hid my burn scars any way I could.

Then one day, one *really hot* day, a few years after the burn, I was taking a walk on the Santa Monica pier. I was meeting a date, and I was a few minutes early so I walked around. There were jugglers, singers, all sorts of other acts begging for attention and money. Not having any to spare, I did my best to stay away from them but watch at the same time. As I stood watching a juggler spin empty glass bottles of beer, a couple came up next to me. Since I was standing with a crowd, I ignored them. When I checked my watch I realized it was time to meet my date. Turning, I saw the couple. At first I politely smiled as I tried to get by them, but when I got a look at the girl, I stopped in my tracks. Half of her face was beautiful; the other half was scarred with burns, worse than anything I had suffered. One eye was even cloudy and blank— she must have lost her vision as well. I wanted to push by her, but I kept staring. After looking hard, I could tell she was wearing a wig; she probably couldn't grow hair on the part of her scalp that was burned. Swallowing, I forced myself to look at the man with her instead of the woman's burns.

The man had his arms protectively wrapped around her shoulder; he was smiling and laughing at the juggler behind me, until he noticed me staring. I still couldn't move. He was a good-looking man, big and strong, probably an actor, and yet he was with this woman who was deformed, worse than I was. As my eyes kept scanning them, I noticed they both had wedding rings on.

"Hey, move along, dickhead," the man said as more of a suggestion than with anger. The woman glanced at me and looked away, she must have been used to the stares. I was stuck though, I couldn't move away. For some reason I wanted to reach out and touch the burns, it was as if I felt connected to her.

"Buddy, I'm being nice here, but this is your last warning, move along." As he said this, I felt the sweat pouring down my body. The nerves and excitement of seeing this woman, along with the turtleneck I was wearing, was making me pour sweat.

"I'm..." I tried to respond, but couldn't. Instead, I pulled down my dickey to show them my scars. The woman looked at them, then to her husband.

"It's okay," she whispered, to both of us I think. Letting go of her husband she stepped over to me, reached out, and pulled the dickey over my head.

"Don't be ashamed..." The air on my now-exposed skin felt amazing. As she smiled at me, I couldn't think of anything to respond with.

"Besides, it's hot as hell out here, you'll sweat to death." With that, she stuffed the dickey in my pocket and went back to watching the juggler. I smiled at her, whispered a hardly audible thank you, and slipped past them.

As I walked down the boardwalk I felt like everyone was looking at my neck. It was the first time I was in public without it covered. When I started to look at people's faces, I realized no one was looking at me. I might have had scars, scars that people will always look at, but I was nowhere nearly as badly off as that poor woman I saw, *and* she was married, happy, and in public without hiding her face. Approaching my date, part of me wanted to run away so I could hide and put my dickey back on, but I fought the urge and went right up to her. Amazingly, she didn't look at my neck for the first hour we talked, and even when I saw her notice it, she didn't even ask. And most shockingly, she seemed to like me, scars and all.

After that day I started to gain more confidence. It wasn't easy, not by a long shot, but little by little I got more confident and took more risks in being myself. Slowly but surely, I realized that the more confident I was, the less people seemed to notice the scars. When you wear long sleeves in 90-degree weather, they can tell something is wrong. Dressing like a normal person, acting like one, and not trying to hide the scars… works much better.

As the confidence grew, I started wearing short-sleeved shirts, shorts, and eventually, went to the beach. People always looked, people will *always* look. But I got used to it. That is not to say that my scars still don't bother me to this day. While I have learned to live and accept my scars, I still am conscious of them. When I do interviews, I try to have them shoot me from my "better" side, the one with fewer scars. It's not a huge deal, and it's not because I want to hide the scars. I just don't want people watching at home to be looking and talking about them rather than paying attention to the performance.

When it comes to my day-to-day life, I usually don't think about my burns. I dress normally and don't ever try to hide them. At conventions or fan outings, things are a bit different. At a typical convention I might shake 2,000 hands and take a few hundred pictures. Normally, no one notices the burns then; it's when I sign items that they really take notice. When you sign something or someone, people do nothing but stare at your hands writing. My hands are scarred pretty badly. In the beginning of my career, people would always ask what happened to my hands. It got so annoying, I started to wear gloves. People got so used to me wearing them, they are now my trademark. When I get asked why I wear them, I usually give a snide remark like *So I won't leave finger prints when I kill you.*

When my acting career started to take off, my burns ended up helping me in numerous roles. Playing a villain so often, nothing adds menace like some tough scarred-up big guy with a pissed-off look. There have been several movies that have had me take my shirt off just to show the burns, giving the character another layer of depth. The viewer, who doesn't know anything about me, starts to wonder why the character is burned and builds their own backstory about it. There has never been a role that I was turned down for just because I was burned, and for that I am thankful. However, I do think that I haven't done many commercials in my career because of the scars. The advertiser probably doesn't want anything to distract the audience from their product. I can understand that.

When it comes to my burns helping me get roles, they almost changed the history of horror movies. In the early 1980's, I got a phone call from my agent. He wanted me to take a meeting with some young up-and-coming horror movie director about a film he was planning. The lead role was a burn victim, and he wanted to cast an actor with *real* burns in the role. When I showed up for the meeting, I was surprised to see the director was Wes Craven, who I had recently worked with on *The Hills Have Eyes 2*. We chatted about the movie he was prepping about a child killer who gets burned by the parents of his victims and then comes back to haunt their dreams. He was very passionate and excited to tell me about the role, but I could tell instantly that I did not fit the look he wanted, I didn't have *enough* burns, and I was bigger than he envisioned. Little did I know at the time that he would go on to make one of the best horror movies in history, and that I, as Jason, would forever be linked to the franchise.

Oddly enough, right around the same time, I did an episode of the television series, *V*. I played a henchman of the alien, Willie, who was played by Robert Englund before he got the role as Freddy. We didn't really meet each other, and no one would have ever guessed that 30 years later, the two of us would be doing conventions around the world together as the world's two favorite killers!

BURNING AGAIN

You would think that after being the victim of a horrific burn that I would have a fear of fire and all sorts of flames. I should be swatting at flames, trying to keep them away from me, screaming *Fire Bad*, like Frankenstein's monster. For some reason, after the burn, fire did not scare or even bother me. Lighters did not send a nervous twitch down my spine, and campfires did not keep me 100 yards away from my friends roasting marshmallows. I honestly looked at fire like any other person did. The only aspect of fire that bothered me those first years was the heat. At times when I got too close to a fire or another heat source, my scars would heat up more quickly than the rest of my body, forcing me back a little.

The lack of fear, I believe, was from the fact that I did not blame the fire for my accident. Fire was simply an element doing what it does—burn things. It was an accident, an accident of my *own* fault. If I should be scared of anything, it should be of myself. Instead of being scared of anything, I choose to be more cautious in my stunts. Having experienced firsthand the pain that not checking every aspect of a stunt can cause, I became overly cautious and thorough with *every* stunt I did. Some stunt coordinators will try and do everything a director asks them, even if they think it's not that safe, in order to please the boss. I, on the other hand, would never put anyone's life or safety at risk, no matter how good it looked on screen. There is always a way to do it safely and make it look good. This work ethic I embraced is why I started to get more and more jobs and eventually stunt coordinating jobs.

Directors, producers, and actors realized they could trust me to keep their crew safe and to get some great-looking shit on the screen.

Though I was comfortable with fire, I shied away from fire stunts for some time. It wasn't that I was scared of doing one; it was just I didn't want to risk getting burned. I couldn't go through that pain again. As I started getting a lot of work, I was offered fire stunts often, but I kept turning them down. Then, one day after a particularly rough car crash scene I did, I watched a friend do a fire stunt on the set as I rubbed my sore shoulder. Watching him burn, get put out and get up, I realized how much easier they are than other stunts. The reason I say that is while they are dangerous, they take much less of a toll on your body. High falls, fights, car crashes, and many other stunts cause your body to endure harsh impacts, even when done safely and properly. With a fire stunt, there is a lot of preparation, but the actual burn usually only lasts seconds, and your body feels nothing and takes no impacts. Besides that, fire stunts pay *a lot* of money. With that in mind, I decided to say *Yes* the next time I was offered one.

That next year, a fellow stuntman and good friend, BJ Davis, whom I had worked with several times, asked me to work on a Michael Dudikoff film called *Avenging Force*. I had done some decent stunts at that point in my career, but this film—this was the one that changed my path in life. BJ was the first stunt coordinator to believe in me enough and trusted me to do some major stunts in the film. I did a few high falls, one from the top of a crane, a huge car chase scene, fights, and finally… my first fire stunt. At one point during filming, BJ came up to me to talk about the next day's shoot.

"The scene where they blow up the house, two people need to come out of it on fire. I'm going to be one of them, and I'd like you to be the other one." He was checking some ropes as he said this, casual and cool. I felt my heart rate speed up a bit, even though I told myself that I would be fine doing one. With a hard swallow, I agreed and he patted me on the shoulder.

The next day the set was closed due to the explosion that was going to happen. Only key crew and BJ and I were allowed anywhere near the house that was rigged with explosives. We went over the routine, the safety backups, and prepared our fire suits. When it was time to shoot, an announcement was made to clear the entire set. Everyone scurried off except for BJ and me who were left inside of the house that was about to blow up. BJ was off to my left in front of the window he was to jump from; taking a look at him, I closed my eyes and took a deep breath. I could feel the fireproof gel oozing its way down my body; it felt cold, but I knew it was about to get all too hot. When action was called, we lit ourselves (since the house was going to blow up, we couldn't have a safety crew stay inside). Listening to the countdown, I stood still, the fire creeping over my body. A tiny voice in the back of my head told me I was going to freak out, that this was too close to what happened all those years ago, yet when the countdown hit one, I burst through the door, right on cue. The explosion of the house ended up being so big that in the final film, you can hardly see BJ and me coming out of the house. As I hit the porch still on fire, waiting for the crew to put me out, I started to laugh to myself. It wasn't nerves that were making me laugh; it was because the stunt was fucking great. I loved it and I knew right at that moment that I would never hesitate to do another fire stunt in my life.

Avenging Force ended up changing everything in my life. The stunts I did on it earned me enough respect in the industry that I was then able to do any stunt needed; I no longer had to *prove* myself. It also changed me financially. When I flew out to the set I had $175 to my name. I didn't even know if I would make it through the filming without going broke. Having done so many stunts on the movie (stunt men get paid per stunt they do, as well as a day rate), when I got home, I was able to deposit $20,000 after taxes. Before that movie, I lived day to day, fighting to get new gigs and to make enough money to barely, just fucking barely, survive. After that, I was never broke again, and I almost always had a steady stream of work.

Billboard Stunt, Music Video for The Band B'z

A few years later I did the best fire stunt of my career and, I like to think, one of the best fire stunts ever in film. Of course it was in *Friday the 13th Part VII*. The character Tina has Jason trapped in the basement, and using her telekinetic powers, she sprays him with gasoline and lights him on fire by exploding the furnace. You almost never see the actual ignition of a character on screen. Usually this is because a stuntman does the fire burn. They have to cut away from the character so they can switch out the actor for the stuntman. The second reason is that it is hard to get a realistic-looking ignition. In *Part 7*, since the situation is in the world of fantasy, the ignition makes sense and looks great in the film. I can't think of another movie that has such an enjoyable on-screen ignition. After I got lit, I ran around on fire so long that the flames actually start to go out—you can notice that in the film if you look carefully. Right before I drop, the flames start to fizzle. At the time of filming, it was one of the longest fire stunts in history.

Since my burn, I have done many fire stunts and people always ask me how I could do it after going through what I did. There are two answers for this… the first reason is that being scared of anything in life is a waste of time. The second is I fucking love stunts. Except for when I am no longer physically be able to do it, nothing could ever stop me from doing the one thing I love the most in my life.

YEARS AFTER THE BURN, THE REAL PAIN BEGINS

As I tried to get my career off the ground, I was flying back and forth from Sparks to Hollywood on a regular basis. I'd go out to try and make connections, get gigs and work, but when I ran out of money, I'd drive back to Sparks to work and save up so I could go back and try again. In 1979, I got my first job on a movie, called *In God We Tru$t*. A stunt coordinator named Paul Baxley hired me to drive a semi-truck in an action scene. It was simple—all I had to do was back up to block the cars driving. Yet, I still fucked it up. They had given me a walkie-talkie to listen for my cue. I was excited because I had never used one before, so I held it in my hand and eagerly listened for my time to go. The minutes ticked by, I heard cars driving behind me and yet, no cue. I wasn't going to go without it, so I waited. After an obscene amount of time, a crew member ran up to my window and started screaming at me.

"What are you waiting for? You fucked up the shot!"

"You guys didn't give me the cue!" I yelled back defending myself. I even held up the walkie-talkie to show him that I had it right in my hand. The guy grabbed it out of my hands and looked at it.

"Goddamned moron. You never turned it on." He spun the knob on top, it made a few crackling sounds, and he threw it back at me. I could feel my face burn hot with anger... at myself. Here I was on my first movie, and I screwed it up. I just knew I would never get hired again, I'd be known as the *guy who couldn't even use a walkie-talkie.* No one would want to hire me. After that film, I couldn't find work for a few weeks so I headed home to make some money. At the time, my dad was having some health issues; he already had had two heart attacks. It was comforting knowing I could be around now and again to help out and make sure he was alright. My mother and I even took a CPR class together so we could administer it in case he had another attack.

There was a sleazy commercial agent, who I had at the time, who was trying to get me work. I had been in Sparks for a few weeks with no leads at any stunt work, so when he called and said he got me an audition for a Coors Light commercial, I jumped at the opportunity. Having been working pretty steadily in Sparks, I didn't want to leave for too long. I booked a flight out on a Thursday, the audition was Friday, and I was to fly back Saturday morning. I flew out and did well in the audition even though I didn't know why I was there, being a stuntman and not an actor. I stayed with my friend, Mike, and we hung out that night after the audition and had fun; it made me miss being in Hollywood. Having an early flight, I went to bed sooner than I normally would. Then, at one o'clock in the morning, the apartment phone rang. Not being my place, I ignored it until a few seconds later when Mike turned on the light next to the couch and nodded towards the phone. He couldn't even say it was for me. Half asleep I sat up, knowing whatever it was, it couldn't be good. For the life of me I didn't want to answer that phone; I didn't want my world to change and come crashing down on me again. With a sweaty hand I picked up the receiver and said *Hello* as softly as I could.

"Son… your father, he had another heart attack. I did the CPR, Kane, I did it, but he didn't make it." My mother sobbed and said a few other things after that, but I didn't hear what. I couldn't think or pay attention; I just kept picturing my father giving me a hug, wishing me luck on my audition and saying... *See ya later, Doc.* He always said that when I left, whether it was to get milk at the store or if I was leaving for weeks at a time. *See ya later...Doc.* I was *not* going to see him later, and I would never hear him say that again.

The next morning on the flight, I kept going over and over the situation—what if I had been home? I was a hell of a lot stronger than my mother. Would I have been able to keep him alive with my CPR? Why did it have to happen the one fucking time I go out of town on an audition? I was furious at everything and everyone—he was only 63, damn it. The next few days were miserable... helping my mom with the funeral arrangements while trying to be the *strong* one. Having to deal with family whom I didn't want to see and worst of all, saying goodbye to my father. My dad had stipulated that he wanted to be cremated in the event of his death, so I went up in a small plane with his ashes and scattered them above Mt. Rose near Lake Tahoe, the same place I would scatter my mother's ashes almost exactly 25 years later. As I sat with that small box in my lap, I swear I could hear him say *See ya later, Doc.* As I poured his ashes out the window, I said out loud, *See ya later, Dad.*

A few days later, I heard back from the agent; I hadn't gotten the role. The odd thing, 30 years later and that was the *only* audition I have ever gone to for a commercial. The hardest part about losing my father was that he never got to see the success I had. He would have been so proud of me, seeing me up on the big screen, getting to tell his friends that it was his son up there. There have been times when I sat in a limo, waiting to walk down a red carpet to go to a premier, when I thought of my father. He was a hardworking man who never had much in his life; in fact, I don't think he had ever ridden in a limosine. *Damn it*, I would have loved to take him with me in a limo to a premiere. My father was such a good man. So good he did something I can't imagine ever doing. My mother had been married before she met him—her first husband died. When she married my father and I was born, my father suggested to my mother that my middle name be Warren, after her first husband. *That's* how good of a man he was.

Honestly, I think having to go through the pain and trauma of my burn with me took years off his life. The stress of visiting his son in the hospital every day for a year, only to see him get worse, put too much stress on his heart. I don't blame myself, but like all of us, I can't help but wonder *What if?* What if I didn't get burned? Would he have lived longer?

In the months after my father's death, I stayed with my mother. I was worried about her and didn't want her to be alone. She had taken it pretty rough and became a zombie of sorts. She would be fine one day, chatty and excited to do something, and the next she would sleep late, hardly eat, and say only a few words. The roles had reversed. I was now taking care of her. Even though the care I was giving her was hardly a fraction of what she did for me, it still made me feel good that I could be there for her in some way. Those last few months I stayed home was the last time I was able to be…normal around her. When I felt she was ready to be on her own again, I moved to California permanently and that is when the problems began.

This is without a doubt, the hardest and most embarrassing thing in my life to talk about. I debated for a long time whether or not to put this in the book. Mostly I stayed away from the idea; it's too embarrassing and hard to talk about. But I finally realized that telling my story might help me deal with it and hopefully, if anyone out there is fucked up like I am, it will help them to know they are not alone as well. Therefore, I'm putting aside my ego, biting my lip, and telling the darkest, most painful aspect of my life… the mental issues the burn injury caused me.

It took a long time for it to seep in and form in my brain, but once it was in, it was there to stay. And once it was there, I could never control it. This insidious "thing" was an odd form of post-traumatic stress disorder (PTSD), a form that I have not been able to find another person with. Often after traumatic incidents, such as my burn injury, people suffer from PTSD. Lots of times it manifests into nightmares and fears. It can also turn into depression and cause pulling away from friends and family. Mine, on the other hand, formed slowly over the years and made me, well, in a way, fear my family. It wasn't that I was scared of them—I wasn't; I just honestly felt like they were all contaminated with…with something that I couldn't come into contact with. I was terrified of getting near them or letting them touch me, for I thought they would get me sick or something.

This fear did not come on as a sudden thing right after the incident. In fact, when I got out of the hospital, I lived with my parents for some time. This irrational fear was a slow-building compulsion that set in when I moved to California, as I had time away from all of my family members. The longer I was away from them, the bigger the seed got—it grew and flourished until finally, I couldn't face them. Many years after the accident when it was all behind me, I started making excuses to not go home and visit. When family wanted to come and visit me, I would tell them I was busy shooting that week or that it just was not a good time for me. Little by little, I pushed them away.

This slow, sudden break wasn't a conscious thing. I didn't realize what I was doing or what was forming in my mind. I just kept telling myself that I was too busy to get around to visiting or that I needed a break from people, though in the back of my mind, I knew something was wrong. My father's death somehow closed a door in my head. It was as if a certain chapter was over in my life and my brain, subconsciously, moved onto a different phase. This translated into an absolute aversion to my family. Even though I wanted to see them, I just fucking couldn't do it. I'd rather touch a filthy, disgusting homeless person than my own mother who raised and took care of me in my time of need.

This odd repugnance cumulated in my not being able to see my family unless there were some very, very strict rules followed. In order for anyone to come visit me at my home in California, they could not touch me when they arrived. When they got to my house they would have to go directly to the garage, stand on a towel, and strip naked. They would then have to walk through the house fully nude and get right into the shower and clean themselves for an extended period of time. While they did this, I would wash the clothing they were wearing along with everything they brought. Combs, brushes, any solid items would also be sanitized. When I finished cleaning everything and they were out of the shower, I could finally give them a hug and enjoy their company. I ended up calling this the "process." It was a routine that everyone thought was ridiculous and stupid, including me... and yet I couldn't help it.

It fucking horrified and depressed the shit out of me having to make my mother go through that routine, but I had *no* choice. If she didn't do it, there was no way I could *ever* have her in my house. Thankfully, she understood this and loved me enough to go through the "process." If she hadn't, I would have never had my mother in my home in the last few years of her life, and she would have never met her grandchildren.

The really strange part was that once they went through this routine, I was completely fine being with them. In fact, the few times that my mother came out and did this, we had a fantastic time. One of my nephews, Gregg, my sister Pat, and my mother were the only ones to ever go through this process. My other sister and family members thought it was pretty much ridiculous and refused to do it. Some of them were so offended by what I made my mother do, saying I *humiliated* her, that one sister even stopped communicating with me. She just couldn't understand it, yet her husband had a fear of hospitals and didn't *once* try to visit me when I was lying in a bed dying only fifteen minutes from their house. Someone who is that afraid of something should understand someone else having an issue. Basically the two of them just wrote me off. Years later, a guy in Germany e-mailed me asking to verify some personal items of mine that he had bought on eBay. Thinking it was some movie props or something, I said sure. He ended up sending me pictures of my old wallet, high school ID, a driver's license, my personal scripts from *all* the Jason movies, and a few dozen other personal items that were in my mother's house. Only family members had access to my mom's stuff after she died, and I find it very sad that they thought it was okay to sell my personal things without my knowledge.

Doctors, psychologists, and therapists have not been able to help me get over this fear of mixing my personal life with my family's lives. They have even had a hard time diagnosing the exact symptoms I have, though they do mostly agree in *theory* that it was post-traumatic stress syndrome caused by the burn injury and subsequent recovery. They believe, and I agree, that since I saw *only* my family when I was in the hospital, that I subconsciously associate them with the pain I suffer, which makes sense. What doesn't make sense to me is that if I associated them with the pain, then why after they were cleaned and "sanitized" was I fine around them? The mind works in fucking weird ways. Whatever the reason is, I gave up trying to figure it out a long time ago.

This compulsion of mine destroyed my relationships with all of my family members. Everyone thought it was ridiculous, that I should just get over my issues and move on. They just didn't understand. My mother and Pat were the only ones who didn't give up on me. Even to this day I only talk to one of my sisters, and even then, it's not as often as it should be. This damn curse is one-hundred times worse than my burns and having to walk around forever with scars. It is, hands down, the worst thing to have ever happened in my life. I know it's hard for people to understand, but unless you have some sort of obsessive-compulsive disorder, I don't really think you can. You want nothing more than to overcome and conquer it, but you just can't. People on the outside can look at me and say *Just hug her. She is your mother, for goodness sake*, but that is not how it works. I have no control over it and trust me, I tried everything to get rid of it and nothing has ever worked. It's why I have none of my parents' family left in my life. Thankfully this compulsion did not apply to my wife or kids since they came into my life afterwards. I love them more than anything and couldn't imagine having to put them through anything that difficult. Having kids made me understand the absolute love that my mother had for me. I now understand how she could spend every day in a hospital for a year and how she could spend months dressing my wounds and bathing me, only to have to be put through a "process" later in life to see her child that she did all that for. I understand, because I know without a doubt that I would do any of that and more for my kids.

My mother and I were always close, but this problem of mine put a small rift between us. We still stayed in contact by phone often, but it severely limited the amount of time that I saw her over the years. And I hate that; I wish I had more time with her, though I am happy that she got to see my success in life, unlike my father. The best part was that she was so damn proud of me that she would tell strangers everything I had done. If you made eye contact with her, she would go on about how her son was Jason. At the end of filming *Part 7*, we all got crew jackets that looked like a letterman's jacket. I got one for my mom that said *Jason's Mom* on the front instead of a name. She loved the fucking thing. It would be 90 degrees in Nevada, and she would wear that thing to the grocery store, just hoping someone would stop her and ask about it. If they did, she had pictures I autographed for her ready to give them as a souvenir. At times it was a bit embarrassing, but it just showed me how much she loved me.

As she got older, her tunnel vision got worse, and she started having trouble driving. She quit driving all together when on, no lie, Friday the 13th, she got in a small fender bender. As she went to exchange the information with the man, she saw that his insurance card said his first name was *Jason*. She threw her hands up right there and never drove again.

Mom was able to see pretty much all of my success; she lived twenty-five years longer than my father and passed away two days before my 50th birthday, which was odd since my father died 17 days before my 25th birthday. To this day I regret pushing her away as much as I did. She was such a great woman and didn't deserve to be treated like that. I'll never be able to forgive myself. The fact that there was no way for me to control my problem does not help the guilt I feel because of it. I fucking loved her, and I miss her every day. There is nothing I can do now to make up for how I treated her, but I try to love my own family as much as I can, because it is what she taught me—how to love.

Me, Mom and my Sister, Pat

Though my family is almost nonexistent in my life, my condition still plagues me. I cannot and will never be able to go to Sparks, Nevada. I wish I could visit it, but in my mind, it's... off limits. So is Marilyn, the photographer I was with that horrific day, even though she wasn't a part of my life. Certain things are as well. An airline, for instance, that my family all used to fly is absolutely out of the question to ever use again. There is no way I can fly it... and in my mind it's so bad that when Mike, the author of my biography, flew down on that airline for the cover shoot of this book, I couldn't touch anything he touched. I couldn't touch the props on the set that he did. He accidentally sat in the chair I was supposed to use for the photo shoot, and I couldn't use it anymore. Mike was the only one who knew of the condition, and luckily, he knew that when I nodded at the chair that it had to be replaced. He made up an excuse and had it switched out. The only way I could touch him in the pictures was to wear my gloves. It sounds like a joke, but it's a fucking curse. The fact that I can't touch something that someone else touched, just because they flew on an airline that my family used to fly decades ago, is torture. I wish nothing more than to be able to get rid of this... but I'm afraid it will be with me forever.

FIGHT
INTERMISSION
II

ROUND TWO

During my first year in college at Reno, I used to hang out at this bar called *The Library*. One night I was hanging out with my old childhood buddy, Tracy, when this guy started giving me some looks. It took me a while, but I realized it was the same asshole that sucker punched me the week before when I was trying to break up a fight. There was a random fight and I tried to pull these guys off each other, and this guy just punched me in the head. The fight got broken up after that, and I let things go. The night I saw him again I didn't want to cause trouble, so I ignored the guy and went about my business until he walked over to me and started giving me shit.

Back in those days in Reno, you were either a Cowboy or a Long Hair. The Cowboys wore boots, tucked-in plaid shirts and hats. The Long Hairs were like me, the guys with shaggy hair who dressed like hippies. The Cowboys never liked us, not that we did anything to them. This guy walked over with his hands in his pockets and started making some stupid ass comment about how he figured I would have gotten a haircut after he knocked the shit out of me the week before. That did it—I wasn't going to fuck around. I turned and swung and smashed his nose flat into his face. The guy was out cold instantly. He fell backwards, slamming into the floor, his hands still in his pockets. The guy was fucking knocked out, and he didn't even get a chance to take his hands out of his pockets. I won that round.

A MONSTER'S METHODS

Acting terrified can be a tricky thing. Anyone can scream, but getting that look of sheer terror in your eyes can be hard. Therefore, if I'm playing a violent killer in a movie, I always do my best to stay away from the actors when I'm in costume on set. If I hang out and chat with them in full make-up and then try to scare them, they will be too comfortable with me to be scared. That's why I always keep my distance while on set, especially the first day or two. Keeping what the monster looks like away from the actors until they shoot helps build some genuine fear in the actors.

Kane as Victor Crowley, Hatchet

This technique was documented in full effect in the special feature on the *Hatchet* DVD called *Meeting Victor Crowley*. In the piece, you can see how scared, in real life, the actors were before they started their first scene with me. Up until that point they had yet to see me in make-up.

It wasn't only the fear of what the make-up was going to look like, it was also the fact that they thought I was fucking nuts. I don't think I would really argue that fact, but the reason they think that is because to get into character I usually scream, grunt, and bang and kick things. For some reason, even when I'm doing a serious role outside of the make-up, screaming helps me clear my head and focus. If you watch the behind-the-scenes of *Hatchet*, you get to see this firsthand.

Regardless, if I'm friends with people on the set or not, if I'm playing a killer, I try to stay away from my victims at all times. I just think the more they are scared of me, or the more they think I'm an asshole, the better their scare will look on screen. At times this makes me look like a real jerk, ignoring the cast like that, but it's my method and what works. I did this the most in *Jason X*, with all of them being Canadian. Avoiding them every day made me seem like some stuck-up American actor who didn't want to talk to them. I would have loved to hang out more, but if I'm going to kill them later... I have to stay away.

One of the main things I do before a scene is yell. This yelling builds up my energy and gets me pumped, especially if I'm doing a violent scene. It's sort of like how a football team all jumps up and down and whoops and hollers before a game.

On the other hand, it also calms me down. Sometimes the yelling will settle the nerves in my system and allow me to be calm before they roll the camera. Either way, most likely you'll find me yelling before a take. It's as if by yelling, I let the monster inside of me take over for a bit. My eyes turn darker and look harder as I'm ready to kill.

Kane as Dennis Rader, B.T.K.

The best way for a scare to look real on film is to actually have the person in the scene scared shitless. On numerous films, I have set up things with the directors to scare the actors without them knowing I'm going to do so. In *B.T.K.*, the director's wife, Caia Coley, is sitting in the kitchen. In the script it calls for her to jump at a noise. I hid behind a wall and waited for the right moment... and *BANG*, I slammed the wall right behind her. She jumped a mile as she wasn't expecting anything, thinking she was filming the part *before* she got scared. The jolt got a genuine reaction out of her. While it made us all laugh on set, it also made for a scene that was much more genuine. I did this same thing in *Ed Gein* when Priscilla Barnes is supposed to jump at the phone ringing. Instead of having the phone ring, the director set me up to hide near her and bang the wall. Again, it got a great reaction.

Kane as Ed Gein, The Butcher of Plainfield

Always messing with people on set, and never really letting anyone know if I really am crazy or not, makes them a bit uneasy when they are about to film a scene where I am killing them. This uneasiness translates to the screen as real fear in their eyes. *He is sort of crazy—what if he takes it too far and really hits me?* Though I would never do something like that, I love people thinking I would or could, because it makes all my kills that more interesting.

If I'm doing a really emotional scene where I have to cry or be upset, music will usually put me in that place. Certain songs from my past will bring back memories and feelings that will pull out the tears I need for the scene. At times, even a person's face with the right eyes would help. Certain eyes can help me get lost in memories as well. For instance, on the set of *Cut*, I asked the wardrobe lady to sit down in front of me, right out of the shot, so I could look at her during a really emotional scene I had. Looking at her face helped me get those tears. I'm not sure what it is, but looking into the right set of eyes can make me cry.

Actors have tons of methods and techniques to get out the emotions they do, but for me, I had no formal training. I never took a single acting class in my life. My talent, if I have any, comes naturally—well that, and getting to be on set and watch some amazing actors throughout the years. Watching Charlize Theron on the set of *Monster*, getting to work with her day in and day out, was like getting a master's degree in acting.

Scene with Charlize Theron, Monster

Being the stunt coordinator on the film meant I was on set every day. I got to watch Charlize do pretty much every single scene in the movie. To see such a stunningly beautiful woman destroy her body and image just to get the role done right showed me the dedication she had. She was so convincing that standing next to her, talking to her, and working with her every day, you didn't think it was her; you thought it was the real killer. I was so fascinated by her acting that I was glued to every word she said. Even though it was later in my stunt career, it was the beginning of my acting outside of the make-up career, so I soaked up everything I could.

Many people have asked me over the years how I get the intensity and rage in my face when I'm on screen... they want to know how to do it. Really, it's just natural. It's something inside of me... that wants out. I am closer mentally to a killer than normal people are. That sounds ridiculous, but it is actually what I truly believe. I have that anger and rage inside of me that psychos have, only instead of going down that dark path in life, I was lucky enough to have good parents and to find an outlet for it in movies. In fact, after I shoot a scene where I'm being violent and angry, I feel a sense of relief wash over me. It's a calm, as if I released the demons inside of me and the rage is gone... for the moment. Who knows what would have happened if I didn't get into this business? I'd probably be serving 20-to-life.

THE FAME GAME

For a long time I didn't consider myself famous at all. I thought I was just a guy with a cool job. Then as I started to get known better, things started to change for me. One of the first times that I realized that my life was different was when I was walking through a video store and saw the cover of a movie I had a small part in. It was called *Steel Frontier* and starred Joe Lara and Bo Svenson. Originally I was hardly acknowledged in the credits as I had a pretty small role. Ten years later, and my name is emblazoned across the front cover as if I was the main star. It's not like I became a household name, but I still had a cult status where my name could help sell movies.

While I have reached a certain status of celebrity, I can still walk through most any crowd and not get noticed. People don't wait for me outside of my house to get a picture of me throwing out a trash bag or hope to get a picture of me at a club. The only place that *everyone* knows me is at conventions. Of course I get stopped from time to time, but usually I can live a normal life. Oddly, the place I get noticed the most is at airports. Since the TSA gets to read my name on my driver's license, a lot of them recognize it and ask if I'm an actor. I like this level of status. It allows for me to live a normal life, at the same time as getting to taste the life of a celebrity.

As I start to get more roles without having to wear heavy make-up, maybe I'll start to get noticed more and more. In fact it's already starting to happen. For years, horror fans picked me out in crowds, but no one else. Now other people are starting to notice me. I was walking through a hotel one day when a worker stopped me and asked if I was an actor. I said I was. He was trying to remember from what movie, so of course I said *Friday the 13th*? Surprisingly he said *No*. Then his face lit up, and he said, *B.T.K.! That's it! You're the guy from that movie!* I was blown away—it was the first time I got noticed from a role out of the make-up… and it felt great. Now that my kids are almost grown up, I'm fine with being recognized more. Just don't ask for an autograph if you are pissing next to me in the stall. I don't want to talk to anyone with my dick in my hand. Sadly, this has happened to me on several occasions. Thankfully the Paul Newman syndrome hasn't kicked in yet. There is an old rumor that Paul was once asked for his autograph while taking a piss, and from that day forward, he never signed another thing. Speaking of bathrooms, I once had a guy try to take a picture of my dick by putting his cell phone over the stall I was pissing in. I tried to grab it but missed and the guy ran out before I could zip up. That incident bothered me some; I can't imagine what big celebrities have to go through.

The fame part of my career really started after *Friday the 13th Part VIII* came out. Being the lead character in both of those movies got me noticed, and I started to get invited to celebrity events. Small ones, but cool stuff nonetheless. There was a celebrity tennis and golf tournament in Columbus, Ohio, that I was invited to. I was thrilled; I never thought I would be invited as a celebrity to anything. The golf game went alright, not too many fans were on the links, but people still eyed me, mostly wondering who I was. That night there was a big event where all the celebs were to walk into this big arena, one by one, as they were announced. Fans filled every seat, and it was standing room only. As I waited in line with the other celebrities to come out of the tunnel, I could hear the round of applause each person got. Some got huge, booming applause while others got polite claps. The guy in front of me, some soap opera actor, got a decent response. Then when I was called out, there was just some small clapping, but when I got halfway out of the tunnel, the place went insane. The clapping and screaming was deafening. I couldn't believe it. People loved me! There were women screaming everywhere, I felt like I was one of the Beatles. Suddenly, roses started to fall at me— *holy shit.* This was amazing. As I turned around to pick up one of the roses, I saw who the applause was really for… tennis star, Andre Agassi. He had decided to come out, unannounced, and was right behind me. I felt like an asshole. Picking up the rose I politely handed it to him and kept walking, trying not to show the fact that I was embarrassed as hell. I might have been gaining some notoriety, but of course I was nowhere near the tennis superstar's fame. It was a lesson learned in humility.

Of course being a celebrity, no matter how big, has its perks. Fans send me stuff in the mail all the time, which is more than flattering. Companies offer you products they want you to try out. Filmmakers send you DVD's of movies that won't be out for a while to get your opinion or a quote. A lot of times you don't have to wait in line at a restaurant and get a great seat. Hell, half the time they even comp your meal. Hotels treat you better than average. They'll check on you to see if you are alright and need anything, let you use facilities they normally wouldn't, and even let you check out extremely late without charging you. People fly you around the world to do signings. A guy once flew me out to Attleboro, Massachusetts, to go with him to his high school reunion. Come to find out each year he would fly out a different celebrity to go with him. He was actually a great guy, or I could think that because he paid me ten grand just to hang out with him for a night. He and I actually became partners on a hidden camera video called "Candid Farts," starring my old high school buddy, Steve. I happen to think that someone farting in public is funny. We filmed tons of scenes of people's reactions to other people farting in front of them. It's hilarious and hopefully will be on DVD soon. One of the best things about being a celebrity is that people will kiss your ass, even if they don't like you. It's a good life, but it also has its downside.

Some of the bad shit that comes with being a celebrity is the lack of privacy. Even though I can walk by most people without being recognized, I still had to get a private phone number, an unlisted address, and make sure I lived in a community where people couldn't just drive up to my house. Not that I ever felt threatened, but there are some odd and sick fucks out there who won't leave you alone. They see your movies and somehow think you are their friend just because they have seen you on television. Danielle Harris, whom I love, had a horrible instance of stalking from an obsessive fan which got extremely dangerous. Thankfully I have never had to deal with anything that extreme.

When I started to become well-known, I got a P.O. Box for fan mail. The stuff was becoming overwhelming, and I didn't want it coming to my house or to my agent's place. After setting it up, I'd go in once a week to check it. Usually I would stand in the lobby and read through a lot of the letters and open packages. I'd get some wonderful letters, some odd ones, and a lot of gifts. I have also gotten some great artwork of the characters I have played over the years, and a lot of it I have even hung up in my house. At the same time I have gotten some sick, odd shit. The worst one I ever received came in a nicely wrapped little box. The handwriting on the shipping slip was so tiny I had to hold it up to my face and squint to read it. I shrugged and pulled the brown paper off the small box.

Inside was a neatly folded letter and something small wrapped in bubble wrap. I unfolded the thick letter, thinking nothing of it, wondering what a fan had sent me now. The handwriting was again tiny—I mean so freaking tiny it seemed like some sort of art project. I literally had to hold it inches from my face to read it.

Dear Mr. Hodder… Kane,

I have been wanting, or more so, needing to give this to you for some time. It is important, vitally so, that you have something that is so close to me… that it's part of me. When I first saw you as Jason, I knew you were the one that needed to have this.

At this point in the letter my eyes were hurting from the tiny print, and mind was racing as to what the fuck the guy was talking about and what could be so important that I had to have it. I put the letter down and grabbed the small wad of bubble wrap which looked professionally wrapped. It took me a few tries but I pulled back the tape and unfolded it. Inside was a small vial; it looked to be one of those sample perfume tubes. It didn't have a name on it and no markings, so I held it up closer to my face to see the liquid inside. It was milky white. I calmly put the vial down and went back to the letter.

Kane, knowing you have my semen means the…

Not much stuff bothers me, but to know that I was just holding some dude's spunk freaked me out. Instantly I ripped up the letter and threw it in the trash violently. As for the semen, I wanted to smash the thing, but then the shit would be all over the place. Using the box it came in, I nudged it into the trash. Sick bastard… why the fuck would you send someone your jizz? I mean really, why would I need that? Christ. How the hell he even got his shit into such a tiny tube I'll never know. I was so disgusted by this, that to this day I wear rubber gloves when I get my mail now. Seriously, every time.

Looking back now, I wish I had kept the letter and read the whole thing to find out why this man chose to give me his spunk. It would have been interesting, and I could have printed the whole thing here. This sort of thing is why the big celebrities don't open their own fan mail. They let their underpaid assistant deal with the vials of semen. Along the same lines, though not as gross, I was once asked at a convention by a group of gay guys if they could buy my underwear off me. They offered $500 bucks for the pair I was wearing at that moment. They wanted me to go to the bathroom, take them off, and give it to them. They even had the cash in hand. I might be money hungry, but I turned it down. Who knows what their plan for it was?

The other downside to fame I have experienced are jackasses. There have been countless times I have run into these macho men who purposely try to instigate a fight with me.

My First Autograph Session with Lar Park Lincoln

The fact that I'm one of the most notorious killers in the world makes these guys puff up their chests and act tough around me. Either they want to be able to say they got their ass kicked by Jason, or they think they'll beat me and be able to say they kicked Jason's ass. These dicks usually try to egg me on by calling me names or saying that I'm really a pussy. I might have a short fuse, but these guys are just idiots so I usually can ignore them. Getting pissed off is what they want anyway; if I gave in and started a fight with them, they'd be winning, even if I kicked their ass.

Sometimes the characters you play make you a bad guy in a person's eyes for real. It's as if they can't differentiate the fact that you are not really Jason or a bad guy. They see you and think you are evil or a monster just because you scared them in a movie or they didn't like it. Those people usually just walk past me, but I have had people stop and say things like *You're an asshole.* Usually I'll laugh and ask... why? Then they'll respond with something like, *in B.T.K., you were so terrible to other people.* I usually laugh at this point—hell, if they hate me because of a movie, then I did my job.

Though I have had a few brushes with the ugly side of fame, I wouldn't trade it for the world. It's an amazing life getting recognized for doing something you love so much. The work alone is the reward, but getting to be somewhat famous on top of that, well, that is the biggest bonus you can get.

NAME DROPPING

Everyone loves celebrities. At functions people talk about the latest movies and shows before gushing about how much they love the lead actor or actress or how they hated them. They grace the cover of every magazine in the racks; they are on our televisions every second with channels and shows dedicated to their lives that are none of our business. For some people, the chance to see a celebrity for a split second is worth hours standing outside of a theater or studio, no matter what the weather. They just want anything and everything to do with the people they have fallen in love with on screen. Whenever I get into a long conversation with people I have just met, certain questions always come up. *What celebrities do you know? Who have you worked with? What's so and so like? Is he a dick? Is she really that funny? I heard so and so looks awful out of make-up—are they?*

Usually I don't mind answering those questions. People want to know and I'll tell them if I know the answer, but I'm not a name dropper. People in Hollywood, or worse, people on the cusp of the industry, love to drop names every chance they get. *Well when I worked with... I once did a commercial with... I met....* And so on. People feel if they have somehow graced the same room as a celebrity, even for a tiny moment, it makes them all that more interesting. And maybe it does, but I'm not one to just throw out names so people will think I'm cool. Of course having worked in the industry, it's impossible *not* to throw around names once in a while when having conversations, but I'll never just drop a name for the sake of it. In fact, some celebrity biographies I have read have dropped ten names a page as if hearing a certain actor did a movie with Tom Cruise will keep you flipping the pages. In my book, I did my best to only mention names when necessary, but for those of you who *need* to hear about them… well here it goes. The one and only time I will name drop.

Over the years I have gotten to work with most name celebrities whether it was in a small capacity as a stunt player in the background or rubbing Will Smith's legs in a closet. Early in my career I got to work with greats like Chuck Norris in *Lone Wolf McQuade* and Tom Hanks and John Candy in *Volunteers.* I worked on two films with Viggo Mortensen before he became a megastar. On *Nothing But Trouble* I worked with Chevy Chase, Dan Aykroyd, Demi Moore, and John Candy one more time. *Lethal Weapon 3* with Mel Gibson was nerve wracking for me. Patrick Swayze was fantastic to work with as well as Brad Pitt, who I think is one of the most talented people in Hollywood. The guy has a stuntman's mentality. On *Se7en* his hand smashed through a car window; he needed numerous stitches, but he refused to go to the hospital, wanting to finish the scene first. (That is why he has a cast on his hand for a good portion of the movie.) Add that mentality to his talent and that is how you get a superstar.

I once did a charity golf tournament with Leslie Nielsen and the mayor of Detroit. It was a blast. Leslie was hysterical, cracking one-liners with a straight face. He had this little *fart in a can* thing he would keep hidden in his pocket. Squeezing it would make an amazingly realistic farting noise. Every once in a while he would make the noise and pretend nothing happened. The funny part was that no one said a word every time he farted; they all thought he was a poor old man who couldn't control himself. It was hysterical! People who know me know I love a good fart joke, so I begged Leslie afterward to tell me where to get one of those things… It took a while, but he told me and I have had a blast with it! In fact that's how I ended up making that hidden camera show with my buddy Steve called *Candid Farts* where we go into an elevator and other places, make the farting noise, and film the reactions without people knowing. We sold the video to Spencer Gifts; they ended up stocking it for years.

In *Batman Forever* I got to work with Jim Carrey, Nicole Kidman, Chris O'Donnell, Val Kilmer, Drew Barrymore, and Tommy Lee Jones. In one scene I played a thug as Two Face's (Jones) driver. Before we rolled film I said, *I'm Kane Hodder. I worked with you on a Steven Seagal movie.* He just looked at me and didn't say a word. Maybe he was just having a bad day, but when you do something like that to a person, they will think you're an ass forever. Needless to say, I'm not a big fan of Tommy Lee Jones.

One of the only on-line shorts I did was with Madonna. It wasn't as exciting to work with her as I thought it would be, probably because one of her bodyguards was a dick. He came up to me before the shoot and told me to not look Madonna in the eyes, no matter what. What the fuck is that about? I don't care how famous you are, you are not God. And to be honest, Madonna was very nice—I think the bodyguard made that up himself.

The movie *Four Rooms*, also with Madonna, had an entire slew of great actors and great directors. Working with Quentin Tarantino and Robert Rodriguez was amazing. If I could do a movie with any directors in Hollywood, it would be with either of them. In *The Fan*, it was Robert De Niro and Wesley Snipes who were the big shots. *Gone in Sixty Seconds* starred Nicolas Cage and Angelina Jolie while I did some car stunts. On *Children of the Corn V*, not only did I do a full body burn while falling from a tower, I also worked with Eva Mendes in her first role, where she earned her SAG card.

Full Body Burn, Children of the Corn 5

In a movie called *Brittle Glory*, I doubled one of my idols growing up, Tony Curtis. It was a tiny scene where I had to stand on the edge of a building wearing a super-hero costume that Tony had on. In *A Night at the Roxbury* with Will Ferrell, I got to piss on Chris Kattan's face in a scene that got cut out of the movie. In *Enemy of the State*, I got to work with the legendary Gene Hackman and one of the most talented people in the world, Will Smith. One day while a couple stunt guys and our boss, Chuck Picerni, and I were getting into our car in front of the hotel, Will came out. He asked if he could ride to the set with us so he wouldn't have to wait for his car. Of course we said *Sure*. In the car, all of us were awkwardly silent as we were in his presence. Will said a few things to get us talking, but we were full of grumbles. Then suddenly *Gettin' Jiggy Wit It* came on the radio. At the time, it was the number one song in the country. Will made a quick joke about the crap they played on the radio these days. We all busted out laughing and a conversation finally ensued.

A few days later I got to work with Will on set, though instead of getting to kick some ass in a fight scene or jumping out of a building, I was in a closet on my knees with Will in his underwear. It was as awkward as it sounds. Will had to shoot a scene where he gets stuck in a closet and the building is on fire. I was the safety on the stunt so I had to prep Will for the shot by rubbing fire gel on his legs to protect him from burns. As I applied the gel to his thighs, I couldn't help but think that I was on my knees in a closet in front of one of the world's biggest stars. Millions of women would have killed to be in my place.

Actors seemed to have a good camaraderie with stunt men. They respect us and don't feel threatened. This usually results in a lot of actors hanging out with the stunt guys. One day on the set of *Enemy*, a bunch of us stuntmen were hanging around bullshitting. Gene Hackman came over to our group, started chatting for a bit, and out of nowhere said *So I heard you guys have a video of Pamela Anderson?* One of the guys ran and got the tape for him. As Gene walked away with it, I thought, now that's a fucking man. The guy was almost 70 years old at the time and he could probably kick most of our asses... and he still wanted to see some porn.

Chuck Picerni also took me to Florida to shoot *Just Cause* with Sean Connery, Laurence Fishburne, and Ed Harris. One day a few of us stunt guys decided to go golfing on our day off. We had six people and the course only allowed groups of four at the most. As I was talking to someone, the guys made the groups up and I got stuck in the two man group with my friend, Johnny Martin. The golf marshal told us we could play with another guy who was waiting. I was a bit pissed that we had to play with some stranger, but at least we were going to get to play. As we walked over to him, we realized it was Ed Harris—well, now that wouldn't be bad. At the second hole, Ed chips the ball, digging up a bunch of grass. He got so pissed he threw his club and it landed, taking a chunk out of the green. Johnny and I politely smiled. Ed apologized, fixed the green, and left. We tried to talk him out of leaving, but he just waved us off and walked off the green. He must have been embarrassed, but I wish he had stayed, for if anyone understands a short temper, it's me.

One time I was the best man at my friends, Jason and Starr's, wedding. What was special about that? Sid Haig officiated it, in his full Captain Spaulding make-up from *The House of 1000 Corpses* and *The Devil's Rejects*.

If hearing stories about celebrities gets your juices flowing, then I hope that was enough of them to get you excited. I could keep writing about all the people I've met and worked with, but I'd have to double the length of this book, and it's more important to me to tell my story and not just the stories I have about meeting other celebrities.

PART III

STUNTMAN

BUILDING A RESUME

In 1980, I decided to make the move to California permanent. My family wasn't too happy about it, but no one gave me shit. They understood it was something I had to do. As I looked for a place to live, I stayed in a cheap motel for a few months.

My First Address in California

All I had was a suitcase of clothing and a toothbrush. As far as I was concerned, it was all I needed. I had made the move and was able to stay in the town I *had* to be in to get work. It was a slow start at first, but little by little I started to get small gigs on shows by *hustling* as much as I could. In a way, we stunt guys were trying to sell ourselves to the film industry—that's why we called networking and talking to others in the business to get work *hustling.*

With all the hustling I did, I hooked up with Frank Orsatti who got me some small stunts on episodes of *The Incredible Hulk.* Then Gary Baxley got me some jobs on *Dukes of Hazzard.* From there I got to do stunts on *V, Time Express, Enos,* and others. Slowly but surely, I made enough money to get a small apartment. Saying I could *afford* it was an overstatement, but I was getting enough work here and there that I could at least hope to make rent each month (with slight help from my parents here and there). The place I got was a studio in the famed Oakwood Apartments, where numerous celebrities stayed in the beginning of their careers.

I kept my small studio apartment as cold as a meat locker. In truth, I picked the place because it had air conditioning. After my burn, to stay comfortable, I had to stay in places that were downright freezing. Visiting me used to drive people nuts. They could only stay in my place for a few minutes at a time without going outside to warm up. It sucked for dates, but at least I had an excuse to offer to warm them up. Even to this day, I still get overheated rather quickly. Parts of my skin are like leather, the pores are sealed shut, so it doesn't breathe well.

The best part about the apartment was its vicinity to the studios—it's practically in the backyard of one. It made it easier to hustle and try and to get jobs, though the jobs were few and far between those first few years. It was rough, but I was doing what I loved, so I was happy. The other great thing about living in Oakwood was the people. It was full of starving actors, comedians, and countless other Hollywood hopefuls. I used to play pool with a young comedian. The goofy bastard always had me cracking up. His name was Howie Mandel. Another guy I had played pool with a few times asked me to help him move some heavy furniture in his apartment one day.

When we finished, I saw a couple nice guitars he had, so I asked him if he played. He picked one up and started playing it and singing "Hummingbird don't fly away, fly away"! I was blown away when I realized the guy I knew as Jimmy was Jimmy Seals of Seals and Crofts. I listened to their music in high school.

When a new neighbor, another actor, moved in across the hall from me, we quickly became friends. His name was Jack Coleman and he was working on *Days of Our Lives* at the time. One day he took me to the set and introduced me to a bunch of people. They liked me, and with a little bit of hustling, I ended up getting a job as the stunt coordinator on the show.

Working on *Days* was fantastic. They regularly needed to do stunts, so I got great experience. I got to flip a car, fall off a cliff, and most importantly, hire a lot of my own people, which came in handy
down the line.

Overall I worked on the show for four years; getting to do stunts on a steady basis for that long was great. As it was still early in my career, I wasn't the most seasoned of stuntmen. I made a lot of mistakes, mistakes that could have been fatal. Thankfully, I only ended up with a few bangs and bruises and made it out alive and as a smarter, safer stuntman. In fact, I have always said that if a stuntman is going to die doing a stunt, it will happen in the beginning of their career. Of course there are freak accidents that can cut anyone down at any time, though 90 percent of the time for a stuntman, it will happen in those early years. There are two reasons for this. The first is that when you are young, you think you are invincible. This mentality pushes a young stuntman to do things he probably shouldn't, because he thinks nothing could happen to him. The second reason is experience. When starting off, a stuntman doesn't have enough experience to compare situations to, to know what will work and what won't. It's that experience that is the most vital part of the craft.

The years I worked on *Days*, I gained valuable experience and also had some sense knocked into me. One day we were gearing up to shoot a car flip scene. We only had two cars so we had to get all the shots we needed before we did the flip since we couldn't use the car afterwards. The director wanted to get some shots of the car speeding by the camera and swerving that would lead up to the flip before we totaled the car. Thinking nothing of it, I got in the car along with a stunt woman. We were both doubling the two soap stars. Since we were doing some simple shots of speeding past the camera, I didn't think anything of the fact that I wasn't buckled in. This was in the early '80s before the seat belt laws and craze went into effect. Most people never wore them. Passing off the scene I was filming as not a real stunt, I didn't think twice… that is until I lost control of the car. Being on a dirt road, when I swerved the wheel a bit too hard to the right, the wheels lost their grip on the road. When I tried to swerve back, it was too late. The car veered off and hit a tree head-on.

If I had a seatbelt on, I would have been fine—maybe a bit of muscle strain from tensing up, but fine nonetheless. Instead, my face ended up breaking the windshield. I literally hurtled over the steering wheel and planted face first into the glass. My top teeth went right through my upper lip, my face got bruised up, but luckily my nose was intact as well as the rest of my body. Shaken up, I turned to the stunt woman… of course, she was fine—she had worn her seatbelt. I felt like an idiot and was in a shitload of pain as I was helped out of the car. They wanted to rush me to the hospital, but I refused. I needed stitches badly, but I wasn't ruining the day of shooting because *I* made a mistake. Soaps hardly ever shot outside; if I left the set it would have shut down production, and they would have lost a day of filming. Besides, leaving would have been too embarrassing.

Car Flip Stunt, Days of Our Lives

After convincing the producers I was alright, we kept shooting. The entire time, which was hours, my lip did not stop bleeding. It slowed up some, but it never stopped. After I did the car flip, which I very carefully strapped myself in for, we were done shooting.

Without hesitating, I went to the hospital and got the stitches I needed. Sometimes in life you have to be stupid so you can learn a lesson—this was one of those times. Another time I was a bit foolish on the set of *Days* was during a helicopter stunt. One of the main characters, Stefano, was kidnapping another character named Marlena (I believe they are both still on the show). He was taking her in his helicopter. I was to double Roman, who was trying to stop him. The scene called for me to run out and grab the skid of the helicopter as it was taking off. The pilot was supposed to go up a few feet and then bring it back down so I could jump off. Well, things don't always work as planned.

The director wanted me to grab on with just my hands and not throw my arms over it for support. I was fine with this, but the only problem I had was how the hell could I clip myself in for safety? Since he wanted to do it in one take and not cut to me hanging on the skid, clipping in would be damn near impossible, so I said *Fuck it.* He was only supposed to go up a few feet anyway. Well, the pilot wasn't stunt trained, he was a regular helicopter pilot doing something like this for the first time. The first part went smoothly. I ran out, grabbed onto the skid, and he started to go up. As I hung there, I decided to make the stunt look more daring by letting go with one hand as if I might fall. As I did this I happened to look down... only to see I was 80 feet in the air hanging on to a helicopter with one hand! I started to panic as I grabbed back on with my other hand. Yelling to the pilot was futile; over the thunderous noise of the blades no one would hear me. Keeping my grip I held on, my fingers aching. Helicopter skids are massive, unlike a pipe that you can wrap your hands around easy and lock in. With a skid, your hand can really only cup over the top. I didn't know how long I could hold on for. I just hoped the pilot realized that I was still dangling.

After a few seconds of panic and pain in my hands, arms, and shoulders, he finally started to lower the helicopter, only he didn't go all the way down. About 25 feet off the ground, he hovered. After another minute I just let go. The crew measured it afterwards—from the bottom of my feet to the ground was 23 feet. Thankfully, or more so amazingly, I didn't break anything on the fall, although I do think I compressed my back, starting my lifelong battle with back pain. The situation ended safely, but it could have been far worse.

Helicopter Stunt, Days of Our Lives

And all of it could have been avoided if I took the time to find a way to safety myself to the chopper. If I was hooked to it, it wouldn't have mattered how high or how long he was up there, I would have been fine. Another lesson learned.

One of the major things I learned from *Days* was to never, ever, take someone's word for something. One day we were set to shoot a simple scene of two characters taking a dip in a pond, frolicking and kissing. Even though it's just them swimming, you still have to have a stunt coordinator on hand, so I was there. They were to shoot the scene in this underground spring-fed pond during February in California.

The owner of the land told me it was only four feet deep all the way across so the actors would have to stay on their knees and pretend it was deep. I trusted the man, but figured I should test it out anyway. Getting into the water I was shocked at how cold it was. It couldn't have been warmer than melted ice. It was freezing, and my teeth started chattering in less than a minute. As I started to walk out, I suddenly fell off into a deep pocket, not even ten feet from the shore. Four feet, my ass. The entire middle was so deep that diving down I couldn't touch the bottom.

Getting out and drying off I told the director that they might not want to film there because it was deep and frigid. He talked to the actors, and they both said they were fine with it. I was then told to go and relax at craft services while they did the scene. I didn't feel comfortable doing that, so I got in the water with the actors and stayed out of the camera's view. I had to fight the pain of the cold just to pay attention to what they were doing. When I heard the actress say *Help*, I thought I was hearing things. Then suddenly, she bobbed under the water, came back up, and called out *Help* again. Fighting off the cold, I dove forward and started swimming towards her just as I saw the douche bag actor, who was a foot from her, swim away instead of helping her because he was so cold and having trouble, too. I scooped her in my arm and swam us to the shore. Turns out, she got so cold her body shut down, and she couldn't move any longer. That day I decided to never take anyone's word when it came to safety. And to this day, even though I have people I trust wholeheartedly, I will always check every aspect of a stunt myself.

TASTE OF FAME

On *Days of Our Lives*, there was a long plot line about a serial killer called the Salem Strangler. Eventually my buddy, Jack Coleman, was revealed to be the malicious character and killed off the show. It wasn't long before he got work though; he ended up getting a major role on a little show called *Dynasty*.

As *Dynasty* quickly became one of the biggest shows on television, Jack's fame and wealth skyrocketed. Having money, he wanted to leave the apartments and rent a house, and he asked me if I wanted to rent a house with him. I jumped at the chance to get out of an apartment and said *Yes*. He ended up renting a cool house near Griffith Park in Los Angeles. I was now paying less than I was at Oakwood and got to live in a real house. We got along great and our schedules were fantastic. Every summer, Jack would go to Martha's Vineyard for the summer, so I'd have the house to myself for three months even though I was paying the same rent as I did all year long. Jack also had Lakers tickets, so I got to go with him or if he was busy, I'd get the tickets. There was even one year he gave me tickets to the Olympics. Now that's a good friend.

Living and hanging out with Jack, I learned a lot about fame. Everywhere we went, Jack got noticed. We'd be out to dinner and people would come over to the table the second Jack put a mouthful of food in his mouth to ask for an autograph. He would smile, cover his mouth, finish his bite, and then gladly sign a napkin for the fan. No matter what, he stopped and signed that autograph or took a picture. Standing off to the side or taking a picture for the fan, I noticed how happy and thankful these people were getting to meet a celebrity they loved. It was these early experiences that influenced me to be the same way with my fans. Jack knew that the fans were the reason he stayed on the air and, ultimately, got him his paycheck. Not only that, he knew how special a moment it was for them to meet a star... and ruining that was something he couldn't do.

There were a few times Jack and I were out where he would be stopped for an autograph, and then the fan would ask *me* for an autograph... just because I was with him! As his fame grew, Jack's fan mail started to pile up. One day, he offered to pay me to start to answer them for him, and having a lot of free time on my hands, I agreed. On the days when I wasn't working, I would sit at the kitchen table and answer letter after letter. At times it got tedious, but he was paying me after all, so I stuck with it. It was amazing how much mail he got. People loved the show and wanted to tell him. Reading these letters I got to see and understand how important an actor can be to a fan. Responding to these letters helped me learn that fans are the most important thing in the world—without them, there would be no stars. This philosophy has stuck with me to this day.

After a couple of years, Jack and I moved to another house in the Hollywood Hills. It was a fantastic house, and we had the same deal. He got the big room and paid most of the rent while I got the smaller room. Around that time, the job at *Days* sort of disappeared. Not really sure why, but one day the calls just stopped coming. Never got a real reason, though I think they found a cheaper guy at the time. It didn't worry me much though because I got another job as a stunt coordinator on the soap, *Santa Barbara*. It was another good experience and more importantly, a stunt coordinator credit. There weren't as many stunts on the show, but it was still rewarding and got me some more experience.

During that previous summer, I got a job on a Chuck Norris movie through some friends who worked with Chuck's stunt coordinator, who was also his brother, Aaron. We all went down to El Paso and sweated our asses off as we did numerous stunts on the movie, called *Lone Wolf McQuade*. It was one of my first big movies, and it was great getting to work with Chuck Norris.

One day I got a good fight scene with Chuck. My gut was in knots; I wasn't nervous about what I had to do—I was confident in my ability. I was just so excited to get a featured scene with Chuck Norris. I did well enough that years later, Chuck had me on a few episodes of *Walker, Texas Ranger*. Chuck's son, Eric, was the stunt coordinator for the show and hired me several times to come in and play a bad guy. When *Lone Wolf McQuade* was wrapped, I went back to California, confident that more work would follow after working on a major film. It still wasn't as easy as I thought it would be.

SUPER MARIO

During those first few years in the 1980's, I was getting work, but not steadily enough that I ever had any savings. I was living pay check to pay check and still having to do an odd job here and there to get by between stunt gigs. I was having fun though and loving every minute of it. After the Chuck Norris movie, my next decent role was in a cheesy comedy called *Hardbodies*. At first I was excited because I got to do a tiny, tiny bit of acting in it. Little did I know it would become the most embarrassing role of my life. It could have had something to do with the fact that my credit was "older geek." I had a few words to say to one of the main characters, played by Grant Cramer, which led into a chase scene on the beach and into the water. Two guys and I chased the character across a stage. I dove at him and missed, then he jumped on a motorized surfboard, and we jumped on jet skis and chased him through the water until I got caught up in a fishing net. The chase itself is pretty cool, but with the 80's music and my dorky acting, it's ridiculous.

When we filmed it, I thought I looked pretty cool with my curly hair and mustache and hat, but looking back now, I look like Super Mario. Thankfully, the film disappeared for a long while, but now with the Internet, of course, a fan found it and put it online to show everyone my crowning moment!

The next big gig I got was doing some stunts on *The Hills Have Eyes 2*. I doubled a character called the "Reaper" doing some motorcycle stunts and a big fall through a glass skylight. John

Bloom, who played the Reaper, was seven feet tall. Even with the height difference, it wasn't a problem, visually, to double him. Falling through the glass, you couldn't tell how tall I was, and driving on the bikes there was so much movement that my height didn't matter much. It was a short shoot for me, but it was also the first time I got to work with Michael Berryman. To this day we remain friends and still work on films together.

Around the same time, I was flown out to Mexico City to do some stunts in *Volunteers* with John Candy and Tom Hanks. It was the first time I had been flown to a foreign location, and I loved it. Both John and Tom were such a pleasure to work with. One night in Mexico, Tom even took all of us stunt guys out to dinner as a show of appreciation for our work. I would be lucky enough to work with John again years later on *Nothing But Trouble*. I hate the fact that he is gone. Five years after shooting *Volunteers*, I ran into Tom in an airport lounge at LAX and he remembered me. I know this because he came up to me first. Both of these guys are among my favorite actors I have ever worked with.

The next year I did a movie called *The Patriot*. It was shot in Santa Barbara so I didn't have to travel far which was nice, but I missed the fun of going somewhere new. My buddy, Rick McCallum, whom I had met while working on *Lone Wolf McQuade*, was working with me on the movie, and in one scene the two of us were standing on the edge of a ship.

Greg Henry's stunt double was supposed to swing down and knock the two of us off into the water at once. It was set up so one of his feet would hit each of us, and at that moment, we would throw ourselves into the water. As the double started to swing down, however, I noticed he was angled a bit too much towards Rick.

Stunt from Ship, The Patriot

"I think he is going to hit just you..." I said as I prepared myself for the impact that I didn't think was going to hit me. Just as Rick was about to answer... wham! The double slammed his entire body into Rick; he didn't even skim me. As Rick went flying 20 feet out into the water, I had to fake that I got hit and throw myself backwards into the ocean. Swimming up to the surface, I had to gasp for air as I was laughing so hard. Rick, on the other hand, had this stunned look of shock on his face; he definitely wasn't ready for the blow he had just received.

With these bit stunts in decent-sized movies, along with my coordinating on *Days of Our Lives* and *Santa Barbara*, I finally made enough connections to get my first stunt coordinating gig on a movie.

MY FIRST HOUSE

It was 1985 and my career was finally taking off. While I had been stunt coordinating for years on television shows, I had yet to do a movie. That's why when I got the stunt coordinating job on *House* it was a huge break for me. On set I did everything I could to make sure there were no accidents and that the stunts looked incredible. The film was about a creepy, old, haunted house that a famous horror author inherits. With his son missing, he soon finds out that the house might be responsible. The film, odd as it was, became a cult classic and even spawned three sequels. I can't take any credit for its success, but it was satisfying that the first movie I coordinated became a classic and not some dud that disappeared. The odd part is the connection this movie had with the *Friday the 13th* series. Sean Cunningham, who created the series and produced it, and Steve Miner, who directed *Part 2* and *Part 3*, directed *House*.

During the filming, I doubled the star, William Katt. In one scene, he hangs from the roof and climbs across it to get to a window. Being too dangerous for a star, I did this stunt. If you look carefully in the movie, you can clearly see it's me with a corny wig on. It was a pretty easy stunt, and it went smoothly like most of the other stunts on the film, though there was one stunt that left me...a little sore. Near the middle of the movie, William Katt kills a giant purple witch and chops her into little pieces. After stuffing her into trash bags, he then buries her in the backyard. The script called for the bag to start moving as he dug the hole. Instead of having the special effects team build something to make it move, I volunteered to be in the bag.

Putting on the rubber suit, I figured I would be fine in the bag when William had to hit me with the shovel to stop the witch from moving. Before I got in the bag, I showed him how to hit me with the flat of the shovel so it wouldn't hurt that much. He understood it and was ready for the shot. When the director yelled *Action*, I started to twitch the way they wanted me to and William started to hit me. The first few blows didn't affect me that much, but then suddenly he got really into the role. He started to slam me so hard that he lost track of what part of the shovel he was hitting me with… which ended up being the heel of the shovel, the hardest, worst part to get hit with. Keep in mind it was a real shovel. Whack after whack, he beat the shit out of me. Inside the bag I started cursing him as I could feel welts forming by the second. By the time the shoot was over, I felt like a team of Clydesdales ran over me.

William Katt Beating the Shit Out of Me, House

The film was a decent success, enough so that it warranted a sequel the next year. I was brought back as the stunt coordinator again and even got a small bit part in the film. During a costume party scene, a giant ancient warrior walks through the party and knocks into me. Wearing a gorilla costume, I whip off the head and yell at the guy for pushing me. The giant pushes me quickly, and I flip over a banister and land on the couch below. It was a bitch of a fall since it wasn't that high, and I needed to do a full flip before I landed, but I got it done successfully and looks pretty good in the final film. One of the biggest accidents of my career happened on this film as well.

There is a scene in a temple where the main character is supposed to swing on a rope across the set. The actor was to jump off a 25-foot ledge, swing across the room, and land on another 25-foot high ledge as well. Being the coordinator, I needed to test it. Jumping off, I swung to one side with no problem, though the G-force pulling me down was much harder than I expected. On the way back I started to swing too close to the set wall… and sure enough, I slammed right into it. I wasn't clipped in, so I went flying. On the way down, I hit the set several times before slamming into the ground. It jacked up my leg so badly I could barely walk, yet, thanks to great genes, I didn't break a bone. In fact, I am proud to say that I have never broken a bone in my entire career, or my entire *life* for that matter. Not one broken bone. When my mother was 78, she fell down a flight of uncarpeted, brick stairs and didn't break a bone—talk about great genes. It's funny, people always ask me how many bones I have broken. They expect that, being a stuntman, I would have a list of a few dozen, and when I tell them none, they never believe me. Sadly, some stunt guys think that broken bones are a badge of honor. They brag about how many they have snapped as if getting hurt is better than doing the stunt. In reality, all that it shows is that you or something fucked up and you got hurt.

After that particular fall, my soon-to-be wife, Susan, came to the set. Before she found me, one of the other stunt guys ran into her and said, "Jesus! We thought Kane was dead when he fell. It was horrible!" This scared the shit out of her, but she eventually learned to deal with being the spouse of someone with a dangerous job for a living. The leg took a while to heal, but there was no permanent damage, and I was able to keep working on the movie. This injury resulted in me realizing something incredible about myself regarding pain. Because of the horrific pain that I endured for such a long time as a result of my burn injury and subsequent shitty medical care, I developed an amazing tolerance for pain. Nothing in life can ever be as painful as that was, so now I deal with less painful things as if they are nothing. I had surgery for a hernia while I was awake. I had both of my shoulders operated on without being put out. I still have dental work done (including drilling), without any novocaine at all. I'm serious. It's not that I'm trying to be a tough guy; it's just not necessary for me. Nothing could ever come close to the burn pain, so life is easy now.

Though the second film didn't make half of the first movie's gross, they decided to make another sequel, even if it had nothing to do with the first two. This time though they changed the name to *The Horror Show* and downplayed the fact that it was a sequel to the *House* movies. Once again I was lucky enough to be brought on as the coordinator. One of the stars of this film was Lance Henriksen. He was great to work with and for years he used to tell the following story. He would say, *Kane and I were doing a scene together and the whole time we were acting, Kane was looking me right in the eye. RIGHT IN THE EYE!!! THE WHOLE SCENE!!! Then people would say, "Yeah, So what? Isn't that what you are supposed to do when you act?"* Then Lance would answer *Yes, but Kane was ON FIRE AT THE TIME!!!*

When it came time to do a fourth film, I was once again the stunt coordinator. The big stunt I did in this one was to flip a car with a pipe ramp. Since you are flipping a car at high speed, you can never be sure what position the car will be in when it makes the first contact with the ground. I hit the ramp at about 55 miles per hour, and unfortunately, the first impact was flush on the roof of the car. That is the worst way that you want the first impact to be, and consequently, I ended up with a pretty good concussion. It would not be my last. In this movie I also did an un-credited cameo as "the human pizza," and I sang on film for the first time in my career. Pretty embarrassing.

Sean Cunningham and the *House* series were great to me and my career. They really helped me jump start my stunt coordinating which opened a lot of doors in the future.

HOW PRISON CHANGED MY LIFE

After *House*, I went and filmed *Avenging Force* in New Orleans, the movie that changed my career for good. After that I shot another Michael Dudikoff film, *American Ninja 2* in South Africa.

Jumping From Roof Stunt, American Ninja 2

Most ninjas are small, compact, and stealthy... I'm big and lumbering, yet I played a ninja in almost every scene. *Ninja* was great because I got to do countless fighting scenes, drag a guy behind a truck, and ultimately flip that same truck with a pipe ramp again, this time into a gas station that explodes all around me just as I land. People usually think when they watch the movie that nobody was in the truck when it lands because the explosion around me is huge. If you watch carefully, just as the truck flips, you can see my white crash helmet in the cab of the truck. Once again, BJ Davis let me do a lot of big stunts in this movie, and it was a great experience.

My career really picked up in 1987 as I was privileged enough to coordinate three movies. One of those movies that year was called *Prison*—the movie that would change my life forever. This giant blond-haired Finnish guy named Renny Harlin directed it. It was his first American film, and none of us knew if this guy could direct or not... Of course he proved he could and went on to direct films like *Die Hard 2*, *Cliffhanger*, and *The Long Kiss Goodnight*. On *Prison*, he did an amazing job with the budget he had. The budget was so small that I had to do most of the stunts myself because we couldn't afford to bring any other stunt people in for the shoot.

There were a decent amount of stunts in the film. One of the best was a high fall I did from the fourth tier of the cell block with sparks shooting off my back. Another stunt I did impressed the cinematographer, Mac Ahlberg, so much he ended up getting me the stunt coordinating job on the movie *Ghost Town* which filmed that same year in Tucson, Arizona. The stunt that impressed him involved crashing a car through an exploding gate, then sliding the car sideways to a stop right on a precise mark within three feet of an unmanned camera. Mac was worried about getting the shot all in one take without destroying the camera, especially since we could only crash the gate once. When I nailed it right on the button, it blew his mind. The shot looks great in the movie. It's just too bad you can't find the thing on DVD in America yet.

John Carl Buechler, the amazing make-up effects artist, was working on *Prison*. Having seen a few of his films, I knew of his work and was excited to meet and work with him on this movie. The finale of the story called for a rotting corpse in an electric chair to rise out of the ground. Buechler had been working on the costume for weeks, especially building it around an actor. At the last minute, the actor could not do the part. I'm not sure why he couldn't do it, but I volunteered to take his place. The costume was extremely tight since it wasn't built for me, but I could get it on. The process to put the entire suit on took over three hours. I had contact lenses, dentures, and enough foam latex to cover a house. It was uncomfortable, but I loved the way it looked and couldn't wait to perform in it.

Kane as Ghost of Charlie Forsythe, Prison

As the scene was being prepped, Renny was talking to Buechler about how to make it look even better. One of them came up with the idea of putting live night crawlers all over my body. When I heard this, I suggested that they put them in my mouth, so when I screamed, worms would fall out. You can't really see the worms well in the final product, but the fact that I was willing to go out of my way to make the film better impressed Buechler so much, and that I worked well in tons of make-up, that when he got the job directing *Friday the 13th Part VII*, he wanted no one but me to play the legendary Jason Voorhees. Since no actor in the previous six *Friday* films had played Jason a second time, Paramount was willing to at least consider me for the role, saying *If he can be intimidating and scary when we see him film in person, we'll consider him.* What? You asked for it, motherfuckers!

FIGHT
INTERMISSION
III

ROUND THREE

There are times when fighting someone can feel fucking amazing. Not that I would ever just go and punch someone, it's all about the situation. One time in college, I was at this club called Bahama Mama's. The owner of the club was Steve Lehman, who is a friend of mine to this day. Some asshole knocked into me on the dance floor. I ignored him and went about trying to seduce the cute young lady I was dancing with. The guy, on the other hand, wanted to show off for his girlfriend, so he grabbed my shoulder and spun me around. *You made me spill my drink asshole*, the guy barked in my face while giving his girl a look that said he could take me. I told him to back the fuck off, he bumped into me, but the guy wouldn't let it go. We started to argue and yell more, so we decided to take it outside. We were smart enough to not fight inside; if you did, the bouncers would stop it quickly and you'd get kicked out for the night. Outside, you could fight and if you won, go back in.

Once in the side parking lot, the guy started to dance around a bit like he was some fancy-footed boxer. A small crowd gathered and pointed at him as if he must know what he was doing. I stood still waiting for him to attack, and when he did, he didn't try to use some pro boxing move. Instead he tried to kick me in the balls like some coward (not sure why so many people have tried to do that to me, but it never works). His foot hit my knee instead, and while he was distracted with his legs, I pulled back and cracked him one right in the face. I hit him so hard, it killed my hand, but regardless, he went down and was out for the count. It felt pretty amazing. The crowd

237

roared. I wanted to shoot my arms up like Rocky and jump around, but I figured it would be cooler to just walk away and slip back into the club like nothing ever happened. This round goes to me.

THE NUMBER 13

The number 13 has followed me through my entire life, mostly in good ways. Besides the obvious fact that my fame came from the *Friday the 13th* series, there are numerous other things that have occurred with the number 13. Now I'm not a person who believes in stupid psychic stuff or that if my palm itches I'm going to get money. To me, most of that crap is ridiculous. Still, I can't deny how much the number has played a role in my life. Here are some examples:

- When I graduated, I was ranked 13th in my class.
- I wear a size 13 shoe.
- I have 13 upper and 13 lower teeth.
- My burn happened on the 13th. (The one bad thing)
- My wife was born on the 13th.
- The street I live on has 13 houses on it.
- I've starred in four *Friday the 13th* films.
- I found out officially that I was Jason on January 13, 1988.
- I recently found another strange coincidence. My son, Jace, is a lifeguard and he works at the club that I work out at. His boss is a good friend of mine named Rain. She was born on the exact same day that I was burned. Not the anniversary of it, that exact day! July 13, 1977. Weird.

This is probably all coincidences, but I can't help but wonder why this number, a number that is supposed to be bad luck, keeps popping up in my life. Hell, ninety percent of the time it has brought me good luck, so I guess I shouldn't complain.

WARNING: DO NOT
TRY THIS AT HOME

First and foremost, I'm a stuntman. It's what I got into the industry to do, and it's what I'll do until I can't walk anymore. I love stunts, and the rush and adrenaline you get from falling or being lit on fire is incomparable to anything in the world. I have done so many over the years, I could literally write a book about each stunt and how much preparation and training goes into them. Most of them go well, some don't. As for myself, I have been lucky to not have been in too many major accidents in my career. As I said before, I have never broken a bone in my body, and I'm proud as hell of that. Other stunt guys love to brag about how many bones they have broken as if it is a badge of honor, but really, it just shows you fucked up. Even if you are prepared though, things can still go wrong. Hopefully they don't, and you end up making the audience's jaw drop at your death-defying feat.

Instead of writing about the countless stunts I have done over the years, I have filtered through my spotty memory and put down some of my favorites here. Some will show you how shit can go wrong, others make me laugh, and some were just flat out painful.

When I was doing an episode of *Alias*, another stunt guy and I had to chase Jennifer Garner through an alley. Jennifer can run—I mean fly. She is fast as hell. We had to run at full speed just to keep up with her. In one take, the guy behind me clipped my back heel, tripping me, and sending me face first to the ground. It hurt like hell and messed up the entire take; of course, he wouldn't admit he clipped me, so it made me look like an asshole.

One of my favorite scenes I ever did was in an episode of *Nash Bridges*. I played a guy who shoots up a beauty salon. Don Johnson shoots me, and I go flying through a giant ten-by-ten foot window. It looks amazing. The only problem was you can't make a candied glass window that big. They had to use real glass and rig it with squibs to blow up just as I hit it. What no one realized was that the store logo in the middle was painted on with latex paint—meaning that when it tried to shatter, the glass stuck to it instead of breaking into small pieces. I landed on massive shards of glass that should not have been there. One of the shards went right into the back of my thigh. I didn't want to, but the production manager made me go to the hospital. It ended up being only four stitches, which was embarrassing. Don kept teasing me about it for the rest of the shoot. I would have done the same thing.

In a TV mini-series I did called *Dream West*, I had some cool stunts. I flew off a tower that gets blown up, did some crazy fights, and everything was fine. Then in one scene, where all I had to do was play dead, I get hurt. I was lying on the ground while a guy flew over a cactus next to me and landed on the other side. Well, when he went to do the stunt he hit the air ram (a device that throws you) wrong and landed on the cactus, which ended up tipping over. They both landed on me. It was this huge cactus with barbs the size of french fries. Thankfully I decided to roll onto my stomach at the last minute, because all the barbs stuck right into my ass. (Can you imagine if I had stayed lying face up?) A crew member had to use pliers to remove them. The first one he pulled out hurt so much I asked him how many he got, and when he said *only one*, I almost shit.

High Fall Explosion Stunt, Dream West

I once did a Taco Bell® commercial with Jack Palance. It was great to work with the movie legend, but the stunt I had to do kicked my ass. It was a one-day shoot, and I was doing a stunt of flying out a window and landing. Only thing was they wanted to get it from all these different angles. Well, to pull me through a window they put me on a pulley system which jerks you backwards through the window. I had to do it 14 times. When I finished, I had whiplash from the numerous sudden thrusts backwards. Then, after all of those takes, I had to stand on an apple box and fall at Jack's feet. My neck hurt so much I could not lift it off the ground, literally. I had to roll over and push myself up. It was worth it though - the commercial played constantly, and I made a boatload of money from it. Not bad for one day's worth of work.

Pacific Blue had me do a fight scene with this tiny guy who was five feet tall... and he ended up beating me! It was so unrealistic, I begged them to rearrange the fight to make it believable that this little guy would beat me, but they wouldn't change it. You win some, you lose some.

In the movie, *Zandalee* with Nicolas Cage and Judge Reinhold, I doubled Judge. There was a boat chase scene where his character gets knocked off the boat at high speed. Of course, I did the stunt. The boat was going so fast, I skipped across the surface and it looked great.

In *Ghost Town*, a little-seen 80's movie, I got dragged behind a horse. That is one scary stunt to do. You can't be positive where the horse will go and what will happen. My arms got all torn up from being dragged a good hundred yards, but it looks good.

In *Ghoulies Go to College III*, I played a janitor who gets knocked into his mop bucket and falls down a set of stairs. When doing a stair fall, you have control of your body. In this case I had my ass in a bucket and had to roll down, hoping the bucket would go down just right. It was complicated, but looks pretty comical in the final picture.

In *Project: Metalbeast*, another very little-seen movie with Barry Bostwick, I played a seven-foot-tall biomechanical werewolf. Buechler did the make-up and it looked great, but it was the hardest character I ever had to play. I had to be on stilts the entire shoot; the damned things killed my legs and being in the make-up on top of it, it was hard.

In countless movies like *Gone in Sixty Seconds*, *Demolition Man*, *Lethal Weapon 3*, and numerous others, I got to do car stunts. Car stuff, slides, skids, small crashes, and jumps are the easiest jobs for stuntmen. We love them; we get to sit in a nice air-conditioned car and just drive around all day. And they pay well, too—wish every day could be a car stunt.

For some reason I tend to play a security guard or a cop in a lot of films, probably because of my size. Guards seem to be the guys who get tossed around a lot in action films, just like I was in *A Low Down Dirty Shame* with Keenen Ivory Wayans. I had a scene in a mall where Keenen picks me up, flips me over, and slams me on the ground. Since they were shooting a wide shot, we couldn't use a pad on the ground and a back pad looked too bulky, meaning I had to be slammed onto a marble floor with no protection, over and over again. On one of the takes, he grabbed my arm and the gun I was holding flew out and hit him in the head (I think he has a scar from it). This pissed him off, so he started to slam me harder and harder. The next day, my organs felt sore. Literally. It was the only time it ever happened to me in my life, but my entire insides hurt. They must have been slamming around in my body.

One of the trickiest stunts I have ever done was in *Fair Game* with Billy Baldwin and Cindy Crawford. The scene called for four of the bad guys to fly down over a speeding train in a helicopter, jump out, and land on the train while they were both moving. With the complicated set up, we couldn't use safety gear because if one of the vehicles went the other way, it would tear us in half. We had to literally just jump out of the copter with guns in our hands, land, and start running across the train, while it was moving. On the first take, the head guy (my old friend Chuck Picerni) climbed down to the helicopter skid and jumped, the second guy (Chuck's brother, Steven) did the same thing, then the stuntwoman Sophia Crawford, jumps from the deck. I was like…*Shit.* Now I had to jump from the deck—if I didn't, I'd look bad. Jumping from the skid was easier, because it gave you at least four feet less to fall, and you could hold on before you jumped (four feet added to 15 or 20 is a big difference). From the deck, you just had to go for it... so I did. We all stuck it and it looked great.

Of course being a movie, we had to do another take to get it from other angles. Again, the same thing—the first two guys stepped down to the lower rail and Sophia didn't, she jumped from the deck. I had to do it again, as well. It worked, but we had to reload and do it again. Again, same thing. By this point, I thought we were pushing it. How many times can you jump out of a flying helicopter onto a moving train and have it work perfectly? We took a lunch break and the director decided he needed a few more angles, so back on the helicopter it was. Only this time, it had rained during the break so now the train was wet. *Of course.* We did it again, and amazingly, none of us slipped. For the final take, the helicopter flew in really close to the train so they could get a good shot of us landing. This one was easy as we only had to jump down a few feet. With all the footage they had, they should have gotten a great scene of a tricky, awesome stunt; instead, for some unknown reason which pissed me off, in the final film, they used the one take where we flew in low! All of that for nothing! That's movies for you.

SO, YOU WANT TO DO STUNTS?

Countless times, someone has asked me how to become a stuntman. Well, the simple truth is it's not that easy. It's one of the hardest disciplines in film to break into, especially if you don't know someone or don't have family in the line of work. There are some stunt schools still around, but most of them are outrageously priced and don't teach more than the basic stunts. They will give you a base knowledge, but stunt work is not like other professions. It's not like going to school to become a lawyer where you walk out the door and you *are* a lawyer. Becoming a stuntman is 50 percent about who you know and 50 percent about proving yourself. Without knowing someone in the industry, it is hard, practically impossible, to get someone to take a chance on you. If you do get that chance, you are going to start off small, maybe getting pushed in a crowd or falling off a chair. Prove you can do that well and safely and you might, *just might,* get another job. The next one might be a bit tougher, a fight scene or a stair fall. Then the cycle continues as you work your way up bit by bit by bit. If you are really interested in the industry, study the craft, follow the rules, and don't be an idiot.

Stunts are not about seeing who has the biggest balls. Jumping off your friend's roof into a pool is NOT safe or even cool. Smashing a table over your head is just going to hurt you. Trust me on this, because I WAS that guy. Professional stunts are done as *safely* as possible. Things can always go wrong, but the people who do them study every possible outcome and make sure nothing can go wrong that they can prevent.

Lighting yourself on fire or going down a hill in a shopping cart will only prove you are a reckless idiot to the industry (regardless of *Jackass,* as much as they make it look unplanned and crazy, they are still professionals who know what they're doing). Getting yourself hurt only proves that you don't know what you're doing. Remember, I have worked in the business for over 30 years and never once have I broken a bone. The true test of a stuntman is to do a stunt and *not* get hurt. Those are the people who get hired.

If you really want to be in stunts, find a stunt person to talk to. See if they will help you out and show you the ropes. That way, you learn from professionals. That doesn't mean to ask me the next time you bump into me at a convention. I'll be more than happy to give some advice, but I couldn't give you much more than what I've stated here.

PART IV

THE RISE AND FALL OF JASON

THE AUDITION OF A LIFETIME

When John Carl Buechler got the job as director on *Friday the 13th Part VII*, he gave me a call and asked me to come down to film a screen test as Jason. I was extremely excited. I had always loved the series; the thought of getting to play a legendary killer was like being told I might win the lottery. I never had aspirations to be an actor, but this incarnation of Jason didn't call for *just* an actor, he also had to be a stuntman... it was a perfect combination for me.

Messing up this audition was not an option, so I enlisted my friend and fellow stuntman, Alan Marcus, to help me out. We didn't have time to work up a routine and practice it, but it was alright. We had worked together for years, and I knew he would go along with whatever I did. I started wondering to myself if I could look and act like a violent, homicidal maniac. Then I remembered a time back on Kwaj when I kind of got that reputation for real, and it was all by accident. It was during my junior year and when we were setting up for a school theatrical production or dance or something. For some reason, I had a four-inch pocket knife that I was messing around with—slashing at people and pretending to stab them (seems oddly foretelling now). I did this several times with people when Sam Ice (one of my basketball teammates who witnessed my hanging off the hotel balcony in Hawaii), threw his hands up in a mock defensive pose just as I lunged at him with the knife. Well, I stabbed him through the hand... accidently, I think. He ended up getting a bunch of stitches, and everyone talked about how horrible I was

251

because I had stabbed him. It blew over eventually, but it was bad for a while. I guess, in a way, Sam Ice was my very first victim.

When I arrived at the studio for the Jason audition, I talked to Buechler for a few minutes and then threw on a makeshift Jason costume. In the room there was a table of studio execs waiting for me. Like I became known for, I felt it natural to stand outside of the room, yell, and hit the walls to get into character. I don't know what their reaction was to it, but they definitely had to hear me. Next I sent in Alan to act like he was walking through the woods on a casual hike. When he reached the middle of the room, I walked in, stopped a few feet inside of the door, and looked at Alan. Then I took two quick steps and grabbed him, lifted him off the ground, and threw him aside. From there I dragged him around the room by his hair, tossed him a few more times, and finally… I walked over to the table the execs were at, grabbed it, and flipped it over. It was hilarious. They jumped back, clenched their papers to their chests, and genuinely looked frightened. Sparing their lives, I went back to beating the shit out of Alan until one of the suits spoke up and said that was enough and we cut the cameras. Poor Alan, I jacked him up pretty good. It was worth it for him, though, because he ended up getting a lot of work as a stunt double on the film. As for me, though I felt like I nailed it, you never know with studios, so I went home and waited by the phone.

When I arrived home later that week, I had a few messages on my machine. The first few were just friends—one was my mother checking in, and the last one was from Buechler saying *I'm calling for Mr. Voorhees.* The second I heard that, I knew I had gotten the part. That night I went out to celebrate. On the way home I stopped by a sporting goods store and bought a machete... I figured I needed to get use to the feel of it in my hand. Little did I know it would feel so damn good.

MAKING A KILLER

Throughout the 80's, I had been a huge fan of the *Friday the 13th* franchise and saw them all in the theater with a buddy of mine, Rick Bell, from Reno. We rooted on Jason, waiting anxiously for his next kill. I always loved the concept of him and how he killed, but I never really thought his character was done justice. He was always so stiff and almost robotic that it just didn't seem natural. When I was officially cast in the role, I went back and watched all the films, taking notes on what I *liked* and didn't *like*. Though I loved the movies, there wasn't much in the *like* column regarding the character after I analyzed him. Most of the time when Jason was just standing and staring at someone, he looked like a statue. I wanted to stay away from that and help add life to the character I loved.

What I felt the character was missing was some depth and emotion, which is beyond hard to pull off when you wear a mask and have no lines in a movie. You can only act with your body movements and your eyes, or in his case…eye, which is incredibly hard to do. The word *natural* just kept popping into my head. I wanted what I did to feel natural, and to do that, I knew I had to let out my inner demons.

As the shoot date got closer, I stood in front of my bathroom mirror and practiced my movements. I ignored my face and focused on my body, eyes, and head angles. It was then that I realized that Jason never looked like he was breathing, which is *why* he looked like a statue. Realizing this, I looked in the mirror and started breathing heavily. At first I tried just breathing as hard as I could in the mirror, but it didn't read. After a little practice, I found that heaving my chest up and down read great. Having it down pat, I decided to use it during filming… little did I know it would define my version of Jason for years.

A few weeks before production, I got fitted for the suit and had the molds for my make-up done. It was only the second life cast I had done of my face, and coincidentally, the first one I had done was by Buechler as well. When you do a life cast, they completely cover your face in alginate—a gooey, liquid plastic. Every inch of your face is encased. You can't hear for shit, you can't see a thing, and you can only breathe through your nose. Sometimes they will use plastic straws in your nose, and other times the actor has to signal the make-up effects guy to clear the gunk from your nostrils so you can breathe. If you are the slightest bit claustrophobic, this process is impossible. There are a lot of famous actors and actresses, one of whom who made himself a big name in martial arts movies, who have freaked out and torn off the latex as they had it done, ruining the molds. For some reason, I always enjoyed the process. Some people like going to the spa—me, I like having my head encased in goo. For some reason, it relaxes me. I think it might be because I can't see or hear anything; it's calming and peaceful. When Buechler was doing my make-up for Jason, I was a bit too comfortable. So much so in fact, I fell asleep. I don't know for how long, but Buechler loves to tell people that I started to snore while I was in the chair.

When the full mask and prosthetics were done, I was called in to try them out to see how it fit and what adjustments needed to be made. It ended up looking great, but there was only one problem… Jason only has one eye. The make-up completely covered my right eye. Normally, it wouldn't be that bad, but in the one good eye, I had to wear a contact that was blurry as hell. I moved around to try and see how I could do stunts, but there was no way. You don't realize how much you depend on both eyes for depth perception. With sight in only one eye, I could easily misjudge a jump or fall, which could have been a catastrophe. In interviews I never admitted to this—I always said I couldn't see shit, but the truth is I told Buechler that I *had* to have more vision. He didn't want to screw up his make-up job, but he understood. To solve the problem he bore out a tiny hole in the covered eye so I had a pin prick of vision. It really wasn't much at all, but it made an amazing difference with the depth perception. Without it, there was no way I could have done all the stunts I did in the movie.

The first thought I had when I started putting on the costume for the first time was *Jesus, this is a lot of latex... at least I won't need many pads.* The costume, a two-piece suit, covered my entire body in a thick layer of gray latex that looked like rotting flesh on the outside. First, I would put on the legs which were like pants with suspenders. Then I would slide into the upper body, and it would connect together. With the bodysuit on, it was time to get in the make-up chair. The process took, on average, three and a half hours to apply. The first time I had all the make-up on, I looked into the mirror in awe. I was unrecognizable... instead, Jason was standing in front of me. When I put the hockey mask on over the make-up, it probably sounds stupid, but it felt magical, especially since it was the best-looking Jason yet. Looking over the details, this tingling sensation of excitement rolled over my body, for I knew from the second I caught my own eye in the camera... that I *was* Jason.

It sounds really corny saying something like that, but it's true, having on the full make-up and mask felt so right to me. Not that I was going to go out and actually kill someone, but I felt like I was really Jason. Looking down at my rotting hands and the tattered clothing on my body, I felt the monster take over me. All the rage and anger that I always held inside took over my body. I naturally started to breathe heavily, I gritted my teeth together, and I clenched my hands. I was ready to kill.

JASON IS BORN AGAIN

Friday the 13th Part VII is about a young psychic named Tina Shepard (played by Lar Park Lincoln) who lost her father through an accident she caused at a young age. Her doctor, Dr. Crews (played by Terry Kiser) takes her back to the lake house at Crystal Lake where she lost her father. Upset one night, she tries to raise her father from the dead, only to raise the infamous killer, Jason Voorhees. Back alive, Jason sets about killing victims… until Tina tries to fight him with her telekinetic powers. Better yet, if you don't know what it's about, put the book down and go watch *Friday the 13th Part VII, Part VIII, Part IX,* and *Jason X.* Then pick the book back up, and you'll be in a lot better place.

The day we started shooting, I got into the costume, alone, in my dressing room (as much as I could) and prepared myself. It was the first day, and I was pretty nervous because Jason was known around the world. Screwing up was not an option, especially since there was this one producer who seemed to have it out for me. Instead of having a fear of messing up and getting fired, I had a fear of having to prove myself. I felt that if I didn't prove to this woman that I could do this, she would use any excuse she could to get rid of me. Of course, the excitement of getting to play Jason overtook the nerves, especially when I started to get the make-up done.

  After three hours in the make-up chair, I slipped on the mask and was given the thumbs up to head to the set for the first time. A production assistant was assigned to me to make sure I got over there, but I told him to go ahead of me, that I wanted some time. Part of the studio wasn't being used, the lights were off in that area, and no one was there, so that is where I went. I was due on set in a matter of seconds, but I had to have that moment for myself to think and breathe… and let Jason take over. It felt so right, so real standing in the dark, looking off into the distance at the section of light and flurry of activity. It was what Jason would do, watch his victims, pick who would be first, and then attack. I had my eyes set on the producer, but instead of killing her, I planned on impressing the shit out of her.

As I took my first step towards the set, I let the character take over me. Walking with intent, heaving my chest, I fixed my gaze at the set and ignored everyone as I walked on. Until this point, almost no one had seen me in the full make-up.

Jason without the Mask, Friday the 13th Part VII

As I walked by dozens of crew members, I could hear them muttering how cool I looked. Everyone and everything seemed to stop as I made my way to the kitchen set. People were staring at me, and though I had met them all beforehand and worked with them as the shoot got ready, I was no longer Kane... I was Jason Voorhees. People I had friendly conversations with that morning stared at me as if I might really kill them. Even the producer I was worried about looked impressed.

Arriving at the set I stopped, heaved my chest and looked around. Everyone was staring at me. I had finally made it. My entire life I loved scaring people and now, now I was going to get to scare people around the world as one of the most famous killers ever. If I didn't have glue in my eye, I would have cried. When Buechler got us ready to shoot, I didn't say a word—I just nodded and kept the mask on. Unlike a lot of directors, Buechler was fine with this, especially since he trusted me and knew I wanted to stay in character as much as I could for the other actors' sake. With everything set, we were ready to film my first kill ever as Jason.

MY FIRST KILL

The first scene I shot was one of Tina's visions. In the vision, she sees Michael getting stabbed in the kitchen with a tent stake. Michael was played by Bill Butler, whom I would work with again in another horror franchise years later. The scene comes in the middle of the movie, yet it was the first thing I shot. We had Bill rigged up so he could hang freely to look like Jason was holding him up by his own strength. The second we were in position and the camera was rolling, I felt Jason taking over me. The character just came out of me, I felt and thought what he would at that moment. There was this sort of satisfaction that washed over me, a feeling I could imagine Jason feeling. Sort of like a junkie taking a hit of his favorite drug. It felt amazing... but the feeling quickly fades and you want more. Thankfully, I had years of it ahead of me.

On Set of Friday the 13th Part VII

To this day at conventions, people bring me pictures to get autographed of my stabbing Bill's character, Michael, with the tent spike. It's a great still from the movie and every time I see it, it brings me back to my first kill. Those first few weeks on set were shot in a studio in Los Angeles. The exteriors were later shot in Mobile, Alabama. During the time in the studio, we shot everything from the big fire stunt in the basement set to the stair fall. The fall through the stairs during the lead up to the climax, even 20 years later, looks amazing. To get the shot, the crew had to build a section of fake stairs made of balsa wood. Underneath was a fall mat for me to land on. Originally in the script, it called for the light to swing down and hit me in the chest, and then I would roll down the stairs. By this point in filming, I felt comfortable enough with Buechler to suggest changes. With the fall, I suggested that the light hit me in the face. I was wearing a hockey mask, after all. I also thought it would be more exciting to fall through the stairs instead of rolling down. John loved the idea and couldn't believe I would do that.

We measured out the stairs and figured the trajectory to see how many stairs needed to be made out of balsa wood, which is a super-light wood which breaks at the slightest touch. We really only had one chance to get it right for time's sake as they would have to build the stairs all over again. Usually when you do a fall, you flail your arms and scream, and being that Jason wasn't a normal person, or even human anymore, I figured the best way for him to fall was like a tree. When action was called, I fell straight back, moving as little as possible. On screen it looks great, but in reality, I cracked my elbow on the real stair edge, almost breaking it. And...I almost knocked myself out. Falling stiffly like I did, I ended up drifting further than I thought I would. When I got up and looked at the stairs,

I found out my head had smashed through the last fake stair, meaning I was inches from nailing my head on solid wood.

Something I did, and never even realized that I did it until the film came out, was how I would turn my head towards the victims before following them. In a scene, I would merely turn my head sharply to where the victim was and then turn my body to follow him. It was something I just did naturally, but it ended up being a thing the fans loved. While it came naturally, it might have been due to the minimal vision I had. Looking before I walked made it safer. Walking through the woods at night is hard as it is, but doing it with a quarter of your normal vision is rough to say the least, so the head turn saved my ass and made for a great character quirk.

DON'T FUCK WITH ME AFTER
A ROOF FALLS ON MY HEAD

With the interior shots done, we headed out to Mobile, Alabama, to shoot the exteriors for the movie. The location was chosen for the price more than the look. It was a decent location, though, and the crew and I were all excited to be out of the studio. The first day I arrived I went to the filming area and checked it out to get a feel of the land and how I would need to prepare for it. Afterwards I went to a temporary hotel; the one we were to stay at for a few weeks wasn't going to be ready until the next day. We ended up getting stuck in this shitty little motel, but it was only for one night so it wasn't a big deal. As I was settling in for the night, reading the script and making notes for the next day, I got a phone call from the production manager. He was calling to let me know that one of the trailers with equipment caught on fire on the drive down to Alabama. Of course it had to be the truck with all the new crash pads I had just bought. Brand new pads I bought *just* for the production.

Calmly, I hung up the phone, got up, and punched the wall... leaving a massive hole. Seeing the damage I caused, I did my best to calm down and not break anything else. The next morning when I checked out, I embarrassingly told the manager what I did and told them to charge me for the damages. A few years later, by coincidence, a fan stayed in the same room that I did that night. He came up to me at a convention and told me that in his hotel room there was a big hole in the wall that had a picture frame around it and a small plaque that read *Kane Hodder who played Jason Voorhees in Friday the 13th punched a hole in this wall!* I'm not sure if the place is still there today, but I thought it was pretty cool they did that... even if they did charge me to repair the wall when they didn't really fix it.

Sometime after punching a hole in the wall, things on the set were going smoothly, and it was time to film the scene where Tina uses her powers to collapse the roof onto Jason, which was a rather big stunt. It was another scene we wanted to make sure we got right the first time because of the amount of work that was involved in it. The crew built a small section of fake roof using balsa wood again, though to make it look like a real roof, they had to use two-inch by six-inch pieces. They were still light and should break, but the problem was they set them on end, meaning the thick part was going to land on me. Two inches of balsa wood is easy to break, but at six inches and being on edge, it starts to get the strength of normal wood. There were also real shingles on top of the fake wood. Shingles are thin and flimsy, but if you ever try to pick up a stack of shingles, they are heavy as hell. To top everything off, the outside ten feet of the roof on each side was built with real wood so the frame itself would hold. Only the middle five feet was balsa. We all figured that the roof would fall on me, and I would safely break through the balsa wood area... We were wrong.

As I prepped for the shot, I thought about how I would probably have to really act that the roof was crushing me down since it would be so light. When action called, I walked out and did the movements as planned. If I had expected the roof to have actually been heavy, I would have braced my knees more and curled my body as the roof hit me. Instead, I stood there, straight as I could to let the impact look like it smashed me down. No acting was needed though, because when the roof landed on me, it crushed me. It was so heavy that it drove me into the ground, cut my forehead through the mask and latex and... almost knocked me out completely. It was so damn brutal I couldn't even believe it. In the film you see me come out of the house over the view of Tina's shoulder. Lar's stunt double actually played Tina in that shot, just in case shrapnel from the roof went flying. The collapse was so vicious that you can actually see her jump with shock in the film. Come to find out, the roof weighed in at over 700 pounds! No wonder it crushed me.

That night after shooting, my body was aching and I was miserably tired having been shooting late every single night. That particular night we wrapped just after four in the morning. Being so late, the production allowed me to use one of the set cars to drive myself back to the hotel since no one else was going back at the time. A few miles from the set, this car sped up next to me and started swerving all over the place. I slowed down to let the guy pass me, worried that he might swerve into the car, when all of a sudden he cut right in front of me. Thankfully I was awake enough to slam on my brakes and avoid an accident. It pissed me off so much my adrenaline started pumping.

Of course the guy didn't just speed off into the sunset; instead he slowed down to a ridiculous pace. I tried to keep my cool, but when the guy kept swerving and almost went into the other lane as an oncoming car went by... I lost it. Pissing me off when I'm already in a bad mood is not a good thing to do. With the road clear, I swung into the other lane and pulled up next to the guy. Rolling down my window I screamed and motioned for him to pull over. The guy yelled at me as well, but I couldn't hear what he said. Amazingly, the guy actually pulled over. The two of us jumped out of our cars like two hard asses ready to throw down. The fact that I was almost crushed to death by a roof, was exhausted and cranky, fueled my anger to a boiling point. On any other day I might have just ignored the guy or flipped him off…but that particular night I was in no mood to fuck around.

"What the hell is your fucking problem?" the bastard slurred at me. Part of me settled down as I realized the guy was just a drunk asshole, but as I turned to get back in the car, I thought about how he almost crashed into an oncoming vehicle. I couldn't let him back on the road. If he killed or hurt anyone I wouldn't be able to live with myself. Turning around I took a breath, ready to try and negotiate with the guy to see if I could trick him into sleeping it off in his car. As I put my hands up to show the guy I wasn't threatening, he rushed towards me, planted one foot and tried to kick me in the balls with the other. Being sober, I was able to move out of the way of his wobbly efforts. Though he didn't connect, I was back to being furious. *Try to attack me? Kick me in the nuts? No fucking way.*

As the guy straightened up, I took two quick steps towards him and swung. I landed a solid shot to his temple, a string of saliva shot out of his mouth as his head whipped around. Before I even finished the follow through on the swing, he was on the ground. Holding myself back from attacking him, a sudden dread came over me as I realized the guy wasn't moving. *Shit.* He was out cold. For a full minute I stood over him, waiting for him to get up and start swinging, but he didn't move. *Shit.* Worried about a car driving by and seeing me standing over a body, I quickly picked the guy up, made sure he was breathing, and laid him down in the backseat of his car. Part of me thought about going to the police, but I was worried about being held for assault since no witnesses could say they saw him attack me first. I didn't want to hold up production on the film, so I tossed his keys a few yards away, jumped in my car, and drove off.

Sleep was fleeting that night as I tossed and turned, worried that I might have caused some brain damage or, worse, killed him. When I woke up that next afternoon I waited for a cop to come knocking on my hotel room door. When none came that day, I made sure to drive by where I left the car... it was gone. That made me feel somewhat relieved, because if the car was there and he was still in the back, things would have been real bad. I have never had any patience or sympathy for people who drive drunk, but that incident bothered me for a long time.

THAT'S A WRAP

As filming wound down, there was only one major scene left for me to film. At this point, I was exhausted from getting hours of make-up done every day, wearing the costume for hours on end and punishing my body with crazy stunts. Little did I know, they saved the hardest part of filming for the last two days… the underwater scene. At that point I had done a decent amount of underwater work in films, though never in major prosthetic make-up. We stayed in Alabama to shoot the scene at some dive tank. Everything was set up, and I wasn't expecting it to be too difficult. Then I got in the water and realized that there was one major problem. With my false teeth in, I couldn't seal my mouth closed when I was holding my breath.

After telling Buechler about it, we realized the only solution was to take off the mask, take out the teeth, and then put the regulator in my mouth. Not the ideal situation. Getting in the tank with the regulator in my mouth, they secured me to the bottom of it with a cable so I would be suspended in the water. Buechler was outside of the tank with a monitor and a microphone. When he talked into the mic it sent his voice through the water so the rest of the crew and I could hear him. When he said roll camera, I had to take the regulator out of my mouth, hold my breath, put my teeth in, put the mask on and then play dead as the camera panned along the chain and up my body. Soon as Buechler called cut, I had to take the mask back off, the teeth out, and then grab the regulator. It was a nightmare. I was under the water, doing that same routine for over ten hours with only one break...and keep in mind I could hardly see as well with my pin-hole eye and contacts.

It took a solid two days in that tank for those few shots. When I was done, I can honestly say I was more exhausted than any stunt I had ever done in my entire life. Constantly holding my breath and being in water for that long drained me beyond belief. It was intense to say the least. Thankfully the shots actually came out great and the picture of me underwater has become somewhat iconic.

When filming was done, it was hard to take. I didn't want to take off that mask and walk away from it. I loved it so much that I didn't want it to end. The last day of shooting, I stuck the mask I used through most of the film in my bag, said my goodbyes, and took off back to L.A. Though it was hard taking off the suit, I couldn't wait to see the finished product. Buechler was nice enough to let me see several cuts of the film before it was released, and man, it was brutal and fantastic. Then came in the Motion Picture Association of America (MPAA). Though I still love the movie, the end product is missing so much great stuff that it still pisses me off to this day. The fans never got to see the full, uncut movie the way Buechler meant for it to be seen. I'm sure if they had, the movie would have been much bigger than it was.

THE DAY I REALIZED
MY LIFE HAD CHANGED

Before *Part 7* came out, Buechler invited me to a Fangoria convention. At the time I had never really heard of them. As much as I loved horror films, I didn't know there were conventions. The second I walked into the doors that day, I knew I had been missing out.

Fangoria's Weekend of Horrors, 1989
Nice Haircut

I felt right at home walking around with people dressed up as zombies and killers. It felt great and I wanted—no, *needed* to be part of it. Strolling through the booths, I bought a few T-shirts, picked up some Jason merchandise, and blended right in with the rest of the crowd. Little did I know at the time that conventions would become a major part of my life and that in a mere hour…I would no longer be able to blend in.

Buechler was hosting a *Friday the 13th* panel and invited me to attend as he was going to show some footage. Not wanting to intrude, I sat in the back of the room and listened to the discussion. I got a kick out of seeing how enthusiastic the fans were, especially since they were going to be seeing *me* as Jason. During the talk, Buechler mentioned me several times and then finally went on to say *By the way, Jason is in the back of the room.* I stood up and waved upon his urgings to see every single face in the room turn towards me and several cameras snap off. Up until this point in my career I had only been a stuntman; I was never the center of attention. While this sudden spotlight felt odd, it also felt great.

A few minutes before the panel was over I decided to sneak out the back; I was getting hungry. As I walked out and gently closed the door, a man's hand quickly stuck through it, so I held it open for him and turned to walk away. As I went down the hall I started to hear some chatter. Turning around I noticed a few people had left, but I thought it was odd, the talk couldn't have been over that quick. A few seconds later, I heard more talking and footsteps, then turning around again, I saw almost 30 people… who seemed to be following me.

Stopping at the concession stand I quickly got in line, wondering why all these people had the same idea I did. As I started to look at the menu board I felt a tap on my shoulder. Turning around, not really having a clue what the guy wanted, I saw a pen and a piece of paper stuck out at my face. I was confused... *he couldn't want my autograph?* Looking away from the man, I realized that the group of 30 people *were* following me! Some were snapping pictures and others were getting their pens ready. Suddenly I was surrounded. I was no longer in line—instead of getting food, I was in the middle of a feeding frenzy... and I loved it.

Though my stomach was growling, I moved the group over a few feet, signed their items, took a few dozen pictures, and answered a thousand questions. Being a horror fan all my life, I had always been passionate about the genre; I just didn't know that so many other people were as well. It was a wonderful feeling, being with people who also loved these films and who wanted to get to know me, because I was now the character they loved. I enjoyed the moment and soaked up the attention and love from these fans, hoping it would never end.

Kane as Jason with Tony Timpone, Editor of Fangoria

Finishing the last autographs, I realized that the movie wasn't even out yet and here I was getting swamped for my signature. It was a different life than the one a stuntman lived for so many years—I just hoped I was ready for it.

During those few months between the release of *Part 7* and the filming of *Part 8*, I signed my signature: *Kane Hodder, Jason #7*. Having gotten the role again the next year I changed how I signed items, meaning, if you ever see that signature, it's rare.

KILLING AGAIN

After filming *Part 7,* I went back to work as a basic stuntman and stunt coordinator. I still loved doing stunts more than anything in the world, but that small taste of being Jason and the fame it brought me kept popping up in the back of my mind. I wanted more of it. Then one day I heard that *Part 8* was going to go into production and that they were going to cast a new Jason. Pissed could not explain how angry I was. I had become Jason, he was a part of me, and I wanted to do it again.

That night I went home and called Barbara Sachs who had been a producer on *Part 7* and worked at Paramount. As calmly as I could, I straight out told her that I wanted to play Jason in *Part 8.* When I finished my sentence, there was a lump in my throat caused by fear. What if they already had cast someone else, what if they didn't like me as Jason? As I waited for one of those answers, she responded with a surprised tone. *Really? I had no clue you would want to play him again.* Of course I went on to gush about how much I loved the character and that I needed to play him again. Come to find out, since no one ever played him twice, they just figured they would cast a new person again. We set up a meeting for me to come in and get the particulars. During that meeting, I was hired to play Jason once again. Walking to my car that day I could feel the excitement and rage build up in my bones again... for I was soon going to get to kill some more teenage bastards.

There was a major lesson I learned from that phone call. If you want something in life, go after it, go get it, and don't wait for it to come to you. If I hadn't made that call, I would not have gotten to play Jason again, and my entire life would have been different. Ever since then, I made sure to not sit around and wait, hoping I would get called back—I went out and made my future.

JASON'S BACK

While the title of the film is *Jason Takes Manhattan*, we actually only shot for two days in New York City; the rest of the time we were in Vancouver, Canada. I have never really cared how much money I made to play Jason. It wasn't about the money. I just loved playing the character. So when I met with Canadian producer, Randy Cheveldave, he asked me how much money I made as the character in *Part 7*. I told him I made SAG scale and would also be happy with that again. He said, "Okay, how about if we give you a 40% raise?" What? A producer going out of his way to be generous? Not common at all in this business. I was elated. I got to play the character I loved so much, and I got a raise! Unreal. Thanks, Randy!

Buechler wasn't on this film and the studio didn't seem to care too much for continuity because my costume looked vastly different than the one just a year before. I mentioned this during the final tests for the make-up. Instead of the chaos I figured it would cause as they tried to fix the problem, I was met with *Oh, well it's no big deal.* There was definitely some frustration, but at the same time, I was just happy to be playing Jason again, no matter what.

Since it was the second time I played Jason, I felt more comfortable that I wasn't going to lose the role halfway through the film and started speaking up, adding to kills and doing what I thought was best for the character. This new-found freedom allowed me to explore more in the character, which was great.

The one good thing about the make-up not being so extensive was that it was much more comfortable on this film. Instead of a ton of latex, I really was only wearing a wet suit under the shirt and pants along with some latex forearm pieces and the head stuff. It made for less time in the make-up chair, which was always nice. They did give me a nice slime look, though. The effects guys would spray me down with a mixture of glycerin and other shit. I was so gooey they ended up giving me my own special "slime" chair because anywhere I sat, no one could sit in it afterwards. I was so sticky, people tried to avoid me at all costs. Of course I got a kick out of this so I would purposely walk into people and "slime" them. This was back when *Ghostbusters* was huge, so I got nicknamed *Slimer* for a while. Regardless of how sticky I was, being back in the suit and on the set for the first time, I was feeling good… I couldn't wait to get back to killing people.

All of the alley scenes in the movie were shot in downtown Vancouver. The place was like a ghost town at night. The sun would set, and there wouldn't be a single person around besides a few bums here and there. During breaks from filming I would walk around in the full costume to get some air and to think about the next scene I had to film. On one occasion, I saw a man down the alley who seemed to be acting a bit sketchy. Being in the dark alley alone, from behind, I looked like a bum—my costume was torn up, after all. The guy started to walk right towards me, so I hunched over and pretended to be digging through a trash can. As I heard him come up from behind I wondered if the stupid ass was really going to try to mug a bum. I didn't wait to find out though. Instead, I turned around and gave him a look through the mask. The man jumped back and yelled *Good Christ* then stumbled and ran away. I had never heard that phrase used before, and it struck me as funny. Scaring people in a movie is one thing, but doing it in real life when you can see the reaction, it's great. Seeing that guy run away put me in such a good mood, I had to concentrate during the next scene to get my anger back.

Another time while walking around the streets in full costume, I found a bum collecting cans. Being the asshole I am, I walked up behind him and just stood there, breathing heavily. When he turned around his jaw dropped down, and he let go of the can. His hands went up to his eyes and rubbed them. *You're not real. You are not real.* He kept saying as he backed up, keeping his eyes locked on me while he pulled his cart away. The entire time I stood there, not moving an inch besides my breathing and, maybe, a tiny head tilt. The man finally stumbled around the corner. As he disappeared, I could hear the shopping cart speed up. Part of me felt like I should have been feeling bad for scaring a bum, yet it cracked me up.

The rest of the time we filmed outside in the streets and things went smoothly. There was no real trouble and since the town shut down, there were no crowds watching to deal with. Besides, the outside stuff wasn't that extensive, so we mostly shot inside. During one of the outdoor scenes, the script called for Jason to kick the main character's dog. I thought it was pointless and didn't have anything to do with the story, so I refused to do it. Besides, Jason is a killing machine; he wouldn't just kick a dog for fun. A dog is no more a nuisance to him than a fly, so why would he go out of his way to do such a thing? I had this conversation with the director, Rob Hedden, and he agreed with me. For some odd reason this tiny conversation, just one of thousands that actors have with directors, got blown out of proportion. People started making up stories about how I menacingly said to Rob from behind the mask that "Jason wouldn't do that." Animal activists started sending me letters and asking me, a *fellow animal lover*, to support them. It even made it on to my IMDB page, and it's become a legend of sorts. Of course it's based on truth, but in the end it just wasn't that big of a deal.

One of the outdoor shots I loved in *Part 8* was the boxing scene with the character, Julius, on the roof. Normally Jason just dispatches his victims in a hurry as if he has somewhere to go, which is great because it shows his rage and need to keep killing, although every now and then, you need to slow down for a second. This is something you don't see Jason do too often. To have a chance to get to stand there and fuck with a victim was great. The actor, Vincent Craig Dupree (VC), really worked himself up in the scene to try and make it look like he was really boxing Jason. The best part for me was that I didn't have to do anything to make a great scene. All I had to do was stand there and move back a tiny bit with each punch. Poor VC. Since he ended up throwing 66 punches per take, he didn't need to act exhausted at the end of the scene; he was. Of course Jason can only play with his prey for so long before the temptation to dispatch them takes over. With one strong punch, bam, his head goes flying off. The fact that it is scientifically impossible for this to happen is what makes it so funny. And not only does it fly off, it goes flying off the building and lands in a dumpster. Great shit. Hitting the head did take me by surprise, though, because the thing was ten times harder and heavier than I thought it would be. I thought it was just foam, but it ended up having some sort of solid structure inside and hurt like hell. Two films later, we paid homage to this scene by having Uber Jason punch off a robot's head.

Poor VC. He also had to endure my wrath in a scene where I attack him in a phone booth. I was supposed to punch through the glass and grab him. For some reason they decided to use real glass instead of breakaway glass. When I punched it, the window fell into the phone booth instead of breaking. It landed on VC's head and shattered, and he ended up falling and cutting up his hands on the glass as I grabbed him. Fortunately it wasn't serious. Not wanting to risk the shot again and thinking it looked good enough, they decided to use the shot in the final film.

VC Dupree Putting Up a Fight, Jason Takes Manhattan

JASON TAKES A CRUISE

In a few interviews, Rob Hedden has said that his original script took place mostly in New York City. It had scenes in Madison Square Garden, at the Statue of Liberty, and all over Manhattan. While I do believe him, I never got to see that script. The script I saw was pretty much what the end product looked like. When I picked up the script at Paramount Studios, I was so excited to read it that I walked over to a courtyard within the studios and read the entire thing. I was a little disappointed that there weren't more scenes in NYC, but there were a lot of kills and that was what mattered to me. It would have been amazing to film all over the city and really make it live up to the title. Sadly, being a horror movie, the budget was not astronomical, and we were forced to *fake* NYC in Vancouver and to set a lot of the film on a cruise ship.

A lot of people have complained about this over the years, but in the end, I don't give a shit. It's still a fun movie with a lot of interesting kills in it. Is it the best Jason movie? No. But it's still Jason wandering around and killing people? Yes... and isn't that what we want to see after all?

On most of the Jason movies, the costume wasn't that comfortable, and I could almost never take it off. Not being mega-blockbuster budgets, there wasn't time or the money for me to take off the costume during breaks or for meals. In fact the only movie I ever worked on that I was able to get entirely out of the costume for a meal was *Nothing But Trouble*, the Dan Aykroyd movie that also stared Demi Moore, Chevy Chase, and

John Candy. Dan played two characters in the film, including the town Justice of the Peace and the giant mutant baby, Bobo. When there were shots of both Bobo and the Judge, I played Bobo since Aykroyd's face was more recognizable in the Judge make-up. The budget was so huge on that film I was able to get out of that massive costume just to eat lunch. It was an amazing luxury and it spoiled me. Unfortunately on the Jason films I had to keep the make-up and the costume on for up to 20 hours a day. It was exhausting.

NYC Billboard, Jason Takes Manhattan

The only way I could get really comfortable while taking a break in the suits was to lie down flat on my back or recline as far as I could in a chair. While filming on one of the ships, I had an hour or so break, so I found a small room that no one was using and laid down on the floor to take a nap... in the full costume. Of course I was covered in the gooey, glycerin stuff that made me look like I had just come out of the water (why

Jason never dried off I have no clue, but at least it looked cool).
I was worried about shit sticking to me from the floor, but I
needed a break and figured I could worry about it later.

While lying down in the dark, rusty bowels of the ship,
I dozed off. In the middle of a dream about killing someone
with a screwdriver, I felt a tugging at my pant leg. Being out of
it, I figured it was a production assistant trying to wake me up
because I was needed back on the set. I grunted that I needed a
minute, but the tugging didn't stop. Fucking kid was
persistent—I ignored him. Then I felt a tugging at my waist…
another at my shoulder and one on my chest. What the hell
was going on? As I lifted my head to see who was trying to
wake me up, I was met with a tiny, wet nose, whiskers, and
black beady eyes looking at me. It wasn't a production
assistant; there were rats…all around me. They smelled out the
glycerin and were enjoying a nice little treat… me. Getting up I
kicked them away one by one and went back to the set, realizing
I needed a better place to take a nap. So much for a luxury
cruise.

TRAUMATIZING LITTLE CHILDREN

Parts of the New York City sewer scene at the end of the film were shot in an abandoned high school gymnasium in Vancouver. The crew built sets and made it look pretty real, especially for being inside of a school. They did this for safety because flooding a real sewer would be practically impossible. Whenever I took a break during filming at this location, I went out back of the school and sat in a chair. It was a nice peaceful area with a big field that allowed me to be by myself so I could relax.

After being eaten by rats on the boat, I decided staying in a chair outside would be a much safer option. I would stretch my legs straight out, put my arms on my stomach, and leave my mask on. One day as I started to drift off to sleep I heard some voices in the distance. Being tired, I didn't move, I merely opened my eyes and looked through the mask. It was two kids riding bikes—they looked to be around 12. They were in the field, but getting closer. Being the sick man I am, I decided to not move and wait for them to get come near me so I could scare them. I used the *statue scare* many times on people, and it always worked. When people can't see your face or eyes and you are not moving, they assume you are not real. Jumping out of a statue pose is a classic scare.

The kids stopped when they saw me. They were about thirty yards away, but I could hear their conversation clearly. At the time, everyone in town knew that the new Jason film was shooting nearby. *Look, it's one of the dummies for the movie!* one of the kids said with excitement. *Let's go play with it,* the same kid said. At this point I was getting excited; this was going to be one killer scare. *No way... We'll get in trouble,* the other said, being the smart one. I could only see the upper half of their bodies. When I saw them get off their bikes and bend down, it took me a minute to realize they were picking up rocks. A second later I heard a rock whiz by me. Then another hit my leg. They were small rocks and with the costume on, it didn't hurt. Then one hit my mask with a heavy clink. I didn't budge as the two cheered and started to walk closer as they gained confidence.

Several more rocks landed near me, a few more hitting my mask. Finally, the kids were about ten feet away from me, getting the courage to touch Jason. It was time. It was slightly awkward to get a good pounce from the position I was in, but it didn't matter, the mere fact that I moved would scare the shit out of them. Jumping up, I grunted, screamed, and started to reach for them. I have never heard screams so loud come out of children before. They were so scared, they ran right past their bikes. I followed them just as far as the grass and stopped. Suddenly, they both turned around, remembering they had forgotten their bikes. Standing a few feet from their bikes, I heaved my chest and stared at the ringleader. Neither of them said anything; they just stared at me, not believing this was happening. Pushing it a bit further, I grabbed both bikes, one in each hand, and threw them a few feet. The kids couldn't take it... they turned and ran.

Laughing to myself, I went back to the chair and sat down. It might have been mean, but it was hysterical. Besides, those kids got a great story to tell that no one would probably believe. The best part was this happened on a Friday, and when I came back in to film on Monday, the bikes were still there. The kids were too scared to come back and get them. I can't imagine what they must have told their parents about why they didn't have their bikes anymore. Throughout the shoot at this location, I got the chance to scare several more kids out back. Word about the shoot had gotten around, so kids were showing up all the time. Kids would appear, I'd scare them, and the ones who didn't run off, I'd take inside to let them watch us film for a while. Eventually it got so crazy I couldn't go outside anymore as dozens of people were coming down to the set!

The dummy trick always worked, and I used it often as a quick, easy way for a scare. We shot the diner scene in Vancouver at a real diner. While they were rigging the doors for me to smash through, I decided to take a seat at the bus stop right outside of the restaurant. As the bus pulled up to let a passenger off, someone on it said *Hey, look at the Jason dummy!* Just as it was starting to pull away, I jumped up and lunged for the bus. The fuckers all screamed as if they were on some Universal tram ride through hell. Getting a kick out of this, I repeated it several times as different buses stopped on their route. I'm a sick bastard, but I love it. I think the lesson here is if you ever see a dummy of something, be careful, you never know, it might be me.

Of course I didn't only scare people when in costume. At the hotel, I became good friends with the night desk manager as I would come in at all hours of the night after shooting. We'd bullshit before I'd head up to sleep. One night I came in and his back was to me, he was sleeping in his chair. I snuck up to him, grabbed his neck and put him in a chokehold while screaming loudly. He jumped, kicked, grabbed at my arms, and cried. When I let him go laughing, he ran away, fell over and pushed himself up against the wall, tears running down his face... and that was when I realized it wasn't the normal guy; in fact, I had never seen this guy before. I quickly apologized and explained the whole situation to the man who didn't seem to want to talk. After a few more apologies, I went up to my room. Can't imagine what the poor bastard was thinking when it happened. Probably would never fall asleep on the job again. The funny part is that I never saw him at the desk again.

One day I stopped by Barbara Bingham's room to see if she wanted to have lunch. As she was putting on her shoes I went on her balcony to see the view. As I was out there, I realized that VC's room was below and Scott Reeves was above; I had to fuck with them. Being the mature man that I am, I went and got a roll of toilet paper and soaked it. Wading up wet balls I threw them on each of their sliding glass doors. It was hard to get some to stick to Scott's door as it was above me, so I made the world's largest spit-wad, about four pounds at least, and threw it up there. It stuck with a thump that sounded like a watermelon smacking the window. Later that night, I saw the two of them in the restaurant talking about how they had all these spit balls on their windows and couldn't figure out how something like that could have happened. The next night I was in my own room on my balcony, which was below VC's (which is why they didn't suspect me. There was no way I could reach all the way up three floors to Scott's window). I saw that VC's door was open so I made another spit wad and threw it through it. Laughing to myself, I was suddenly hit in the shoulder with a peach, then a wad of wet paper followed by a bucket of water. I guess they got their revenge.

The night I scared the kids, karma kicked my ass. When Jason gets hit with the toxic waste at the end of the film, you see him starting to melt and he pukes. For some reason it looks like a puppet on film, but that was actually me. My entire life I have been able to puke on command. I don't know why, but I can trigger the gag reflex in my throat by simply flexing my neck muscles. When I told this to Rob he thought it was fantastic, so instead of making a prop to puke, I did it myself. Of course to puke that much, I had to drink just shy of two pitchers of water. My gut felt like it was going to burst. I couldn't wait for him to call action so I could puke the shit up. When we finally did the take and I got the stuff up, I felt better, but it had already taken its toll on me. Competitive food eaters are nuts, because my stomach was killing me after consuming so much liquid. Not only that, I didn't get all of the stuff up, which meant my body had processed almost a pitcher of water. That night I pissed, literally, every five minutes. I didn't get any sleep; it was miserable. At one point I was thinking about sleeping in the tub so I could just piss and not move. I always knew that actors suffer for their art—I just didn't know pissing all night was included on that list.

During that same shot, it was scripted for Jason to say his first line of dialog ever. As I was melting I was supposed to say *Mommy please don't let me drown.* At the last minute Rob decided to take it out. It would have been cool to say Jason's only line ever, but at the same time I'm glad we didn't shoot it. It would have added another layer of oddness to an already weird ending. At the time of filming I really didn't understand the ending, but I didn't argue much. I didn't feel like I had enough pull as an actor yet to fight for such things. Though I added some stuff to the movie and made a few character adjustments, fighting over an ending was out of my league at the time. In later years, I was told by lots of fans that they liked the ending. What do I know? I'm just a killer.

FUCKING JAZZ HANDS

Like with most of the Jason films, production was pushed through in order to get the film out the next year. On *Part 8*, the shooting schedule was so tight they didn't have much time to shoot a trailer and get it out before the release of the film. To save time and money while we were filming in Vancouver, they hired a crew to shoot a trailer in NYC. It's actually a teaser trailer, meaning that it doesn't show anything from the film and that it "teases" what you will see. I love the concept of the trailer, except for one thing that pisses me off to this day... *Jason was played by someone else.*

When I first saw the trailer, my gut tightened up and I wanted to vomit. I was so pissed that someone *else* was wearing that costume, that someone else was playing the character I loved... it crushed me. In fact I was so upset by it that for years, decades really, I would never admit it wasn't me in the trailer. I didn't want people knowing someone else wore the mask, even if the Jason in it looks like a douche bag. Standing with his back to the camera he looks like he has a load of shit in his pants and when he turns around, forget about it. It looks like he is doing some sort of jazz hands. His arms are open so wide, and he is squatting down like he is waiting to get a big hug from someone—embarrassing to say the least.

For a while I wanted to find out who the guy was who played him in the commercial so I could punch him in the face for disgracing the character I loved. I did ask around, but I never found out who it was. Still don't even know. Probably wouldn't punch him now, but I probably would call him a

Broadway fairy for those damn jazz hands, though to be fair, it probably wasn't the actor's fault. Whoever directed it probably told him to do it…maybe I'll punch that douche.

KING OF NEW YORK

There was only one day I got to film in New York City, which was sad, because it was absolutely amazing. Instead of getting a trailer, to save space on the streets they rented some rooms in a building at the tip of Times Square. It was incredible—the entire time I got my make-up done and got into my costume, I could see the lights of the city blinking outside of the window, calling me down. Back in the late 80's, it was nothing like the Disney World it is today, but it was still a place that was, in a way, the center of the universe…and I was about to film there.

When I was in my full costume, I had a few minutes to myself before the van was going to pick me up. I walked over to the floor-to-ceiling window and looked out. This sense of excitement overcame me. There was something about the flashing signs, the people rushing around on the streets, and the fact that I was above them, watching it all… dressed as Jason, that was magical. Filming in Vancouver was great, but there was never anyone around. This time, for the first time in the series' history, really, Jason was going to be out of the woods and in public.

Not wanting to let go of the view, I reluctantly left and got into the van. I was only being brought about a block down to the center, but they didn't want me to have to walk through the streets in full costume. Getting out of the van, I found myself standing right in the spot I had been staring down at just minutes before. The energy was even higher down there than it was from my inconspicuous perch above. Though it was late at night, there were still a lot of people walking around the streets because it was Friday. As tourists and New Yorkers alike saw me across the way, they stopped their stride, pointed, and stared right at me. I thought it was cool that people stopped to see Jason, and I just hadn't realized how many had seen me until I walked around the van. The second I stepped in front of it, I heard a tidal wave of screams and applause. Staying in character, I turned my head to look at the crowd—I was blown away—there were hundreds of fans lining the streets. As I looked at them, their screams became louder. I heaved my chest and looked from person to person giving them a stare-down. One woman couldn't take the excitement, she jumped over the police barrier, dropped to her knees, and started to do the *I'm not worthy* praise. I might have been menacing, but under that mask I had a shit-eating grin from ear to ear.

Kane as Jason in Times Square, Jason Takes Manhattan

After playing with the crowd and taking some pictures with a group of police officers, we got down to filming in the center traffic island. One of the cops thought it would be funny to do the rabbit ears behind my head in the picture. That really pissed me off. Remember, I take my character seriously. I told him to go fuck himself, and I didn't take any more pictures with NYPD.

In the movie, the two main characters come out of the subway in the middle of Times Square thinking they are safe, only to have Jason walk out behind them. Now if you know anything about New York City, you might realize that there is *no* subway station in the traffic island in the middle of Times Square. There is one a few blocks down, but it doesn't have the dramatic feeling of walking out in the middle. Therefore, the crew built a fake subway entrance and plopped it down on the sidewalk. The poor actors had to squat down and pretend they were walking up stairs to make it look real. They did a great job, too, and almost no one, except real New Yorkers, realized that it was a fake entrance.

The Infamous Times Square Subway, Jason Takes Manhattan

Throughout the night, the crowd stayed to watch us film, loving every second of it. Whenever I had any downtime, I would quickly snap my head in their direction, making them go nuts. The extent of my scenes in NYC were restricted to that small traffic island. Really all I did was walk after my potential victims, kick a boom box, and show my face to a few street punks, though of course, one of the few times that I fucked up had to be that night, in front of hundreds of fans. Again the accident had to do with the whole not-looking-down thing. When I kicked the boom box, I didn't want to look, so I didn't. The only problem was that it stuck on my foot and when I took the next step, it tripped me up. I tumbled right over onto the ground. As embarrassing as it was, it was funny as hell. Makes me wish that the Jason movies had bloopers on the DVDs. Everything else you see in the finished product was shot in Vancouver. That is the magic of movie editing my friends.

JASON VS ARSENIO HALL

A few weeks before *Jason Takes Manhattan* was to be released, I was doing a slew of publicity, when all of a sudden I got a call asking to be on *The Arsenio Hall Show*. They said they wanted me in full costume. I thought it would be a ball, but I said to them... *You know I won't talk, right?* They simply responded with *That's the point.* At the time, his show was huge, and everyone was watching it. I was excited to get a chance to be on it, even if I would be in full costume.

The day we were to tape it, I arrived at the studio and met Arsenio. The guy was great, we went over what we were going to do and then he quietly pulled me aside and said *Look, I'm really nervous around you in that costume, so don't fuck with me... seriously.* I could tell by the way he said it that he wasn't joking around with me. Too bad he didn't know my personality, because if you tell me something like that, you *know* I'm going to fuck with you all I can.

Backstage before the show I got into the full make-up, which was exact from the movie (minus the glycerin slime in order not to mess up the set). Hanging out behind the curtain, I couldn't do my traditional yelling to get into the mood, but it was alright, I didn't want to get too violent after all. As the show went to a commercial break, the previous guest left the set and came back through the curtain, right where I was standing. It was Bo Derek and she literally bumped right into me and screamed. I'd like to say it was an accident, but it wasn't. I knew it would scare the shit out of her. Lots of guys told me that they were jealous that I felt Bo Derek's boobs against me.

When the curtain opened for my introduction, I did my best to act as Jason would in that situation. Of course he probably would have just hacked off Arsenio's head in a second, but I pretended he was in a good mood that day. The second I walked out, I could tell Arsenio was actually nervous, that he wasn't playing up that giggly paranoid laugh… it was real.

Though the episode was only on once or twice during that year, it has found a new life online. On YouTube it has millions of hits, and dozens of other sites boast it as "Jason on a Talk Show!" People love seeing their favorite killer in an untraditional setting. I have to admit, I think the segment was genius. It's funny, so many people ask me how I didn't laugh during the interview. Honestly, I was cracking up under that mask, although when I started to laugh too hard, I forced myself to get in the mindset of Jason… Jason doesn't laugh. The real Kane might have slipped out once or twice with a tiny smile, but overall, I kept the laughs to a minimum. The best part was the ending when Arsenio offered his hand to me. He had no clue if I would shake it or not, so when I pull him forward, it scared the piss out of him.

Kane as Jason, Arsenio Hall Show

The producers on the show and Arsenio, himself, loved the appearance so much that a few years later when *Jason Goes to Hell* came out, they asked me to be on the show again. This time they tried to take advantage of the success of the previous episode by keeping me on the stage the entire time. Oddly though, I was put with the band. The gimmick pretty much fell flat, but it was still great being on the show again and getting to mess with Arsenio one more time, especially since he asked me again not to fuck with him! So naturally, I did. Again.

JASON TAKES A BREAK

When *Manhattan* came out, it wasn't as a big of a success as Paramount hoped it would be. It was the eighth film in the series, after all. It did, however, find a huge following in the home video market and in syndication, like all of the *Friday* movies. You can't go one Halloween or a Friday the 13th without seeing it on television somewhere. With the poor box office showing and having made the series for a decade, Paramount decided to sell the property to New Line Cinema, where it sat cold for a few years. It was the first time in the series' history that a film didn't come out within a year or two after the last. I was upset that I wasn't going to be able to step into the costume right away again, but I knew it would come around eventually.

Though my career was doing well before the Jason films, the series gave it an extra boost. I worked on no fewer than 30 movies and TV shows before I put on the mask again, only four years later. It was a great time in my career as I was always working. I was constantly coordinating, doing stunts, or acting in small bit parts. I no longer had to fight to get a job—jobs were coming to *me*. That is something that every actor or stunt person dreams about.

During those four years I worked on movies like *Deep Star Six*, *Waxwork*, and *Texas Chainsaw Massacre 3* where I got to double LeatherFace. My great buddy R.A. Mihailoff played Leatherface, and I stunt-coordinated the film. Getting to put on that costume and be on film as another horror legend was another highlight in my career. In the film I'm Leatherface

299

about a quarter of the time. For safety reasons, any time the real chainsaw was used, I was in the Leatherface costume. I also did the entire fight scene in the water at the end of the movie. It was great working on the film, but most of all, it was great to kill some people again.

There were a couple of Steven Seagal films during those years as well, *Under Siege* and *Out for Justice*. I worked with Seagal three times total, especially during the peak of his career. He is good at his style of martial arts.

Doubling as Leatherface, Texas Chainsaw Massacre 3

The only problem is that he learned his moves in the real world, where you *actually* hit people. His training was not in traditional stunt training, where you learn how to make it *look* like you hit people. After a while of working with him, I noticed that some stuntmen who were going to do a fight scene would get slightly nervous beforehand and mumble and groan to themselves. I quickly found out why. In stunt fighting, you learn how to pull your punches so you barely touch the person you are fighting with. Most of the time it's about the camera angle and the angle of the punches. After a well-choreographed fight scene, you shouldn't be sore at all (unless you land on the ground in it); with Steven, though, things were a little different.

If someone doesn't pull their punch and you know they are not going to, what happens is you start to anticipate the impact and tighten up. This basically *foreshadows* that the hit is coming and doesn't read well on the film. Steven, more often than not, would make more contact with the stunt guy he was fighting than the person would expect. It wasn't necessarily that he meant to—he just did his fight scenes that way. On each of the three movies I worked with him on, someone went to the hospital. It makes for a very realistic fight scene, but in the stunt world, going to the hospital is the number one thing you try to avoid. Since I expect some realism from victims whom I kill in movies, I would sound like a hypocrite if I were to complain too much about his way of doing a fight. I just feel that the amount of realism that you need in a violent scene is a matter of the proper degree.

As Jason slumbered, there were a bunch of other small horror movies that I got the chance to work on. I did a film with Donald Sutherland called *Younger and Younger, House IV, Ghoulies III*, and a bunch of others. Then there were also a few big films thrown in. I had met and become friends with Charlie Picerni and his son, Chuck, who both stunt-coordinated big budget action movies and they both hired me countless times on various films. I did some stunts and played a SWAT member in *The Last Boy Scout* with Bruce Willis, and ironically, with Danielle Harris who would later go on to play Marybeth in *Hatchet II* and become a good friend of mine. Then I did some stunt car driving in *Lethal Weapon 3* with Mel Gibson. In one particular scene in the movie, I had to drive a car and slide it around Mel while he was on a motorcycle on the freeway. At the time, Mel was one of the most famous people in the world. Let's just say that having to drive a car at a mega star and slide it without hitting him was nerve wracking, especially since it was such a big film that if he got hurt, it would shut down the production. Fuck up a major star, and you'll never work again. Thankfully, I didn't hit him, though years later several people told me that I should have.

Getting to work and do stunts on a regular basis was fantastic, yet something was missing. After getting to be the star of two films, the acting bug had crept its way under my skin. Jason might not have had any lines, but unlike stunts, I was playing a character. I had some small parts in other films along the way, but they just helped fuel the fire. By the early 1990's, I was itching to put that mask back on and to start acting some more. Little did I know that my phone was about to ring and Jason was about to come out of hiding and go to Hell.

HELL...IS A NEW JASON COSTUME

When I got the call to once again play Jason, I hit the roof with excitement. I was pitched a quick idea that I thought was weird and was told that the director was fresh out of school and in his early 20's, but I didn't give a shit about anything, I was going to be Jason again. The best part was that I didn't have to pursue the role for the first time. Adam Marcus, the director, and Sean Cunningham, the producer, talked and both agreed that I *was* Jason. After that it wasn't a question of who would play him. Once again, I was given a decent raise to play the character (even though it wouldn't have mattered) and also the job of stunt coordinator for the film.

With *Part 9* in the *Friday* series, they decided to take it a new direction and to ignore some of the stuff from the previous films, especially the ending of *Manhattan* a few years before. Several producers told me the concept and pitched the make-up ideas for Jason to me, and though I didn't necessarily agree with them all, I nodded and shut my mouth, not wanting to mess up my chance to become my beloved buddy once more. When the script first arrived at my house, I sat down and read it straight through with no breaks at all. At the end of it, I was scratching my head a bit. Jason turning into a snake and eating his way through his sister's pussy to be reborn again in the same body at the same age he died in? *What the fuck?*

Regardless of what the script was like, I was mostly pissed about the fact that Jason wasn't going to be in it for more than a quarter of the film. That is not what fans wanted—fans want Jason; that is what the films are about. Tits, murder, and Jason. Adam Marcus, who wrote and directed the film, was a fantastic kid, but he was just that, a kid. I was concerned at the beginning, but he ended up doing fine.

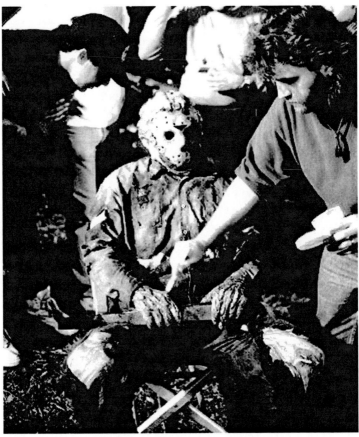

Kane as Jason, Jason Goes to Hell

Feeling more confident in the role, or more so feeling that the chances of getting fired were a lot slimmer than before, I spoke up about Jason not being in the film much. Everyone listened to me and explained that they were trying to explain the mythos of Jason and to take it in a new direction since the series was starting to get stale. Though they took me seriously, I think most people thought I was just pissed that I wasn't going to be in the film much, and they were right. To appease me, they gave me a small part as a security guard in the morgue. At that point, I was known for being Jason, and they knew fans would love to see me out of the costume and killed by a version of myself. I loved the concept and was happy at getting it, so I stopped complaining about shit. I was just the actor, after all.

When it came time for the new suit and make-up, I was blown away at how different it looked. At first it hardly looked like Jason. It was a beefed-up, deformed weirdo. I was taken aback... but I quickly fell in love with it. The final look was great; I looked bigger, crazier, and meaner than ever before. I loved the idea of the mask sort of melting into his face and being part of him. The only problem was it was incredibly uncomfortable. Wearing the *Part 8* suit compared to this thing was like swimming naked in a pool. This suit was like an iron maiden.

The first day I tried it all on, I noticed instantly that they had put the dead eye on the wrong side... I mentioned this, saying it had to be changed. I was met with dumb stares and quickly told that it was *too late*. This made me quite upset; Jason might have looked totally different and the plot was pretty crazy, but I wanted him to at least be as consistent as possible with my version. One thing you learn while working on a film though is not to piss off the make-up people if you are having extensive make-up done. Get on their bad side and they will make your four hours in the chair feel like days and the removal process hurt like a bitch. I shut my mouth.

The costume on this film consisted of a full body latex suit that covered me head to foot. The latex was so thick; it didn't breathe at all. I got so fucking hot in the first few days of filming that I couldn't take it. I never bitch, but there was no way I could make it another day without doing something about it. To fix the problem, they set me up with a cool suit I could put under the latex. In between shots, they hooked it to a hose and ran cold water through it to cool me off. Not only was the suit miserably hot, the mask and make-up was a bitch as well. In the previous two films, I was able to take off the mask when I needed to get fresh air and relax. With the extensive make-up, I couldn't take the mask off as it was built into the latex, which meant I could never get a breath of fresh, cool air. All day long I had to suck streams of air through the tiny holes. It was miserable, probably the toughest make-up I have ever had to endure. Thankfully, I only needed to be in it for 12 days. Compared to the eight weeks on *Part 7*, it would have been a cakewalk... if the suit had been comfortable.

OPENING THE GATES

The opening of *Jason Goes to Hell* is one of the wildest scenes in Jason history, especially at that point in the franchise. Being the ninth movie, Jason having killed tons of people raised the question - why isn't anyone doing something about this? Adam did a great job at writing a traditional *Friday* kill scene, but then turning it upside down and on its head. Put a hot chick in a cabin alone (who was a stuntwoman friend of mine, named Julie Michaels. I got her the role, and years later she returned the favor and got me on an episode of *VIP*). I have worked with Julie and her stuntman husband, Pee Wee Piemonte, numerous times over the years. A strange coincidence is that before Pee Wee was working steadily in the stunt business, he was my stand-in for lighting purposes during the Times Square scenes in *Jason Takes Manhattan*. Anyway, Julie's scene entailed showing the audience some nudity right off the bat; then Jason shows up, chases her... business like always, but not quite. Suddenly, just as Jason is about to catch his prey, the woman dives over a bush, lights come out of nowhere, and a team of agents open fire.

During the ambush scene, Jason gets shot an insane amount of times - how do you stop a monster who can't be killed after all? When we were prepping for the shot, I was rigged with 75 squibs. A squib is a small explosive that is detonated and pops open through your clothing, making it look like a bullet hit you. At the time, being rigged with 75 squibs was unheard of. Usually a person was rigged with a few, or maybe ten, but this, this was crazy. I had them on every single part of my body.

The Machete, Jason Goes To Hell

As we started to film, we really only had one shot to get it right. If it screwed up, they would have to put a new costume on and re-rig it with squibs. One-chance takes are always nerve wracking, but with stunts, you have to do them a lot. As they started filming, I stood in the middle of the field, the lights blaring down at me, ready to pretend to be shot dozens of times. As they called action and the squibs started to explode, I jerked and flinched my body as if I was being shot over and over again. After a minute it started to feel ridiculous and I was thinking this has to look ridiculous. It just felt like I was doing it for ages. In the end, when I watched the dailies (the footage from the day), it looked pretty damn good.

After Jason gets killed, he is rolled into the morgue and I have my cameo out of the make-up. In one of my scenes as a SWAT guard, standing by the entrance to the morgue, I frisk down Dean Lorey. Dean was the writer on the film who also had a cameo. The little bastard kept laughing when I patted him down, which he was supposed to, but it made me laugh. Being me, I thought I'd try to get him back.

Dean is a little guy, so I figured I would frisk him really hard and grab his ass to make him laugh. Well, I grabbed a little too hard and my fingers slipped right in between his cheeks, to a place I never wanted to go. It disgusted and freaked me out more than it did him; hell, I ended up punishing myself instead of getting him back. The thought of the feeling on my fingers still creeps me out to this day.

GOING TO HELL

Being the first Jason film in the series produced by New Line Cinema, which also owned the *Nightmare on Elm Street* series, they wanted to tease the movie that fans had wanted to see for years. With Jason being sucked into Hell at the end of the movie, he was now in Freddy's world for the first time. To tease this, they had the brilliant idea of Freddy's hand coming out of the ground and grabbing Jason's mask, sucking it into Hell with him. Being the stunt coordinator on the film, I volunteered to play Freddy's arm.

To get the shot just right, they built a seat under the set for me to sit in. Because I had to keep my arm crammed up a hole filled with sand, the shit kept falling through all over me, getting in my face. There was a monitor under there with me so I could see the shot above. Once the dog sniffed it just right, I could reach up and grab the mask. It was uncomfortable as hell with one arm stuck up in the air, my face crammed against the floor above me, sand falling in my face, but we got it done, even if it took countless takes. The dog was a good mutt, but it took an insane amount of time to get him to sniff the mask just right. When he finally did, I struck, thrusting my arm up high and grabbing the mask. I even broke one on the way down, which was great. I took the broken mask pieces home with me.

Little did I know this little scene would cause such a stir in the horror world. Regardless of what people thought of the movie, this was *all* they could talk about when it came out. Everyone wanted to know if they were going to film *Freddy vs. Jason*, when it was going to be, what the plot was, and so on. I was asked countless times about it. The sad part was there was nothing solid yet, so I had no good answers for anyone. One fun fact that came out of my grabbing the Jason mask was that I technically had, then, played Freddy on film, which meant I was the only person ever to play three of the most famous characters in horror history: Jason, Leatherface, *and* Freddy.

When the movie came out, it made money, but it was still considered a small failure. Some of the kills are great—the fencepost ripping the girl in half is insane, but the whole body jumping and Jason being anyone, it just wasn't what the series is about. It was a good idea to try to take the series in a new direction, but it wasn't what the fans wanted; they just wanted to see Jason kill people. You take that away and fans are going to be pissed.

In the end, I'm proud of my scenes in the film—the opening is very cool, and the fight at the end is pretty damn epic. John LeMay's character fights Jason in the end and I beat the hell out of Keith Campbell, John's stunt double. He still says that he has never gotten that sore from a fight scene. During that fight, I enlisted the help of my buddy, Alan Marcus, once again. Since I like realism, I came up with the idea of John's character repeatedly punching Jason in the face. Since I was wearing a hockey mask, I had Alan punch me square in the mask. Twenty-eight times. With each punch, I yelled *Harder!* He only stopped because his fist was killing him. Strangely enough, when I was done shooting for the night, I couldn't remember where I had parked my car or what day it was. Maybe working with Seagal wasn't that bad after all.

Overall I think the film is fun, but after four years of no Jason films in the theater, people were itching to see their favorite killer get back out there and chop some people up. Having the real Jason in only a quarter of the movie angered and disappointed the hardcore fans. I think this anger and bad word-of-mouth affected the box office. Though just like the others in the series, it has enjoyed a good life on DVD. I think a decade later, people found the fun in it, especially when they can watch it with other Jason movies, so that way, they don't feel cheated for not getting to see Jason enough. Even myself, I have learned to like it more.

JASON TAKES AN
EVEN LONGER BREAK

With *Jason Goes to Hell* not making as much money as the studios hoped, they shelved Jason for a while. There were still hopes of doing a Jason vs. Freddy movie, but bad scripts and failed concepts pushed that film back farther and farther. About a year after filming *Hell*, I had a feeling that it would be a long time before I got to put the mask on again, so I thrust myself deep into my work like always.

In the eight years between *Hell* and *Jason X*, I continued to work steadily. Stunts and coordinating continued to be my bread and butter, but I was starting to get some small bit roles in more things. I did a movie with Patrick Swayze called *Fatherhood*. There were a few small stunts I did, but I also played a bus driver in one scene. Patrick impressed the shit out of me. I had such a small part on the film, yet he made sure he remembered my name. Every day he would say *Hey Kane, how is it going?* The fact that he went out of his way to remember my name just showed how good of a guy he was. It makes me sick that he had to die so young when some of the other asshole actors live forever.

During those years I worked on some big films as well. Charlie Picerni hired me again on *Demolition Man* with Sylvester Stallone, and I worked for Chuck on *The Fan* with DeNiro, and *Se7en* with Brad Pitt. I was getting amazing work in some of Hollywood's biggest films. And as much as I loved it, I wanted to start acting more. Thankfully, Jason had made me a name in the horror world, which led to a lot of roles in films like *Pumpkinhead 2*, *Project: Metalbeast*, *Children of the Corn V*, and others along with *Wishmaster*. *Wishmaster* was genius casting because even though we had small parts, it put Tony Todd, Robert Englund, and me in the same film. Horror fans went nuts to see Freddy, Candyman, and Jason all in the same film. It was great working with those two guys, and it was the start of a long series of projects and events that we would do together throughout the years.

Also during this time, my two sons, Jace and Reed, were born, making it a special time in my life even if Jason wasn't in it. At first I thought becoming a dad would change my stunt career. I thought I would be more cautious and hold back from doing the big stunts to make sure I was there for my boys, but for some reason I wasn't. Instead I kept trudging on, being afraid of nothing, doing dangerous things day in and day out. I thought about it once, wondering why I wasn't scared to leave my kids without a father. It took me a while, but I realized it was because that is who I am. I'm a stuntman, it's in my blood, it's what I do; it's what I have to do. It's what puts the food on the table; besides, I'm confident in what I do. I know that even if I'm jumping off a building, getting lit on fire, or falling down some stairs, at the end of the night I was going to come home and tuck my babies in.

Having kids did change a lot of things, though. For once in my life, I had a major responsibility beyond myself. I now had two little guys who looked up to me. It made me push even more to act. Hell, acting wasn't going to get me killed, and I wanted my kids to be able to see my face on film one day, not just behind a mask and some latex. I wanted them to be able to look at the big screen and see the face that tucked them into bed at night for years…even if I was probably killing somebody. With this new responsibility, I was ready to keep at my career, no matter what.

On Set with Sons, Jace and Reed, Jason X

On the Red Carpet with My Boys

Eight years after wearing the mask, after countless rumors of a new movie or that *Jason vs. Freddy* was going to be made, I finally got a call saying it was time to kill again. Only thing was, I thought it was a joke.

JASON IN SPACE?

When I first heard the concept for *Jason X*, I thought *Are you fucking kidding me?* I had to ask several times; I really thought someone was trying to pull a joke on me. Jason in space? Yeah, right. When I realized that it was real, I just thought *Oh, shit.* How can you make that believable or even good? People were pissed at the last film as it is, and now you are going to send him into space? *WHY?* Then, the script finally arrived. I sat down with it, huffing and puffing about the premise, not even wanting to open the thing. There was no getting past it though; I had to read it.

In the first two pages, my mind started to change. The premise and set-up was actually pretty good. As I kept going, I started to sit up in my chair—the stuff was great. The script was solid. The screenwriter, Todd Farmer, understood the series and got it right. There were references to older films, ancient mythology, and even inside nods to people who have worked on the series over the years. Instead of trying to do the series over again or take it in some odd direction, Todd took what worked in the series and put it on the pages. He even took the stuff that didn't work and poked fun at it. The only thing he did differently was throwing Jason's ass into space. The script was solid, to say the least, and the thought of playing a cyborg version of Jason was pretty appealing. I loved the character more than anything in the world, and to get to play a beefed-up version... *shit*, I was more excited than ever to put the mask back on.

Out of all the Jason movies I was in, this had the biggest budget and was the most comfortable for me to shoot, as it was all inside a studio. The make-up was also great. Stephan Dupuis, the make-up effects designer on the film, gave me more freedom than I ever had before. For the first time, they used my real neck and ears, making for a lot less latex being applied. The *dead* eye, instead of gluing it to my face like in the other films, was fitted into the mask so it just sat over my eye, making it much more comfortable compared to the heavy pieces I wore in the previous films. The Uber Jason make-up was much more extensive, but still comfortable in comparison—and I felt so fucking bad ass in it, I could have worn it all day.

Kane as Uber Jason, Jason X

By this point in the series, when we started filming, people trusted me as the definitive voice of what Jason would and wouldn't do. James Isaac, the director, really trusted me when it came to my opinion on how Jason would do something. In the script, there was a scene where Jason came up behind one of the characters and snaps his neck like a ninja. I said that Jason wouldn't do it quite that way. He would take his time; he would grab the guy and slowly snap his neck and crush his head. Jim loved the idea, and it ended up being in the final picture. There were multiple times on this film when I would put my own flavor on kills and certain moves.

Filming *X* was the first time that I felt like a *real* star. My name was first on the call sheet (the list of actors and when they get called in—the star is always on top), which meant a lot for me to see. I felt really important this time, more than just the guy behind the mask. It was also the biggest paycheck I had ever received. They realized I was important to the franchise at that point, which got me that salary. They even had a realtor show me apartments in town and let me pick which one I wanted to stay in for the filming. Got a beautiful penthouse in some luxury high-rise, it was great! They even hired a driver to bring me to the set every day. In addition to that, they gave me a car to drive around myself when I had time off. It was amazing… and I was having the time of my life.

The opening scene in the movie was one of the most enjoyable days of filming I ever did. Mostly because it was the most people I ever got to kill in one day while filming; five people in one day, one of whom was David Cronenberg, the legendary director. Being a fan of his work, it was a real treat being able to kill his ass. During that same scene, there was a part we filmed that ended up getting cut out of the movie. A female agent, like David's character, walks into the room and looks at Jason, says a few lines, and grabs his crotch. Didn't make much sense, which is probably why it got cut out. Sometimes I think Todd wrote that scene just for my benefit.

Preparing to Kick Some Ass, Jason X

X was the most technologically advanced Jason film ever to be made—hell, it was one of the most advanced films I ever worked on. There were so many special effects and green screen work, it was amazing. In fact, the film was one of the first films in history to use an all-digital process. We made history with that film.

BREAKING NOSES

Since we were shooting in Toronto for such a long period of time (three months), the entire cast and crew were Canadians, which saved money. Really, I was one of the only people to be from out of town. The director, Jim Isaac, had his family there with him, as well. One day, he decided to bring his son's kindergarten class to the set to tour it... probably wasn't the best idea in the world with me around. Of course I couldn't just shake the kids' hands and take pictures with them. Instead, I had to be the asshole.

As the kids started to tour the set, getting all excited, I decided to hide in the make-up room where all sorts of props and pieces were strewn about. Being in full Uber Jason make-up, I decided to sit on a stool and lean back as if I was a prop—the classic *look like a dummy trick* that I had done many times before. The class came in, and the director pointed out how they did certain things and what the make-up department did. Being sick like me, Jim played along with my gag and said *Here is one of the Jason dummies.* All the boys said how fake it looked as they laughed and snapped a few pictures. Classic boys trying to be tough. That bravado disappeared the second I jumped up.

Having scared countless people, I have never felt bad about it; being scared makes us realize we are alive. This time though, I felt somewhat guilty. As I jumped up and roared, the class scattered, and most of them went screaming out of the room. Several were too scared to move. One kid choked on his gum while another fell to the ground and curled up into a fetal position. The worst one however... well, he pissed

321

himself right there in front of me. I don't think I ever saw such terror in someone's eyes before. The kid stood there, frozen still, his eyes bugging out, and his pants dripping wet. I felt horrible; his friends were going to tease him for life.

When you scare someone in your house by jumping out at them, they get startled, but then they see it's you and laugh. In this situation, these poor kids were in a scary place they didn't know, face to face with a monster who couldn't take his mask off. As all chaos broke loose from my scare, I did my best to not look threatening, which is pretty impossible in that costume. Thankfully, Jim and the other adults scooped up the kids and calmed them down. I'm just glad the kid who choked on his gum didn't die. Afterwards, when everything settled down, we took pictures and the kids relaxed, even if some of them wouldn't come near me. Even the teacher's assistant wouldn't look me in the eyes; of course, she was older so I messed with her and kept using my blood-red eyes to give her the look of death. I ended up giving the pissing kid a piece of my Uber costume for a souvenir. It was the least I could do for humiliating him. I don't blame him if he still hates me to this day. Sorry, buddy.

The only other really big scare I did on the set was to this new make-up guy. It was one of his first films, so I figured I had to fuck with him at some point. I had one of the veteran effects guys make me a mask that I could break. I took it, snapped it in half, and then waited for the right moment. I was in my make-up, waiting to shoot, so I switched the mask I had on to the broken one and then waited by the door for the new guy to walk in. I jumped right in front of the door as he walked in and kicked it to make it look like he nailed me. I doubled over, dropped the mask on the ground and started screaming that he broke my nose. As he stood there frozen in shock, I started yelling about how he just shut the film down and that he would never work in the industry again… poor bastard almost started crying as he checked if I was alright. When I popped up and laughed at him, he just gave me a pissed look and walked away. Welcome to moviemaking, my friend.

Another day on set, a girls soccer team stopped by to visit. One of the kids was the daughter of a crew member. I didn't get to scare these girls as I walked out, not knowing they were around. I did however play soccer with them in full costume. It had to be a hell of an experience, playing soccer with Jason Voorhees. Someone took some pictures while it happened. I would love to have them, unfortunately I never got copies.

Todd Farmer, the great writer who wrote the script, had a cameo in the film. He plays Dallas, one of the grunts whom I kill in the virtual reality chamber. The scene called for me to smash his head into the wall. He begged me to let him do the stunt, but I wouldn't let him. Remember, I like some realism. The wall had a piece cut out and foam put in the hole and painted so it looked like the wall. It was a small part, though, so the stunt double had to hit it right on to make sure he didn't smash his face for real. We rehearsed it several times, and I kept telling the guy that his face was too close to the edge, but he swore he was fine. Now in a film, when someone smashes a head against something, the actor doing the pushing doesn't actually do any pushing; you just sort of put your hand on the back of the head and guide them. You let the stuntman smash his own face so he has control of it. That is the way we did this, though it didn't work out as planned.

Just like I thought, as we shot and I smashed his face, the guy nailed the hard edge of the wall, missing the hole. His nose exploded, blood shot everywhere, and the guy almost collapsed because he hit the wall so hard. After yelling *Cut*, the guy got rushed off for medical help, and the crew stood there staring at me, as if it was my fault. They already didn't like me that much because I was keeping to myself, and now on top of it all, they thought I just broke a guy's nose. Half of them probably still think it's my fault. When another actor's nose got bloodied later in production, it was no doubt they blamed me again.

Even though I was blamed for something that wasn't my fault, I got payback. Lisa Ryder, who played Kay-Em 14, actually hit me in almost every take we did. Lisa and I had a lot of fight scenes together, but for some reason, she didn't know how to pull her punches and hit me over and over again. She was like Seagal. I was starting to expect them after a while, because she was always kicking in the movie. One time she nailed me in the stomach and another time in the balls. Payback is a bitch. The fight scenes look good though, so it didn't matter.

While most of the crew thought I was an asshole for keeping my distance, the mechanical effects guys and I really bonded. One of the main guys was a big bastard. Before each violent scene, I would go over to him and he'd help me get ready. I'd punch and smash him, he'd shove me around and get me all psyched up, almost like two football players getting ready to run out on to the field. At one point I punched, or shoved, each one of the mechanical effects guys, and they all loved it. Really, they were the only ones I hung out with on the set, and I was fine with that.

ONE LAST KILL

The last kill I filmed in *Jason X* was when I kill Crutch, one of the pilots of the ship. He was played by Phillip Williams, who has done a ton of movies since *Jason X*, including one of my all-time favorite comedies, *Tommy Boy*. I walk up behind Crutch, hold a severed head for him to see, scare him, and then smash the back of his head into a control panel. He, too, ended up getting a bloody nose during the kill scene. This time, however, I have to take the blame. I was pretty rough with him. At the time, it was just another kill for me to do. If I knew it would be the last kill I ever did as Jason, I would have… I don't know what I would have done. Maybe savored it more? Perhaps if I knew it was the last time I was going to be Jason, I would have been pissed and really killed the guy. Whatever I would have done, I'm just glad I didn't know it at the time. It would have been a lot harder taking the suit off than it was.

When filming, we didn't have any inkling that this would be the last Jason film… with me at least. There was talk of *Now that Jason has been to space, what the hell do you do next?* But really, on a film set you are never thinking about the next film, you are concentrating on the one you are doing. It never occurred to me that I wouldn't come back. *Fuck*, at this point, I *was* Jason. I didn't think anyone would ever play him again except for me. I wish that was true.

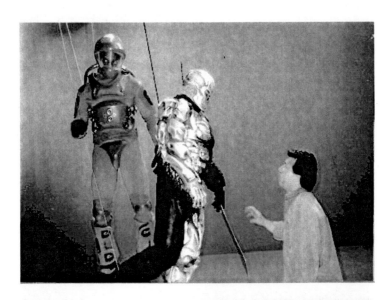

On the Set of Jason X

FREDDY VS...WHO?

Soon after the release of *X, Freddy vs. Jason* got the green light and went into production. At first it was no question that I was going to be in it. When I first heard the news that it was finally going to be made, I was on cloud nine. It was my dream to get to kick Freddy's ass. Ever since I was in the first film almost 15 years earlier, I wanted to make a movie with Freddy. The excitement I had over getting to make this film is comparable to winning the lottery. All I could think about, day in and day out for several months after I heard it was going to be made, was what was the script going to be like? The waiting didn't last long as New Line called me down to pick up the script. I had lunch with a New Line executive, and she gave me the script saying, "We are finally doing this movie!"

With this script I was like a kid on Christmas morning waiting to rip open his presents. *This was the one*, the one we *all* have been waiting for. This time, instead of pulling over and reading it in the parking lot, I forced myself to wait until I got home to read it, so I could savor every word and page to its fullest. In my comfortable chair at home, I put my feet up and disappeared into the world I had been a part of for the last 15 years. The script was good. There were some things I didn't like, but overall, I was impressed how well the writers had woven the two worlds together. There were a few tweaks I would have liked to have made to Jason's character, but otherwise it was really good.

Finishing the script I started to make notes about how I wanted to play certain scenes. Jason was shown in a more sympathetic light in this film, so I wanted that to shine through. Marking a few of the scenes where Jason had emotion, I went into the bathroom and stood in the mirror. Looking at myself, I hunched my shoulders more than normal, tilted my head down, and used the one eye that Jason had to practice conveying the emotion. I don't know how long I practiced it, but by the time I got out of the room, the sun was going down. That night I hardly slept as I thought about the different scenes, how I would play them, and how fucking excited I was to do this movie. It was going to be amazing. *Jason and Freddy...together...for the first time.*

As I waited for a start date on the film I had been waiting forever for, I kept working. Show after show, movie after movie I worked, waiting for the call to tell me that we would start to film on such and such date. For some reason, the call wasn't coming. I started to get worried that the production hit a snag, and that it was going to be delayed or pushed off once again, so I started to make some calls. For a while I got the runaround, and the people I talked to seemed nervous. Then one guy I got on the line from casting...I don't even know who the hell it was...told me the truth... *The role of Jason has been cast. Thanks for your interest, though.* I paused for a second, realizing the guy didn't know who I was. *And they cast the guy who has been playing it for years, right?* hoping he would say my name. My stomach twisted into a knot waiting for the response. *Actually, no, they hired someone who has played the part before.* I will never forget those words: *Someone who has played the part before.* With that, I hung up the phone without responding.

The room started spinning, I wanted to throw up and smash something at the same time. *What the fuck was going on? Was this for real? Did they actually hire someone else? I am Jason. The fans even said that all the time. How could they, why would they, replace me? Four films and suddenly I'm out on the street?* I had put my heart and soul into playing this character! It can't be possible. Falling into my chair I was too wrecked mentally to destroy anything. My heart started throbbing, and I felt a tingling pain across my chest. I had never experienced anything like this in my life; it felt like a mix between a heart attack and finding out that a loved one had just died... and in a way, one just had.

JASON IS DEAD

After the initial shock wore off, I was able to think clearly...almost. Part of me still wanted to smash the shit out of my house, but I had to get the truth first. What if the punk on the phone was wrong? I sat for hours making calls and listening to people nervously confirm what I had heard. Each time I asked why I was being replaced, I got a different story. The one I heard most was that they wanted to have a *bigger* Jason. Ken Kirzinger, who was cast as the new Jason, is only an inch and a half taller than me. Did that difference really read on film? Another one that I heard was that someone wanted Jason to have more sympathetic eyes. *What?* First, Jason only has one eye and for my whole career, people have told me that I have such expressive eyes. The one that pissed me off the most was the rumor that I asked for too much money! I never, ever jeopardized my chance of coming back to play the character by doing something stupid like that. It was never about the money. I loved playing the character. Period. Besides, we never even got to the point of talking money before I was replaced.

I have no hard feelings towards Ken; he is a good guy who was just looking out for his own career. Besides, who would turn down the chance to play a classic character? I do have a problem with the fact that someone had represented him as playing Jason before. That was not hearsay. I was told that directly from someone in casting. Yeah, he did stunts in *Part 8*. He did two quick shots as Jason in the film, one I wasn't allowed to do and the other because we were short on time.

Though I wanted to do it, the producers would not let me do the car stunt where Jason gets hit by the cop car. They thought it was too dangerous if I got hurt and if I couldn't finish filming, the entire film would be ruined. Therefore, they had Ken do it. He did a good job, even if he is only on the screen for a split second... little did I know that one shot would come back to haunt me. The only other scene in the film that he did was of Jason walking out of the subway car and getting electrocuted. We were running behind schedule, so they had Ken do that one shot to try and catch up. I don't like the shot. Though most people don't notice it, Ken didn't move like my version of Jason. He swings his arms when he steps out. I would have never done that—Jason doesn't swing his arms. Every time I see that one scene, it makes me so angry. It ruins the character for me. It might have been a tiny thing, but that is how seriously I take the character. One little thing and I'm not happy.

It was hard swallowing the fact that I did nothing wrong and *still* lost the role. Hell, I must have done a good job. If I hadn't, I wouldn't have been asked back three times. Not wanting to go to jail, I let myself simmer down for a few days before I tried to approach anyone. I tried to get in touch with people working with the movie, but I got the runaround almost every time. It was like they were scared to talk to me.

A rumor started that I lost the role because Ronny Yu, the director, didn't want me. My fans went nuts, protested the production, and even made up shirts that said *Fuck Yu.* Clever as the shirts were and as much as I appreciated the support, I don't believe it was Yu. For one thing, he didn't know who I was. The second thing, and this is what I really don't understand... is that I was told he had NEVER seen any of the Jason or Freddy movies. Even during production, they said he didn't watch them because he didn't want to be influenced by them. Part of me thinks that if he saw me, he might have requested, at least, an audition with me. I hold no grudges against Ronny, for he has even said in interviews that not bringing me back was not his decision.

If it wasn't Yu's decision, then whose was it? The studio's? Perhaps, but even they denied it was their decision. Rumors float around the Internet and through the fan bases, but you have to take them all with a grain of salt. Someone does know the reason, though, and one day I would love to find out the truth... not that it would make it any easier. The bottom line is I wish that I had been given a reasonable explanation as to why I was replaced. That's all. I guess I felt I was owed at least that much. Especially since everyone was dying to see that movie. Even Robert Englund said *People were looking forward to Englund vs. Hodder more than they were for Freddy vs. Jason.*

Months after the news, I sunk into a depression. I became cranky and more of an asshole than I usually am. My family got annoyed with me, co-workers noticed the withdrawal from my normal hijinks, and life seemed like shit. As they were filming in Canada, I got a small role in *Daredevil* playing a bodyguard along with some cameos in *Charmed* and *Grind*. Though I was getting some great work, I was still miserable. Every day on the sets I would think about the fact that someone else was wearing *the* mask at that moment, playing my character. It horrified me. I would do a scene, go back to my trailer to relax, and suddenly start wondering what the hell they were filming, wondering how Ken was going to look and act. It ate me up inside.

It wasn't until I got the job as stunt coordinator on the Oscar-winning film, *Monster*, that I really started to ease up. I was so mesmerized by Charlize Theron's performance of the real life serial killer, Aileen Wuornos, that I started to forget about the fact that they were filming the movie I had dreamed about doing for 15 years. During one particular scene, I saw Charlize get so into her character that when the director yelled *Cut*, Charlize couldn't come out of it for several minutes. She stood there, tears and rage in her eyes. In that moment she was not a beautiful celebrity, she was that killer. As she slowly slipped out of it, I saw her eyes clear and Charlize come back. It sounds fucking cheesy, but as I watched Charlize let herself go to become a monster… I was able to let go of my monster. Her acting inspired me to become a better actor, to try my damnedest to get out from behind the make-up and masks now and then.

Playing Jason was an amazingly incredible part of my life that will always be with me… but he was gone. With the death of his character in my life, it was time to start a new chapter in my career.

Though I was ready to move on, the loss was still hard to deal with. When *Freddy vs. Jason* came out, I refused to watch it for a long time. I didn't want to have anything to do with it. I didn't want to see the movie I should have been in. I didn't want to see someone else wearing that mask. Though I was ready to move forward in my life, there were still a lot of ups and downs, mostly because of how the whole thing went down. I was given the script. I was getting ready for it and then nothing… no one even bothered to call and tell me I was out. If I was brought in, sat down, and told *Hey Kane, you did great for us over the years, but we want to take this film in a new direction. I hope you understand. Heck, we'll even give you a small cameo.* It would have been hard, but nowhere near as hard as not knowing anything. It's sort of like being married to someone for almost two decades only to come home one day and find that she has left you… but with no explanation as to why.

What made me so mad about losing the role is that I know I'm the only person to ever play Jason who took it as seriously as I did. It wasn't just a gig for me, it was a passion. It really was. I would have played him for free—I loved him so much. Hell, if they would have let me, I would still be playing him now. Ken and the others, they liked playing him; they liked being the star of a film. Who wouldn't? But they didn't have the passion and drive I did to keep the character as consistent and evil...

Years later, the pain and anger still has not gone away, especially since fans still remind me about it on a daily basis. I don't blame them; they were angry as well, but at every convention I do have at least three dozen fans come up to me and say *I hate that you weren't in Freddy vs. Jason,* or something along those lines. I grumble about how it pissed me off as well, and sometimes I go into a bit more detail, but none of them will ever know the full extent of how much it hurt me... and still does. The only thing that has helped the wound heal a bit is finding a new character I love just as much...Victor Crowley.

In the end, I got a bit of a laugh when I saw the movie. Though I was spitting bullets the entire time I watched it, I couldn't help but crack up when I saw that I had a cameo in the film—a cameo that, to this day, my fans still don't even know about. Early in the film, two of the characters are waiting for drugs in line at a mental institute. Behind the counter there is a television playing *Texas Chainsaw Massacre 3.* The scene they happened to be showing was an entire scene where I played Leatherface, and low and behold, I was still in the film! It was probably done by accident, but regardless, it was fun to know I squeezed my way into it somehow, even if for only a flash in the background.

FIGHT
INTERMISSION
IV

ROUND FOUR

Deleted due to the advice of my lawyer... Seriously.

ROUND FIVE

The final round goes to my father. My dad loved nickel slots and played them all the time. Being in Sparks, casinos were plentiful. Dad didn't just like sitting at one machine though; he always had to play four or five at once. He'd get a row, put a nickel in, pull the handle down, and then repeat the process all the way down, over and over again. Five machines were better than one. I didn't go to the casino much when I was young, but this one time dad talked me into going with him, right after my 21st birthday, before my burn injury.

Dad was doing his typical five-machine routine while I stood on the other side of the row, slowly putting nickels into one machine, worried I'd lose all my money in a matter of minutes. Out of nowhere I heard my father starting to yell. Scooping up my nickels, I ran around to the other side to see what was wrong. There I found my dad, who was in his 50's at the time, arguing with some young guy around my age. Come to find out, the kid was pissed that my dad was taking up so many machines. Dad told the guy to leave him alone, but he wouldn't listen. *I'm telling you kid, you leave right now or I'm going to punch you right in the nose*, my dad sternly said to the kid. I stood back a bit, feeling a bit embarrassed by my father's cheesy line.

The guy kept it up, and just as I was about to step in, my father stuck to his words and nailed the guy right in his nose. Blood shot from the guy's nostrils as he stumbled back, trying to grab onto chairs for support on his way to the ground. Dad grabbed his little bucket, scooped up his nickels, turned to me and said, "Let's go, Son." I was flabbergasted. I couldn't believe my father just cracked a guy in the face. On the ride home, he didn't seem too proud of it, but he didn't apologize for it, either.

Looking back now, I can see that a lot of my anger, rage, and personality came from my father. While I might have gotten that from him, he also instilled a few things in me, as well. For one, he never laid a finger on me or my mother and always told me that any man who touches a child or a woman is not a real man. I have always followed that rule, and I do my best to look out and protect women and kids as well. My father was a hell of a guy, and I guess we are more alike than I thought. This round goes to Dad.

Fighting is a million-dollar racket; people pay tons of money to watch boxing matches and cage fights. It's in our blood to be savages and fight for our lives, though now that we don't have to fight to survive, we do it as an exposition. In the real world, fights break out all the time as people cannot control their tempers, and I'm one of them. I don't approve of fighting in all circumstances, however. In fact, I wish I could control my temper more. Though I try not to fight, I know I have more rounds in my future.

WHAT A PISSER

I have issues. I'm an asshole with OCD and a fucked-up sense of humor. Even so, this part might take even those who know me best by surprise. My buddies, Rick McCallum and R.A. Mihailoff, love to tell a story about the filming of *Hatchet II* when I busted into R.A.'s room. Without saying a word I opened the door, walked past them, and started to piss on the dressing room wall. The two of them just stared at me until I was finished. Zipping up I smiled at them and walked out of the room. Being some of my oldest friends, they just laughed it off, figuring I was just being an asshole like usual. What they didn't know, was that I *had* to piss in his room.

It all began back on the set of *Friday the 13th Part VII*. It wasn't a conscious decision or something I planned out, it just sort of happened. One day I had to piss, but the bathroom was too far away, and we were about to shoot. Trying to stay in character, I figured where would Jason piss? Being in a studio, I couldn't just go on a tree. Seeing William Butler's dressing room nearby, I snuck into his room and pissed in the corner. He was one of my victims, so why not piss in his room? Jason would piss on his grave; it was sort of the same thing. Originally, I just thought I had to piss and needed a place to do it, but when it came to *Part 8*, I suddenly had this overwhelming anxiety that I *had* to piss in another one of my victim's dressing rooms. This time I chose VC Dupree's dressing room, the boxer from the movie, and pissed away. While filming *Part 8*, I even pissed in a full basket of mail. We were shooting the tunnel scenes under a post office in Vancouver. I couldn't find a bathroom, and I was rushing to get to the set, so I pissed in the post office behind some boxes. As I finished, I realized I had just soaked an entire bin of mail. That one I felt bad about, but I still couldn't help but chuckle at people getting some yellow mail with a foul stench. From that film forward, it became a method, a tradition, or whatever the fuck you want to call it—the bottom line was, if I was playing a killer, I had to do it to one of my victims. At least I always did it to the men.

When I filmed *Part 9*, I didn't have many victims that I personally killed. Since I technically kill myself in the movie, I decided to piss in my own dressing room. It's a fucked-up thing, but hey, that's how I am. It has now been something I have done on all of the movies I have killed people in. It's also the reason I busted into R.A.'s dressing room to piss. For some reason I could never get in the room with him not being there. Worried about breaking my streak, I decided to just barge in and piss, knowing they would think it was just a joke.

As to all the people I have pissed in their rooms—sorry guys, I would have told you, but I have never told a soul in my life…until now.

To the following people, I apologize for pissing in your dressing room:

Friday the 13th Part VII	William Butler
Friday the 13th Part VIII	VC Dupree
Jason Goes to Hell	Myself
Jason X	Jonathan Potts
Hatchet	Josh Leonard
Hatchet II	R.A. Mihailoff
Ed Gein, The Butcher of Plainfield	Jay Wilkins
B.T.K.	Matteo Indelicato

Hopefully this won't scare anyone off from filming with me. Hey, think of it as an honor or that I'm just marking my territory... or just make sure you lock your door. As for you psychologists out there, go ahead and analyze this. I'd love to hear your thoughts about why I do this—right before I piss in your office.

CHOKE

Over the years of taking pictures with fans, I have become infamous for choking people. When I pose for a picture with a fan and they ask me to choke them, I don't just put my hands around their necks. That doesn't look real at all, so I really choke them. The crazy part is the fans love it! People *always* ask me to choke them. Fans laugh at it, exchange stories about it and show off their pictures, though there were a few times where I almost got in trouble choking people.

The Infamous Choke

During one convention I choked this little guy a little too long as his friend was fidgeting with the camera, and he passed out on me. Literally, he fell right at my feet. After he came to and woke up, he was white as a ghost and just slipped out of the room. Another time I had a guy come back the second day of a convention, pointed to his eye, and said *Look!* Half of his eye was bloodshot; I had busted blood vessels. Another time, a guy in a wheelchair came up for a picture. I choked him pretty hard. After the picture was snapped, he rode off not really saying anything. He looked upset, so I asked the guy taking the picture what was wrong. Come to find out, the guy became paralyzed after he was choked so hard, his neck broke. I felt like shit after that. Those few incidents made me back off from choking people for a while, but then, too many fans asked me to do it, and I felt bad saying no, so I started it up again.

And Yet Another Choking Victim

Choking One of My Youngest Fans

I could go on and on telling you stories about how I have choked people, but I think it's better to let the fans tell you in their own words. Below is a small selection of quotes from fans I have choked.

Your life is not complete until you have been choked by Kane!
~Janel S.

I was choked by Kane for a photo at DragonCon 2009. I've been in the Army for 10 years. As such I'm a pretty big guy and in decent shape. Kane hauled me up on my tiptoes by the neck like I weighed next to nothing. AWESOME!"
~Anonymous

I was warned before I met him, but I didn't believe it. The minute he grabbed me, I saw the light.
~Shad Y.

WOW, they couldn't snap the picture fast enough. As much as I love my picture, it pains me to still look at it!!!
~Ace H.

Kane was choking the life out of my brother. I pretended to fumble with the camera and take my sweet time...fun to watch my brother change colors through the camera lens.
~Toby L.

I felt as though my eyes would eject from my skull. His grip could have removed my head entirely.
~Sam H.

It was like having the life choked out of you, but in an orgasmic way. You think "Holy Shit, Jason fucking Voorhees is choking the shit out of me."
~Dennis C.

The first time I met Kane, he choked me so hard I thought I was going to pass out. My neck was red for the rest of the day. It was great!

~Brad T.

Say you're a musician and you get the chance to jam with your heroes. As a Jason fan, this is the only way I can describe what being choked by Kane is like.

~Jai S.

When Kane choked me, I almost peed my pants. My kids still make fun of me when they see the picture.

~Jerry S.

My neck was sore for days afterwards.

~Jeff M.

I have gotten married and witnessed the birth of both of my sons, but the day I got choked by Kane has got to be the best day of my life!

~Dan H.

(Couldn't give a quote, passed out)

~Craig S.

100 KILLS

Over the years I have killed an insane amount of people in the movies I have been in. Instead of listing them all in the book, I decided to compile some of the most kickass 100 kills I did starting with *Friday the 13th Part VII*. While I enjoyed killing every single one of them motherfuckers, there were some who stood out above the rest. I have marked my favorite kills with an asterisk* next to the kill. It's crazy to think I get paid to do this shit...

Friday the 13th Part VII: The New Blood

Total Kills	Film Kills	Kill Method
1	1	Tent stake in throat
2	2	Stabbed with tent stake
3	3	Punched through chest
4	4	*Sleeping bag slammed into tree
5	5	Axe into face
6	6	Pulled underwater and drowned
7	7	Sickle into throat
8	8	Head crushed in hands
9	9	Party horn jammed into eye
10	10	Butcher knife into stomach
11	11	Machete into neck
12	12	Thrown out of window
13	13	Spike stabbed into back
14	14	*Weed whacker into gut
15	15	Axe into skull

Friday the 13th Part VIII: Jason Takes Manhattan

Total Kills	Film Kills	Kill Method
16	1	Spear Gun into gut
17	2	Spear into chest
18	3	Guitar smashed into face
19	4	Sauna rock into chest
20	5	Stabbed with broken mirror shard
21	6	Harpoon into back
22	7	Throat sliced
23	8	*Choked to ceiling
24	9	Thrown and electrocuted
25	10	Impaled on antenna
26	11	Axe into back
27	12	Hypodermic needle into back
28	13	Face smashed into pipe
29	14	*Head punched off
30	15	Strangled
31	16	Headfirst into slime barrel
32	17	Thrown into diner mirror
33	18	Head smashed with wrench

Jason Goes to Hell

Total Kills	Film Kills	Kill Method
34	1	Crushed with bear hug

349

Jason X

Total Kills	Film Kills	Kill Method
35	1	Soldier hung
36	2	Face smashed with stick
37	3	One armed choke
38	4	Choked with chain
39	5	Head smashed
40	6	Pole through body
41	7	Thrown through door
42	8	*Frozen head
43	9	Machete through body
44	10	Back broken
45	11	Face smashed into wall
46	12	Neck slowly snapped
47	13	Impaled on screw
48	14	Throat cut
49	15	Cut in half
50	16	Impaled on hook
51	17	Chopped to pieces
52	18	Head cut off
53	19	Electrocute face
54	20	Sleeping bag slammed against another
55	21	Sleeping bag slammed against another

Ed Gein

Total Kills	Film Kills	Kill Method
56	1	Impaled on hooks

57	2	Shovel smashed into head
58	3	Tree branch smashed into face
59	4	Two handed strangle
60	5	Head cut off with hacksaw

Hatchet

Total Kills	Film Kills	Kill Method
61	1	Disemboweled
62	2	Body torn in half
63	3	Chopped with hatchet
64	4	*Head torn apart by jaw
65	5	Head twisted around
66	6	Face power sanded
67	7	Head cut off with shovel
68	8	Body cut in half
69	9	Head slammed into mausoleum

B.T.K.

Total Kills	Film Kills	Kill Method
70	1	Face stomped
71	2	*Suffocated with plastic bag
72	3	Shot in head
73	4	Strangled
74	5	Shovel into gut
75	6	Shot in face
76	7	Beaten and strangled
77	8	Cop run over with car

Hatchet II

Total Kills	Film Kills	Kill Method
78	1	Tackled and smashed
79	2	Skull chopped with hatchet
80	3	Lower jaw ripped out
81	4	Face sliced off
82	5	Spear jammed into mouth
83	6	Choked with own intestines
84	7	Face smashed with hatchet
85	8	*Face pushed into boat propeller
86	9	Giant chainsaw up from crotch
87	10	Giant chainsaw up from crotch
88	11	Head chopped off
89	12	Crotch chopped with hatchet
90	13	Head power sanded
91	14	*Ultimate curb stomp
92	15	Splattered around cabin
93	16	*Skinned alive

Exit 33

Total Kills	Film Kills	Kill Method
94	1	Stabbed
95	2	Gutted with knife
96	3	Smashed against wall
97	4	Face smashed with hammer
98	5	Head smashed with car hood
99	6	Face stomped
100	7	Eye gouged out

KILL STATISTICS

Kill Total by Sex: 32 Females
68 Males

Kills with Bare Hands: 22

Kills with Weapons or Objects: 78

Kills with Power Tools: 6

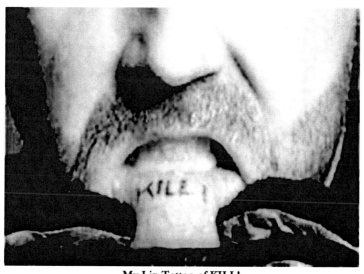

My Lip Tattoo of KILL!

PART V

THE BIRTH OF A NEW KILLER

MOVING ON

In the immediate years after I shed the mask of Jason, I started a gradual shift. Though stunts are in my blood, I tried to focus more on acting. Like always, the stunt work was there, and I loved every minute of it, but with each film, I did my best to try and slip in some acting. Slowly, but surely, it worked. Of course it helped that I was now a known name in the horror world. With that fame, people started asking for cameos, which gave me more acting experience. I did bit parts in *2001 Maniacs, Behind the Mask,* and *Room 6,* where I have a great fight scene with Jerry O'Connell.

Kane as Homeless Demon, Room 6

357

Around this same time I got to work with one of my fucking favorite people in the world - the sick, twisted, amazing Rob Zombie.

When Rob first came out with White Zombie, I was hooked to his music. For several years I listened to every single thing he put out. Then one year I was doing a convention, and Rob was there as well. At this point he was a pretty damn big celebrity. Loving his stuff, I wanted to meet him. I asked one of the promoters to introduce me and he said he would. When I finally shook Rob's hand and said *Rob, I'm Kane Hodder.* He replied with *I know who you are. I'm a big fan of yours, and a few years back I actually waited in line to get your autograph.* When he said that, it fucking floored me. Here was a guy who I was a huge fan of and he was somewhat of a fan of mine too.

Interview with Rob Zombie

A few years later when he became a filmmaker, his true genius really shined. His first movie, *House of a 1000 Corpses*, was one of the most ingenious, original horror movies to ever come out. When it came time to do the sequel, and he asked me to be the stunt coordinator, I was once again floored. Getting to work with Rob was a dream come true. Getting ready to film, I watched *Corpses* a half dozen times to get a feel for his style and what sort of stunts he used in that film. It was one of the first times I ever did that. Normally I just meet with the director and talk about what he wants. With Rob, I actually found myself being... almost nervous.

When shooting started on *The Devil's Rejects*, I could instantly tell that it was going to be another gut-wrenching, gritty masterpiece. Being a fan of the first one, I tried to live up to Rob's vision by giving him powerful fight scenes and great stunts. Early on in the shooting, I was working on blocking out a scene where the character Otis kills two band members in a chicken coop. Rob told me an idea of what he wanted, so I blocked a few routines with stuntmen Chris Carnel and John Ashker. When I thought it was good enough, I brought Rob over to show him what we had put together. At one point in the fight, I thought Otis could take a branch and smash it into the guy's balls. Rob gave me a weird look when I showed him this. In a very serious manner, Rob said *I don't think that is appropriate*. My gut dropped, I was nervous. Here I was working one of my dream jobs, and I just insulted the director by taking something over the top. After what seemed like an extremely long pause, Rob said that it would be more appropriate for Otis to rip the guy's balls off and shove them into his mouth. I started laughing—Rob was just as fucked up as I was. From that point on, I knew I was going to have a good time.

The final product became something that I think is one of the most gut-wrenching, realistic horror films in modern times. It's one of my favorites that I have worked on. Working with Rob helped me move on from the whole Jason fiasco even more. I might not be able to play the character I loved anymore, but I was still going to get to work on some great movies.

REBIRTH

John Carl Buechler changed my life by requesting me to be in *Friday the 13th Part VII*. If it wasn't for him, I wouldn't be known as a horror legend, if I may call myself that. I would have had a great stunt career, but I wouldn't have become what I am today if it wasn't for his support. My entire life and career was changed a second time around, when Adam Green came into my life. Adam got John Carl Buechler to do the make-up on *Hatchet*. They were having a conversation one day where Adam was trying to figure out who to cast in the role of Victor. John suggested me, and Adam said he would love to, but how the hell would they get a hold of me? John opened up his cell phone and gave me a call. A week later, I had the script in my hands.

After reading the script for *Hatchet*, I wanted to do the movie… badly. It was like a Jason film, but with a character with more depth, angrier, and tougher. It brought back memories of the heyday of horror in the 80's when slashers were just about killing and tits, not that torture stuff they sometimes make today—just good old fucked-up ways of cutting people's limbs off. In my first meeting with Adam, I knew right away that not only was he talented, but he was also passionate as hell. I have worked with a lot of filmmakers who have had a lot of fire behind them, but very few had the childlike energy and excitement as Adam. The second I met him, I knew we were going to hit it off.

Adam knew I could play the psychotic killer, Victor Crowley. He had been a fan of my version of Jason, which is why he wanted me in the film. Though I was dying to play the role, I asked Adam to give me a dramatic role as well. He wrote a part in the movie that would be perfect for me to play out of the make-up—the killer's father. Adam somehow sensed that maybe I could pull it off as it had some emotional depth. Maybe. During our first meeting, Adam turned to talk to a producer for a second, and as he did, I made myself cry. It's not the easiest thing to do, but if I work at it, I can make tears come out and look convincing as well. When he turned back and saw me crying, he said *Okay, you convinced me.* With that, he was sold. I had landed the role of Victor's father.

The story, about a horribly disfigured boy who dies traumatically during a Halloween prank after his father hits him in the face with a hatchet, was a story that was with Adam since his youth. At a summer camp he attended, the counselors told a story about a monster called Hatchet Face, but never gave more information than that. Being naturally creative, Adam, hardly a teenager, made up a backstory to go with the name. The concept never left him and years later, he brought it to life in the movies. The fact that he had known the character in his mind for so long made Adam more than just a writer or director—he knew Victor inside and out. Being an actor, having a director who can answer any question about a character you are playing is priceless.

Adam was able to pull off getting me, Tony Todd, and Robert Englund, to appear in the same movie… a horror movie trifecta. Unfortunately, none of us had shooting days together. Regardless, it was great being in another film with them. Besides getting to work with Adam, one of the best parts of the film was working with John Carl Buechler again. For this movie he was back in the make-up chair creating the ghastly monster I was to become. *And,* he got to make his own cameo in the film as the piss-drinking Jack Cracker. I was thrilled that Adam did that because John doesn't get nearly enough credit for the talented work he has done over the years. The character make-up John made was fantastic; it was one of the best-looking make-up jobs I have ever had done. He made Victor look fucked up and crazy. Even the young Victor make-up was so good it scared the piss out of my own children whom Adam let have a cameo in the film. The kids who tease Victor in the truck only to get scared by his face—two of them were my boys, Jace and Reed. Another interesting fact is that when the characters in *Hatchet* hear the far-off wailing of Victor's voice in the swamp saying *DAAAADDDDYYYY!!* it's actually a mix of my voice and my son Jace's voice saying it.

While Jason and Victor are similar in that they kill anyone and everyone, Victor has more of a backstory, which I love. And… he is spastic, unlike the slow-moving Jason. After years of doing the slow Jason walk, it was fun to move faster and be a bit more energetic. I really got into the character, learning his story and *why* he kills. Adam cleverly left some of the story out in the first movie, so he could reveal it in the second one. While he did that for the audience, he was always there telling me bits and pieces of the backstory so I would be able to find more motivation in the scenes.

In the film, there is a major fire stunt that I had to do in the full Victor make-up. With fire stunts, you only get one chance to do them right. They are too dangerous and expensive to do multiple times. Since Victor shows a lot of skin, we had to figure out how to light me on fire while also giving me an escape route out of the costume if things went wrong. We decided to split the back open, so it could be peeled off in an emergency. The wardrobe department snapped it together, and we were good to go. The stunt went off great, and I thought it felt awesome. After they put me out, I got up and expected a huge round of applause, because usually that is what happens after a major stunt. Everyone was clapping, but nothing huge like I expected—I thought it was really good so I didn't know why I didn't get a bigger reception.

Full Body Burn, Hatchet

It wasn't until months later when Adam was editing did I find out why everyone was a bit awkward after the burn stunt. The flap on the back of the suit had come open and was flapping around during the entire take, ruining the shot. Adam was so upset and nervous about it, that he didn't want to tell me at the time. It ended up costing him a ton of money to fix it in post-production by putting computer-generated fire over the flap. It worked so well, though, that you don't even notice it in the movie. When I found this out, I was pretty pissed at myself. I'm the stunt coordinator, and it's my job to make it look real and not a mess. I'm just glad he was able to fix it in post-production. If he couldn't have, it would have ruined that part of the movie. Then again, I could blame the wardrobe department for not securing the suit tightly enough… Wherever the blame is, it worked out in the end.

We filmed most of *Hatchet* at Sable Ranch, a major filming location in California which doubles for a lot of locations in movies. In fact, I was there three summers in a row filming movies: *Ed Gein*, *The Devil's Rejects*, and *Hatchet*. One particular night on *Hatchet*, we took our dinner break and ate like we normally did. I was in full Victor make-up and had some time left on my break, so I decided to take a walk to see who else was filming at the ranch. Come to find out, a porno was filming in the old western town set. I snuck out of the woods, behind the crew. There, all lit up were two people having sex in a barn. The guy had a girl bent over and was taking her from behind. The guy noticed me, but since I was sort of far away, he couldn't really tell what I was. He did see me, though, because I saw his face scrunch up a bit before looking back down at his work. I took a few steps closer, with everyone's back to me. No one could see me but him. This time he started to stare at me, looking around as he tried to see if anyone else was seeing me. Trying to ignore my ghastly image, he closed his eyes and went back to thrusting. I took this as an opportunity to move even closer. This time when he looked at me, I lifted my hand and waved ever so slightly. He had had enough. He pulled out, yelling *Cut*, and pointed in my direction. I high-tailed it back into the woods. From a ways in, hiding behind a tree, I cracked up as I saw the man with his dick slapping around pointing to the woods and the entire crew looking at him like he was nuts. Wonder if the guy ever realized what I was.

Hatchet turned out to be fantastic. Until *Hatchet II* took its place, it was my favorite film that I had starred in. It's pure cheesy, hard core, 80's-style horror. Adam knew what he wanted and nailed it on the head. I was so impressed with him that when we finished shooting, I knew that I would drop everything to work with him again... any time. And in fact, I was lucky enough to have that happen again and again. By bringing a new iconic character into the world of horror and letting me play him, Adam changed my life. Not only do I now have a new character to love and play, but he also allowed me to show my real acting side by giving me the role of Victor's father. Though the scenes were small, they opened up a lot of doors, and suddenly I didn't always have to be behind a mask or just making a cameo, I was about to become a leading man, and it was all thanks to a spunky New England horror fan and his childhood campfire story.

FROZEN

Adam Green and I worked so well together that as soon as we got a chance, we worked on another film...*Frozen*. While I wasn't going to be in this film, besides a much-appreciated cameo, I got to stunt-coordinate the movie. Adam had once again written a brilliant script, this time about three skiers who get stuck on a chairlift when the resort closes down for the week. It's a claustrophobic, terrifying thriller and the hardest movie I had ever had to shoot. Adam, being a stickler for making things look real, insisted the entire movie actually be shot fifty feet up in the air on a real ski lift, in the cold. And when I say cold, I'm not talking about put on a jacket cold; I'm talking put on 15 layers and have a million hand warmers cold. It was miserable.

Ski Chair Lift Rig, Frozen

The conditions were beyond horrifying. Sub-zero temperatures, wind, heights—it was one of the only films I had ever been on where people didn't just stand around and bullshit off to the side. Here, there was no side; we were up in the air almost the entire time. If you worked on the film, you froze your ass off and worked hard, but it was worth it. I have so much respect for the actors and crew for fighting through the conditions. I didn't have to suffer the weather half of the time the crew did and yet, I found it hard being out there. Sitting in that ski lift, those kids really went through what the characters did. In fact, I would clip them into the chairs down at the bottom of the mountain. They would then be lifted up the mountain to the shooting location. From then on, they had no breaks, no chances to go to the bathroom or warm up. They were stuck there. And if they did want a break, they had to ride the lift another 45 minutes up and back down the hill in the freezing cold. They definitely didn't have to act like they were suffering—they were.

One of the most satisfying things on the film, for me, was to hire my friend Chester Tripp, a fellow stuntman, to do some work. Chester isn't a young man, yet he is in better shape than most 20-year olds. When I talked to him about the film and the stunts he would be performing, he went out of his way to set up a wire in his backyard to practice hanging from it and crossing it with just his hands. When it came time for him to double the actor trying to make his way across the cable, I knew Chester would be ready. The only problem was his gloves. It was so cold he needed warm gloves to keep his hands from going numb, yet the thick gloves kept him from getting a good grip on the cable. He had to opt for thin gloves, which meant his hands would go numb rather quickly. Not only that, the ski lodge wouldn't let me safety him to the cable he was climbing. Instead I had to safety him to the chair lift, which meant that if he fell, he wouldn't just drop a few feet. Instead he would drop, snag, then swing back a long way under the chair, which is not the optimal choice for safety. As I watched Chester shimmy out for the first time, I just knew he would fall. With the temperature, the thin gloves, and the strenuous activity, it seemed impossible. Then, Chester surprised me and did the stunt perfectly without falling once. Only one hell of a stuntman could do that under those conditions. His stunt looked so great, it's on the poster for the movie!

Not having to wear make-up the entire time, I was able to talk to Adam more freely than on our previous film and guide the work that needed to be done on the stunt end, which let us bond and work closely together some more. The film ended up being critically acclaimed. I just wish *Frozen* had been given a wide release, for I think it is one of the best modern-day thrillers ever made. It is fucking tense, disturbing, and moving. It's a fantastic film that deserved much more attention than it got.

Chester Tripp's Stunt, Frozen

HATCHET II

When production finished on *Frozen* it wasn't long before we went back to the swamp to film *Hatchet II*. I was in Montreal doing a convention when Adam called me and told me he had finished the script. He said it was the best thing he had ever written. I couldn't wait to read it and asked him to send it over right away. He said due to security reasons he couldn't; he had to give us hard copies with our names watermarked on each page so it wouldn't get leaked. I was a little disappointed that I had to wait, but it was worth it. When I finally read the script, I was pumped. There were twice the kills and more backstory for Victor's dad, which meant more time for me to get some acting in. I was thrilled to get back into psychotic killer mode as I loved playing Victor the first time around. By the time I had the suit on for the second round, I could feel the same passion and love I had for Jason filling my heart. Only this time, I was the *first* and *only* person to play the character.

This time, almost the entire film was shot in a studio where we all had our own dressing rooms. My good buddies Rick and R.A. were on the film with me and, of course, I had to fuck with them a bit, especially R.A. One time I came across him taking a shit in the bathroom, so I quietly snuck in and kicked the door, trying to scare him. Instead I broke the hinge on the door and annoyed him more than anything. We decided not to tell anyone I broke the door and left it at that. Still wanting to scare him, I found an opportunity one day when I heard him in one of the offices talking to someone. I stood outside of the door, got a good stance, and kicked the fucker really hard. Again, this did not go as planned. Instead of busting the door in, my foot went right through it, creating a huge hole and not scaring anyone. The idiot I am, I did this right across from the producer's office, which meant I got caught.

When a maintenance guy from the studio came around, he said I owed $100 bucks to replace the door. The next day I brought the money in and asked if he was going to fix it or replace it (I was leery of this ever since I paid to repair a hole and they framed it instead of fixing it), the guy said he had to replace it. I said *Good* and with that, punched three huge holes in the door, making sure he wasn't just going to patch the hole. The producers just shook their heads at me and walked away. Good thing Adam likes me.

Though the make-up in *Hatchet II* looked amazing, I had two problems with it. The first one was that I started having some allergic reaction to the latex, which blew my mind because with the countless monsters I had played, I had never had a problem. All over my back, painful blisters bubbled up. Each night when they removed the appliances, the blisters would tear open. It was painful as shit. It got to the point where we were not sure if I would be able to film or not. Thankfully it subsided a little bit and I pushed through the pain, not wanting to mess up the schedule. The make-up crew thought I was allergic to the latex, but that didn't make sense because I have had more latex on my body than anyone! It was odd alright—I just hope it doesn't happen again.

The other pain in the ass was how long it took to remove all of the make-up. Robert Pendergraft took over the Make-up EFX from Buechler for this movie. While the make-up looked fantastic, it was much harder for me overall. When we stopped filming for the day, I would go to the make-up department and have them start removing it. The rest of the crew would go out back of the studio and have a few beers with Adam and bullshit. It was the longest make-up removal time I have ever had. By the time I got the stuff off me, I would rush to the back and everyone would be saying their goodbyes. I felt like the unpopular kid being left out of the party each day. Regardless, we all had a great time and had a blast with the movie.

Kane as Victor Crowley, Hatchet II

With the film done, Adam originally planned a straight to DVD release, knowing that the ratings board would cut his film to shreds. Amazingly, the studio got behind putting it out in the theaters and even got AMC to show the movie unrated. We did a shit load of publicity, interviews, appearances, you name it and we did it... all to get the fans out to see the movie. Sadly, they had less than two days to see it before AMC pulled it from the screens.

My Holiday Card with Victor Crowley Grin

Now, I'm not going to go in-depth on this situation or even speculate as to why they pulled it. Hell, I could write a book about the ratings board and how they cut the shit out of almost *all* of my movies, especially the Jason films and how unfair they are towards horror movies when television shows like *CSI* show worse stuff every night. I'm not going to get into that though,

373

because it pisses me off, and it's useless to rant about. The bottom line is AMC took a chance, and I respect that. At least a few people got to see the movie in all of its glory on the big screen.

Before *Hatchet II* even came out, Adam and I were working together once again, this time on a short segment for a movie called *Chillerama*, a collection of short, funny horror films. This time I was reunited with Joel Moore from the original *Hatchet*. Fresh off *Avatar*, Joel put on a Nazi suit and played Hitler while I played another monster, this time, a Jewish Frankenstein called Meshugannah. Our segment was called *The Diary of Anne Frankenstein*, and it had me dancing on screen for the first time. It was one of the oddest things I ever shot, but it was so much fun.

Kane as Meshugannah, Chillerama

In one scene, I'm leaning against an examining table before I'm brought back to life. Joel is speaking in his gibberish German about how hideous of a creature I am to Kristina Klebe, who played Eva Braun. The scene called for her to say he isn't hideous and to grab my crotch. Always having to play jokes, before the scene I took a giant tube and stuck it down my pants so when she grabbed me she would feel this massive member. As she grabbed me, I waited for her to burst out laughing, yet she didn't. Not a word, not a peep about it. Even after the take was done, she didn't mention it. At that point I felt like an asshole if I mentioned it, so I didn't say anything. I never ended up telling her, so poor Kristina thinks I have a huge dick…not that I don't.

Adam Green and Me

I can honestly say that Adam helped take my career in a new path and for that I am grateful. The best part is that I know we'll work together more in the future, and hopefully, I'll be picking up that hatchet again very soon. Adam is one of the best upcoming directors in the business and I'm honored and proud he has taken me along on his ride towards the top.

MORE KILLING

After Adam graciously gave me one of my first emotional scenes on the first Hatchet movie, a door suddenly opened up. Before I knew it, I was the leading man in a movie; of course it was still horror, but a lead role without the make-up, nonetheless. Filmmaker Michael Feifer called me and asked if I would be in a film version of Ed Gein. I thought it would be great. I had read a ton of books on Ed and found him fascinating—America's first serial killer, the man who ate and skinned his victims and dug up dead bodies to use their skulls as soup bowls and other body parts for much worse things. His sickness is beyond bizarre and interesting to say the least. When I asked him what role I would play, I almost hit the floor—he wanted *me* to play Ed. At first I didn't understand, because Ed was skinny, small, and old. Here I am, big, thick, and well, not quite that old. I wouldn't look the part at all, but at the same time, I didn't give a shit. I could worry about it later; it was a lead role without make-up.

Though I had read countless books on Gein and even owned a piece of wood from the porch of his house, I still did some research to find out what made him tick. The man filleted women and peeled their skin off to use for clothing. He was fucked in the head. A lot of people who lived in his town said he was a loner and one oddball of a man, not like a lot of other killers in the world whom you would never expect. Realizing this, I did my best to always, always, look a bit off in each scene. I wanted him to have that glimmer of *I might gut you right now* in his eye which would give anyone the creeps. With that in mind, we set off to filming.

Once again, we shot this movie at Sable Ranch, and I was lucky enough to work with another well-known horror personality, Michael Berryman. I didn't actually kill too many people in this movie, but one of them was Mike. Even though he was playing Ed's only friend, he still ended up being a victim. Feifer wrote a scene where I smash Mike's character's head with a shovel. I can read people pretty well by looking into their eyes, and I can tell you positively that Mike was a little concerned when I raised that real shovel over my head, that I might actually smash him instead of smashing it into the ground right next to his head. I love scaring the scary guys the most. Another scene in the movie, I drive slowly past the deputy who is making out with his girlfriend in his cop car. I give them a creepy look as I slowly drive by. They can't see that I'm also dragging Mike's dead body behind my truck. Feifer wanted me to give them a look like I was extremely uncomfortable. I'm not a trained actor. In fact I have never had an acting class in my life, or any formal training at all. I thought *How am I going to look like I'm very uncomfortable and nervous?* Since I'm a little method with my acting, I did something that nobody ever knew. I took my pants and everything off below the waist and drove past them and the entire crew. Needless to say, I was very uncomfortable doing that. I guess it gave me the look that Feifer wanted. I just read that last paragraph back to myself. I really am fucked up in the head.

Though I had been in countless films at this point in my life, it was a new experience being the main character... and I loved it. The fact that I got to kill more people on film was another perk. The film was fun to shoot, especially since we shot near where I lived and I could go home at night. Feifer was even nice enough to let my son, Reed, have a small part in the film. He plays a kid in the middle of the road who talks to Priscilla Barnes for a couple minutes about catching frogs. While the film was a straight-to-DVD B-horror movie, it found a great following, even if it is not accurate at all. Feifer set out to make a film about a real-life character, but to make it his own. I think he succeeded in that. Since it was my first major role, I'll always be proud of the film.

Like with Adam, Feifer and I had a good working relationship—so well that he invited me to play the role of the warden in his film, *Bundy: An American Icon.* It was one of the first speaking roles in my life where I got to play a good guy. I was a warden. I didn't have to kill anyone. It was odd going to set and not having to put on a ton of make-up or an outfit covered in blood, or strangle someone to death before I headed home for the night. I was thankful that Feifer let me have that role, for it allowed me to act outside of things I have played before. It was also good practice for the next role that he offered me, Dennis Rader, in *B.T.K.*

When Feifer asked me to play the lead in *B.T.K.*, I was thrilled. Again, I had read a ton of books on this real-life serial killer. Unlike Ed, who was always the weird creepy guy, Dennis was a well-liked family man in his community. He volunteered at his church, and worked for the Compliance Department which was in charge of animal control and housing violations. He had a wife and two kids and seemed like a loving, nice man. Only he had a dark side, which made him kill people for almost 30 years. He would bind, torture, and kill his victims; hence why he called himself the BTK killer. In getting this role I was intrigued, because not only did I have to play the crazy killer, which I knew I could nail, I also had to make him likable as well. This was a whole new ball game for me...playing someone who is likable? And the best part was that unlike with Ed, I actually looked like this guy in some ways.

Kane as Dennis Rader, B.T.K.

During filming, I did my best to make him a normal, likable man who had that tiny look every now and then that seemed like he might just snap. I had a great time with the role and really got into every scene, adding my own stuff here and there. Of course, I did my best to actually scare people on the set like I normally do, but in one scene we scared a bystander by accident. In the movie, there is a part where my character picks up a little girl in his van. You think he is going to kill her, but ultimately he gives her a ride home. We filmed this on a suburban street in North Hollywood with the camera in the van for most of the shooting. Down the street, an older woman just happened to be looking out her window. All she could see was the little girl talking to the driver and then finally get in the van with him. In a panic, the woman called the police and reported a kidnapping. She told them that the girl looked scared and that the man was creepy. When the police arrived, they thankfully saw the camera crew before they circled the van and pulled out their guns. It caused a good laugh for all of us on the set, but I took it as a compliment—at least what we were doing looked real!

Other than that incident, everything went great and I believe, or at least like to believe, that I did a decent job. A lot of the reviews talked favorably of my performance, which really helped with my confidence going forth as an actor, and the movie did well in the DVD market. After it came out, fans came up to me all the time to tell me how much they loved those two movies. They said it was great to see me killing, without the make-up on. Since I never had dreams of being an actor growing up and have never being trained as one, to hear that fans were excited to see *me*, blows my mind and makes me feel like I can do anything.

JUST THE BEGINNING

Now in my mid-50's, my aging body is starting to not want to crash cars into walls anymore, but I'm not slowing down. If anything, I'm just getting started. There is a lot of life left in this killer's battle-worn soul. And in some ways, I feel as if my career is just beginning. Though I want to keep my body count rising, I'd love to do a comedy someday and a ton of other roles to challenge myself. Acting is my new love that will take the place of stunts when I can no longer light myself on fire and dive out of a building. While I want to try other genres of acting, something tells me that I won't be able to resist a killer role now and then.

Who knows, maybe when I hit my 70's, I'll have to write another biography to tell the new stories I experienced in the twilight of my career. Hell, maybe I'll break a record for being the oldest serial killer in a movie!

The body count has just begun my friends…

I FUCKING LOVE MY FANS

First and foremost, I have to thank all of my fans. Without my fans, I would be nothing—I'm not an idiot. I know that without you guys, I would not be starring in films and appearing at conventions year after year. Some of you have been with me since I first put on the hockey mask. Others of you have become fans from my later films, while a few of you started to watch my films after meeting me. Regardless, my fans are the best fans in the world. When I lost the role of Jason, tons of you banded together and protested, trying to get me back, and for that, I will always be grateful.

Fan and Friend, Jenni

Other fans come out year after year to see me at conventions, constantly visiting my table, keeping me company, and going out for drinks with me at night. I receive hugs and gifts, you tell me stories and talk about my movies, and I even get to choke a bunch of you bastards.

You guys rent, buy, and watch my movies, which enables me to keep making them. I want to thank every one of you for putting food on my table and keeping me working. Some of you crazy fucks even get tattoos of the characters I have played. And a few of you really dedicated fans have gotten my autograph tattooed on your body, which blows my mind! The fact that someone can like me that much that they want to put my name on their body, forever… shit, I can't even explain how that feels.

With Fans in Mexico

Fan's Tattoo with My Signature

A little while ago a fan sent me a story he wrote about something I did a long time ago. Until I read it, I had completely forgotten all about what I had done. I was doing an appearance at a haunted house when a young man in a wheel chair came up and got an autograph and picture taken with me. Now I don't discriminate against anyone, I choke people in wheelchairs just the same as giant muscle heads, so I treated this guy like everyone else. After strangling his neck, I told him to have fun in the haunted house, he shrugged and said he couldn't go in as it wasn't accessible for his chair. For some reason that pissed me off. Not that I thought the place should be designed for wheel chairs, that would be practically impossible, but the fact that this guy wanted to be scared and couldn't, made me angry. Not even thinking, and not giving the guy a chance to argue, I picked him up and carried him through the haunted house. The guy fucking loved it! Afterwards he thanked me and I didn't think anything of it. I just wanted this man to get spooked like everyone else. After that night I never really thought of it. Ten years later I find out that this act meant so much to this guy and his friends that they wrote a story about it and posted it on a website. Reading that story made me realize that my fans appreciate me just as much as I appreciate them. That's why no matter how tired or pissed off I am, I still try to meet every fan I can and respect them like they have respected my career. I never know when something so small, can mean so much to someone.

The great part about my fans is that you guys don't just come to my table at conventions and shake my hand once. You sick bastards come back year after year, convention after convention, to take more pictures, bring me presents, chat, and let me choke the shit out of you. I love all of you guys, and it means the world to me that you constantly support me day in and day out. I just hope you guys stick with me in the new phase of my career as I do more acting out of the make-up... though I don't think I need to hope—I know you guys—you'll be there.

TOUCHY FEELY SHIT

My career started from nothing. I wasn't raised in the industry. I didn't grow up in Hollywood surrounded by the business. I was just a kid from Nevada, who was raised on a small island in the South Pacific. All I had was a sense of wonder when it came to the dangers of life. Instead of stepping back from the ledges and shying away from things that hurt, I wanted to try them, to test my limits and see how far I could make it. When this attraction to danger met the reality of stunts, a passion was born and I followed it. Knowing no one and nothing about the industry, I made it my life's purpose to become a stuntman. The fire of desire to succeed is what kept me going, even when I was burned beyond belief.

Almost my entire career has been a battle. I had to fight to break in, fight to overcome my injuries, and fight to keep working in the industry that I love. If I had given up after my burn injury and gone back to school, I would have been just another guy working in an office. I'm not saying this to make myself sound like I'm amazing or anything. I'm saying this because I want people to know that no matter what life throws in your face, no matter what shit rains down on your head, if you have a dream, there is no reason you cannot follow it and achieve your goals. And that is not some touchy feely shit; if you want to do something, do it. My life is so fulfilling and amazing, I can't imagine what it would have been like if I had given up when life threw me one of the worst curve balls you could ever receive.

Life is about overcoming challenges, making it to the next level and moving forward, always moving forward. I see so many people all over the world in my travels who have just settled with what they have because it was the easy option. If I took the easy option, I would have killed myself in that hospital all those years ago. If settling in life is alright for you, then fine. But if you ever have a desire in life, a passion, but feel like it is unattainable, think about the shit I went through. Think about someone having to hold your dick while you piss because your arms are bolted in place. Think about not being able to move an inch because excruciating pain overwhelms you. Think about having to overcome all of that before attempting to move forward. Then look at your situation and see if it's that bad. Look everyone, all I'm trying to say here is to follow your dreams... it's fucking worth it.

Kane Hodder

KANE HODDER
ACKNOWLEDGMENTS

There are many people who helped me along the way in my life and career whom I need to thank. I mentioned many of them in the book, but there are some really special people whom I want to point out directly to thank for affecting my life and career in such amazing ways.

First and foremost, I want to thank my wife, Susan, for seeing the potential in me, especially considering that when we met, I was driving an old beat-up police car, living on unemployment, and not doing well in my career. Susan saw past all of that. She saw inside of me and the person I could be. Even though I was a loser, she gave up her life and being close to her entire family on the East Coast to be with me and to give a life with me a chance. To this day it amazes me that she stood by me all those years and loved me even with all of my flaws. I can be a hard person to love at times, and yet, she never stopped loving me. For believing in me, loving me, and giving me two great kids, I love her. I wouldn't have been able to make it this far in my career without her support.

My two sons, Jace and Reed. I want to thank you guys for making life fun and giving me a reason to feel proud. I never realized how incredible it can feel to be a father until you guys were born. I hope your kids make you feel as proud as you make me feel. You guys are amazing, and the world is yours for the taking. Just try not to be too much like me!

391

Dad, for giving me my personality which totally matched his. For never giving up on me when I left college and for simply being a hell of a father. The biggest regret I have in my life is that he never got to see my success in the career that made him worry so much about me.

Mom, for being my biggest supporter in my life, no matter what I did, for always supporting me with everything and every risk I ever took. And for taking care of me, not only when I was a child, but when I was unable to care for myself after my burn injury. *Everyone loved Jason's Mom.*

The lady who took me into her home when I was burned, put me in her shower, and called an ambulance, I owe her a huge thanks. I honestly don't know if I could have done what she did for me. A complete stranger. And if you are reading this, or someone knows who she is, please contact me so I can thank her personally.

Along the same lines, I want to thank the burned man wearing the scrubs who saved my life without ever knowing it. I wouldn't be here without you.

Huge thanks to Mike Aloisi for busting his ass to get my life down on paper.

Tom Morga and Dennis Madalone for taking time out of their lives to teach me how to do stunts at Paul Stader's stunt school in Santa Monica back in 1975. Out of the goodness of their hearts, they helped me train to be a stuntman when I couldn't afford to take the classes.

Gary Baxley, for giving me some of my first stunt jobs on *The Dukes of Hazzard* and *Enos*, along with Frank Orsatti for giving me some of my first jobs on *The Incredible Hulk* and other shows. You guys got the ball rolling for me, and I'll always be grateful for that.

A huge, huge thank you to BJ Davis for being the first stunt coordinator to believe that I could do dangerous stunts. BJ let me do everything I knew I could, but never had a chance to. His faith in me changed my career forever, and I'll always be grateful for that.

Sean Cunningham for giving me my first stunt coordinating job on *House* and sticking with me on many more movies after that. Also, for being the father of Jason!

John Carl Buechler for making me Jason. He is the sole reason I got the role that changed my life forever. Not only did he change my career forever once, he did it a second time by introducing me to Adam Green.

Rob Hedden, director of *Friday the 13th Part VIII*, for allowing me to be the first person to play Jason twice.

Adam Marcus for allowing me to play Jason a third time, especially for wanting me and not making me fight for the role.

Jim Isaac for doing the same thing and making it easy.

Charlie Picerni, Chuck Picerni, and Conrad Palmisano for enabling me to work on huge blockbuster movies. It was a pleasure to be on those sets with you guys.

Mike Feifer for giving me my first leading role out of make-up.

Richard Friedman, for giving me some fantastic character acting roles.

Tommy Brunswick, for giving me my first kissing scene in *Exit 33*.

And last, but certainly not least, Adam Green. I can't thank him enough for how much he has helped change the path of my career. I want to thank him for giving me my first acting scene that had substance to it, which also opened doors for me. For giving me a new horror legend to play. For hiring me again and again. For trusting me. For consistently giving me something new to do on every film. For giving me my first crying scene, dancing scene, sex scene, and always having faith in my stunt coordinating. *Thank you Adam.*

MICHAEL ALOISI
ACKNOWLEDGMENTS

I want to thank Kane Hodder for taking a chance on a new company and a young writer. Once he decided to go forth with the book, he never lost faith in me and supported all of my creative decisions, which is more than any author can ever ask for. As much as he scares the piss out of me, he is a great guy and I'm honored to say he's my friend.

My wife, J.Anna, I would like to thank for having faith in my writing and my dream of starting my own company. And for always supporting every idea I have, no matter how crazy it is.

My wonderful parents, Jean and Al, who have believed in me my entire life, supporting and being there for everything I have ever done.

My brother, Jason, for rushing over to celebrate after signing Kane and who came up with the title of the book before I ever wrote a single word.

Aunt Lorraine and Uncle Tom, for always being my biggest fans.

Jesse Adair for taking some amazing photography for the book cover and for our promotional use. Visit his website at www.JesseAdair.com for some wonderful horror photography.

Sarah Espano for being a creative genius in designing the graphics for our book covers and illustrations, including the AuthorMike Ink logo. Visit www.EnveCreative.com for assistance with graphical design.

Gina Petrone for doing a great job of polishing the final manuscript.

And a big thank you to all of AuthorMike Ink's employees and freelancers who put everything they have into each one of our books.

AUTHOR'S NOTE

While Kane and Michael stand by the fact that everything in this book is true, this is still a work of *creative* nonfiction. Memory can be a fickle thing. One cannot recall every detail of every situation in their lives. Certain situations in the book have been padded to add color and readability. At the same time, every effort has been made to be certain that everything is as accurate as possible. If anything is incorrect and we have offended someone, we apologize as it was not done on purpose. We will make efforts to correct any mistakes brought to our attention in the next edition of this book.

To protect the identity of certain people, some instances and names have been altered. All pictures are copyright of the respective owners, and are reproduced here in the spirit of publicity. Willist we have made every effort to acknowledge specific credits when possible. We apologize for any omissions and will undertake to make any appropriate changes in future additions of this book if necessary.

NOTE ON THE TITLE

Efforts were made to find out if Kane really is the actor with the most on-screen kills in history. While Kane has a very high number, we cannot verify without a doubt that he has more than anyone, mostly because it is a subject that is arguable. Do you count kills that a character makes that are not seen on screen? If the character sinks a boat with 200 people on it, does that count? Hell, in *Jason X*, Jason blows up an entire space community, and who knows how many people were on that—thousands? Do you count that? Also, we looked at it as Kane is the person who has *murdered* the most people, not just killed. Rambo would probably win that title. It's sort of like the title of *The World's Strongest Man*—can that really be proven? If someone has a higher body count, when it comes to on-screen murders, we will apologize...right before Kane finds you and kills you so he can keep the title.

PLEASE HELP BURN SURVIVORS

During the shooting of *Friday the 13th Part VII* when I had time off, I worked out at a local gym near the hotel I was staying in. While there I met a 13-year old kid named Billy who was also a burn survivor. Poor kid was burned worse than me; in fact, he didn't even have any fingers left. I started up a conversation with him and came to find out the kid was a huge *Friday the 13th* fan. When his parents came to pick him up from the gym, I talked to them and invited Billy to the set to watch us shoot. The next day he came down and watched us film the weed whacker scene. They both thanked me profusely, saying it made their day. His mom even pulled me aside and said how much this meant to Billy. Little did they know, it meant more to me than it did to them. Getting a chance to help someone else who went through the trauma I did was the least I can do.

This meeting with Billy really made me realize how much I needed to, and wanted to, give back and help others who helped me. Shortly after our meeting, I started to visit burn camps and meet up with burn survivors whenever I could. Twenty years later, I still visit these camps and talk to people every chance I get. I have a good buddy named Nathan from New York, and I went with him to a burn camp last summer. He is an amazing kid, and I am proud to call him my friend. When I felt like giving up on life after my burns, a burn survivor saved my life by simply being there. For me, seeing that I could have a normal life after my accident changed everything for me. And that is what I want to do for these kids and adults alike who have been burned.

In fact, this means so much to me that my publisher, AuthorMike Ink and I have teamed up with *Scares that Care!* to help raise awareness of burns. Together, we hope to educate children and adults alike on burn safety, how to avoid getting burned, what to do if you get burned, and most importantly, how to live with burns and the scars they leave. If we can help one person not get burned or help them live with their burns and scars, it would mean more to me than all of my years in the industry. Life is about giving back and that is what I'm trying to do now.

And when I talk about burn survivors, I'm not talking about a burned finger after getting a baking pan out of the oven. I'm talking about people who have suffered *serious* burns. Burns that need medical treatment and leave scars. Nothing pisses me off more than when people come up to me and say that they understand and feel for me, because they have been burned, yet they have no scars. If you are seriously burned, you have scars. Those are the people I want to help, people whose burns have changed their lives.

I know the pain they go through and have gone through. Knowing their dilemma, I can talk to them on a personal level. No matter how many times a nurse, doctor, or family member tells you that you will be just fine, you are not going to believe them because they never suffered what you went through. How would they know it was going to be alright if they hadn't experienced it? If someone walks in, covered in burns and sits in front of you, you are going to listen to them. That is why I try and visit burned people as often as I can, to get through to someone who might be in that dark place I was once in.

People are cruel. One tiny thing wrong with you, whether it be a birth defect or scarring from an accident, and they will stare at you, point you out to friends, whisper about what they think is "wrong" with you and, worst of all, tease. It's a horrible fact of life, but it happens, often. Having scars over half of my body for most of my life has made me get used to people looking at me a little funny. The first time a kid asked me, "What is wrong with you?" I nearly lost it. To this innocent kid, I was a freak; it was just in his nature to wonder what was wrong with me, because I was different from him. Going to the beach and taking off my shirt, almost everyone stares and wonders how I got burned. Those first few years were torturous getting used to not being normal. As time went by, I learned how to deal with the image issues—enough to get by, at least. Being able to talk to another burn survivor who has just had it happen, to be able to tell them that it will get better, it just means so much.

Understandably, newly burned people think they are now freaks. While it is true that people will be cruel and stare at them, it doesn't mean their life is over. Look at me. I have a fantastic life and career, and my burns have never affected it; if anything, they have helped some of the roles I have played. Showing and telling this to these people, hopefully, lets them see that they, too, can go out and live their lives the way they want to. They just need to learn how to ignore the comments and stares. It is hard as hell, but it is possible.

In these visits, all I want to do is show them they are not alone and that things can and will get better in life, for I know how dark of a place being a burned person can be. If I could just help one person the way that that man in the scrubs helped me, then my whole ordeal would have been worth it.

"Scares That Care!" is a not-for-profit organization created by horror industry professionals that provides money, toys and other items to help sick children. By teaming up with me, they now are dedicated to helping out burn victims and their families as well. If my burn story has touched you at all, please, please give whatever you can to this great charity to help a child who is going through a horrific experience heal and live a better life. 100% of every dime donated will go directly to helping out a child in need. There is even a link right on their page to donate to my branch of this charity. To donate simply visit their website below and click the donate link.

www.ScaresThatCare.org

HOLLYWOOD GHOST HUNTERS

Hollywood Ghost Hunters
Steve Nappe, R.A. Mihailoff, Kane Hodder, Rick McCallum,
Danielle Harris

For years I have been into ghost hunting and the paranormal. When my friend Rick McCallum and I realized we both shared the same passion, we decided to form our own ghost-hunting team. What we came up with is a group of industry professionals teaming up to become...The Hollywood Ghost Hunters. Originally I was going to put a large section in my memoirs about the team and our experiences, but after a few talks with Mike Aloisi, the author, we realized there was enough material to make an entire book on its own. Therefore, keep an eye out for our book and visit the website for updates.

www.HollywoodGhostHunters.com

A Journal About the Making of
Kane Hodder's Biography, *Unmasked*

THE KILLER & I*

Michael Aloisi

THE KILLER AND I
A Behind the Scenes Journal of the Making
of Kane Hodder's Biography, *UNMASKED*

By
Michael Aloisi

If you enjoyed reading about Kane's life, you need to read *The Killer and I*. With *Unmasked*, you got to see the inside of Kane's mind and how he got to where he is in life. Now, see Kane from a different perspective, through the eyes of a writer, who had to endure a year long journey with one of the world's most famous, cinematic killers!

This odd couple story of a tough as nails stuntman who kills people on screen for a living and a timid writer who has never sworn or drank alcohol in his life will leave you in stitches. Not only will you get a behind the scenes look at Kane's life and how the book was made, you'll also get to read about Kane scaring Mike on a daily basis and all the other hilarious situations he gets Mike into!

*I might be bias, but The Killer and I is one of the funniest things
I have ever read...Even if the title is grammatically incorrect.
If you want to see how I really am these days... read Mike's journal!*
-Kane Hodder

*Please read my journal, I need people to testify at my murder trial...
For I know somehow, someday, Kane will be the death of me!*
-Michael Aloisi

Ask for *The Killer and I* at your local bookstore or buy it online. For autographed copies and sample chapters, visit the website.

www.KaneHodderKills.com

CPSIA information can be obtained at www.ICGtesting.com
Printed in the USA
LVOW10s0731011014

406729LV00001B/1/P